T0249020

Computational Modeling: Concepts and Applications

Computational Modeling: Concepts and Applications

Edited by **Gregory Rago**

New York

Published by Willford Press,
118-35 Queens Blvd., Suite 400,
Forest Hills, NY 11375, USA
www.willfordpress.com

Computational Modeling: Concepts and Applications
Edited by Gregory Rago

International Standard Book Number: 978-1-68285-069-5 (Hardback)

The publisher's policy is to use permanent paper from mills that operate a sustainable forestry policy. Furthermore, the publisher ensures that the text paper and cover boards used have met acceptable environmental accreditation standards.

Trademark Notice: Registered trademark of products or corporate names are used only for explanation and identification without intent to infringe.

Printed in the United States of America.

Contents

Preface

Computer-based simulation is one of the most preferred methods of studying a system today. The primary goal of this book is to collaborate the latest research in this discipline. The topics included in this book on computational modeling are elaborate discussions on many applications of computational modeling, such as three dimensional technology, fuzzy logic, cloud computing, visualization, virtual machines, etc. which are of utmost significance and are bound to provide incredible insights to readers. This book will be an apt reference for a wide variety of readers including students, researchers and academicians.

The information shared in this book is based on empirical researches made by veterans in this field of study. The elaborative information provided in this book will help the readers further their scope of knowledge leading to advancements in this field.

Finally, I would like to thank my fellow researchers who gave constructive feedback and my family members who supported me at every step of my research.

Editor

3D PRINTERS – NEW POSSIBILITIES IN EDUCATION

Joanna Szulżyk-Cieplak[1], Aneta Duda[1], Bartłomiej Sidor

[1] Faculty of Fundamentals of Technology, Lublin University of Technology, Nadbystrzycka 38, 20-618 Lublin, Poland, e-mail: j.szulzyk-cieplak@pollub.pl

ABSTRACT

In the last few years a significant growth of three-dimensional printing has been noticed. Although 3D printers have been around for about 30 years, they were very expensive, that is why they were available in the industry only in the majority . In recent years, prices of 3D printers have fallen more than tenfold, owing to the fact they are used not only in large enterprises but also in all kinds of educational institutions, small businesses or in do-it-yourself men's houses. They are, inter alia, used to construct physical models, so much needed in education. Nowadays, one of the most popular 3D printing technologies is FDM (Fused Deposition Modeling). Relatively low prices of printers in this technology make them available for almost everyone. The paper discusses the technology of rapid prototyping, with particular emphasis on the use of 3D printing and appropriately matched printer to designed laboratory stand.

Keywords: 3D printer, 3D scanner, 3D print.

INTRODUCTION

In recent years, there are many discussions about the problems of higher education, unemployment among graduates, fields of study mismatch to the market, etc. Wondering how to overcome these weaknesses, it is necessary to look for new forms of engineering education, because there is an impression that traditional education, in the changing world, "does not keep up" with fast development. One of the tasks educational system is facing is developing engineering characteristics favoring innovation [1].

Education in the field of rapid prototyping technology perfectly fits this trend. In the United Kingdom, educational programs using 3D printers began to show up [16]. Classes are also more interesting for students, allowing them to broaden their knowledge not only in theory but also in practice. They have a remarkable effect on imagination, so owing to them, children's ideas can be converted into real projects. Three-dimensional printing technology is also becoming more widely used in higher education. Printers are used there not only for research but also for educational pur-

poses. They are not only a curiosity but diversify classes by using 3D technology, which become more attractive and expand the scope of thematic application of the classes [3].

TECHNOLOGIES OF RAPID PROTOTYPING IN THE PROCESS OF DESIGN AND PREPARATION OF PRODUCTION

Rapid prototyping is a term used to describe a set of methods for rapid, precise and repetitive production of elements in incremental technology, usually with the use of a computer. Introduction of rapid prototyping has revolutionized prototyping. Instead of a long, laborious process of creation of models and prototypes it has become much faster. In prototyping, the model is created in layers, which distinguishes it from traditional processing methods, in which elements are created by removing material from a prefabricated product. An important characteristic distinguishing prototyping from traditional methods of processing planning is a changed designing system. Another element which affects the advantage of prototyping over decrement method is the possibility to create complex structures, such as a hollow sphere [3, 8]. Models created by rapid prototyping are made and designed faster than elements in traditional methods. A comparison of these two methods is shown in Figure 1.

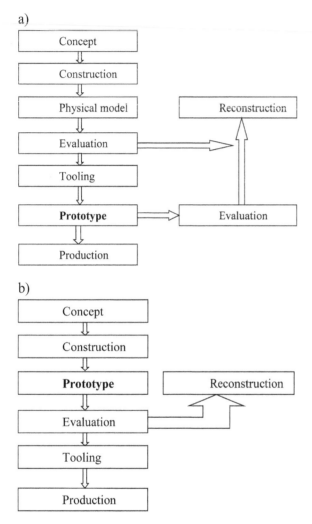

Fig. 1. Scheme of the process of introducing new product to the market: a – traditional approach, b – using rapid prototyping

3D SCANNING

In order to obtain a three-dimensional model of a given object, it does need to be modelled or searched on the Internet. 3D scans allow for obtaining the model. It is a device that carries actual shape, three-dimensional geometry to digital form. This process in some cases accelerates designing and work in some occupations [2, 4].

3D scanning is used in reverse engineering, that is in the process of obtaining information of a given object, necessary to construct its equivalent. There are also other applications of this technology. It is often necessary in medicine – for instance in selecting an ideal prosthesis for an individual patient. It is also used in museums (Figure 2) to create digital models of buildings or small exhibits. Three-dimensional scanning technology is also used computer graphics to create, inter alia, games.

Autodesk 123D Catch gives a very interesting option of three-dimensional scanning. This program allows for scanning on the basis of photos. It is enough to make several or a dozen pictures of selected object. The photos have to be taken all around at different angles. Then, the pictures are sent and analyzed in the cloud, which is an additional advantage because it does not burden our computer. All the process takes a few minutes and eventually we receive the model that latter can be worked on in other CAD software. 123 CAD except the version for Windows is also available for iOS [9].

In the future, having enough amount of money, 3D scanner can be placed on our desk next to the 3D printer – such a set is ra eal three-dimensional copy machine. This refers to the Digitizer scanned made by MarkerBot. This 3D scanner will be intended for home users. Owing to it and 3D printer, everyone, even without designing skills, will be able to duplicate some items quite as easily as photo copier. It is interesting that having digital model, it will be possible to send it to someone who will print it on 3D printer. Unfortunately, this scanner is currently not available for sale [5].

EQUIPMENT AND MATERIALS USED IN RAPID PROTOTYPING TECHNOLOGY

Number of 3D printer applications is still increasing They can print with various materials, for instance: plastic, metal, imitation of glass, titanium, silver or gold, and even chocolate. Scientists are moving much further and are still looking for new applications for three-dimensional printers. The team from University of Southern California developed a method of houses creation in 3D printing technology [12]. In contrast, NASA is working on developing a prototype of 3D printer that will print food. It is one of the stages of preparation for manned mission to Mars. Figure 3 presents the visualization of houses printing [10, 13].

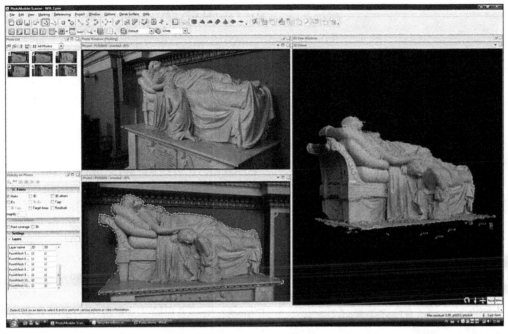

Fig. 2. 3D scanning of the Tomb of Mary Krasinska in Opinogora [15]

Producers of 3D printers are trying to find clients not only in large companies, research or educational institutions, but also in households. An interesting alternative to currently expensive printers is Rep-Rap project [14]. It was developed by Adrian Bowyer at the University of Bath in the United Kingdom. Its main concept is to create a self-replicating machine, in the form of 3D printer. This machine works in FDM technology.

Currently, the produced machines are able to print 70-80% of the parts required to make the next printer. It is necessary to remember that this is the printer to be independently assembled. Unexperienced user will do it in 2–3 days. All schemes, instructions are published under GNU license, that is, they are available on the Internet, for free, and anyone can modify them in any way. Figure 4 shows the "mother" printer and its two "children" [6, 14].

3D printer is needed not only for do-it-yourself enthusiasts. We will find many uses in house:. phone case, and cover for damaged electric kettle, as well as glasses frame, a fragment of broken toy or Lego. Plastic car elements can also be printed – for instance, switch to windows for rare or historic car with parts hard to buy. Only three-dimensional model of the part you want to print is needed. It can be designed by ourselves or downloaded complete model from the Internet. Within 5–10 years, this branch of industry is predicted to significantly develop that 3D printer will be available in a computer store in the same way as an ordinary 2D printer [5].

Fig. 3. Visualization of houses' printing [13]

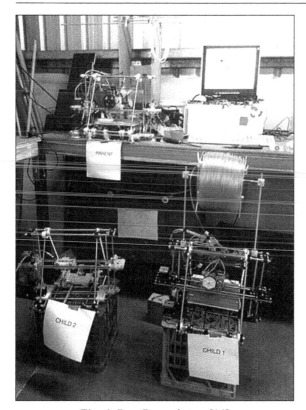

Fig. 4. Rep-Rap printers [14]

LABORATORY STAND FOR RAPID PROTOTYPING

On the basis of the review of 3D printers available on the Polish market, laboratory stand equipped with 3D printer, designed for didactic purposes, e.g. simulation and visualization of technological processes, has been developed. When designing the stand, the following criteria were taken into account: printer cost, printer parameters, printer usage environment and didactic application.

Theoretically, the stand should be a group of devices enabling construction and analysis of complex CAD models. The set matched to the needs of laboratory stand should be so efficient to allow free use of the program for three-dimensional modelling without a problem. This stand should be equipped with CAD software which is easy to use and has transparent interface. The main element of the stand will be a 3D printer working in FDM technology, which is able to print from the following materials: ABS, PLA, PVA, Nylon. Work area of 3D printer should not be smaller than 200 x 200 x 200 mm, and minimum thickness of the layer should not be equal more than 0,2 mm.

3D PRINTER PARAMETERS

When reviewing popular models of 3D printers, the model that meets all design assumptions has been selected. Taking into account work area, which is included in design requirements and a number of other factors, Leapfrog Creatr has been selected (Figure 5). This device uses an incremental technology of model building consisting in layered applying of thermoplastic material through a hot nozzle (FDM technology). The printer can print models not only from the materials listed in the design assumptions, but also from other materials. Minimum layer thickness (Table 1) is much smaller than the assumptive, which is another advantage of selected printer. The selected printer has two print nozzles, which allows for printing of two different materials simultaneously, for instance: from the model material and supporting one. An additional advantage is built-up work area. Owing to this solution, the printed object is protected against external factors such as: wind gusts that affect print quality very adversely. The printer software is free, which eliminates additional costs. Selected printers can work on Windows and Mac. Faculty of Fundamentals of Technology has license it for Windows 7, which is fully supported by selected printer. Among printers in a similar price range, choice of Leapfrog Creatr printer is the best option.

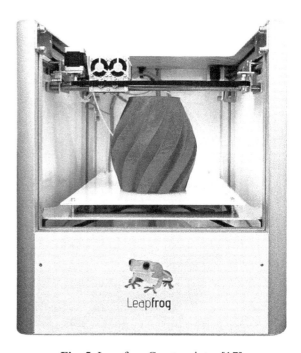

Fig. 5. Leapfrog Creatr printer [17]

Table 1. Specifications of Leapfrog Creatr printer

Outer dimensions (L×W×H)	500 × 600 × 500 mm
Build size (L×W×H)	230 × 270 × 210 mm
Max. print volume	13,7 l
Positioning accuracy	0,05 mm
Layer thickness	0,05 mm
Electrical connection	100-240 V
Material types	ABS, PLA, PVA, LayWood, Nylon, LayBrick
Extruder size	0,35 mm
Speed X and Y axis	do 0,35 m/s
Production speed	ok. 2 cm³/min
Power consumption	400 W
Price	7500 PLN

SELECTION OF STAND ELEMENTS

Efficient CPU with a large monitor is required for comfortable work with CAD software. Therefore, Asus M51AC-PL005S has been selected. It is equipped with quad-core Intel Core i7-4770, powerful graphic card nVidia Ge Force GTX 760. It also has 8GB RAM and 1 TB hard drive. LED Full HD (1920 x 1080 px) Monitor IIYAMAProLiteB2780HSU 27" with time reaction equal 2ms has been selected. The set was also equipped with professional mouse and keyboard Logitech mk710 (Table 2).

Taking into account the fact that Faculty of Fundamentals of Technology has licenses for Windows 7, there is no need to buy it for selected CPU. Since the Faculty has also package AutoCAD Design Suite Ultimate 2013, Autodesk Inventor Professional included in the abovementioned package has been selected as CAD software. It is easy to use, has transparent interface that simplifies the user work, so fully meets designing assumptions. This choice allows for elimination of additional costs of purchasing expensive CAD software license.

Table 2. Preliminary estimate of designed stand

No.	Description	Price
1	3D LeapfrogCreatr printer	7500 PLN
2	CPU Asus M51AC-PL005S	4000 PLN
3	Monitor IIYAMAProLiteB2780HSU	1200 PLN
4	Keyboard and mouse Logitech mk710	350 PLN
	Total	13 050 PLN

CONCLUSION

3D printing technology is undoubtedly new chapter in teaching. 3D printers directly support teaching process. Printed models facilitate better understanding of the creation process. They also enhance students' involvement in the classes. 3D printing allows the students to transfer their ideas into reality. The students who can physically examine their projects, more enthusiastically participate in the classes, and their abilities of spatial imagination are effectively stimulated. Printed models allow the students to learn about the strengths and weaknesses of their projects.

In the study, there was designed laboratory stand for rapid prototyping using Leapfrog Creatr 3D printer. This stand will be used for teaching purposes, such as simulation and visualization of technological processes. During the analysis of popular 3D printers available on the market, one which meets all design assumptions has been selected. Decision was made on the basis of printing precision, built size, quantity and diversity of materials used for printing, minimum layer thickness, as well as additional factors that affect printer selection. Moreover, designed stand has been equipped with efficient computer set including CPU with professional graphic card and high-end processor, large LED Full HD monitor, as well as professional keyboard and mouse.

REFERENCES

1. Bergmann C., Linder M.: 3D printing of bone substitute implants using calcium phosphate and bioactive glasses. Journal of the European Ceramic Society 30, 2010, 2563–2567.

2. Bubicz M.: Raport: szybkie prototypowanie cz. I. Projektowanie i Konstrukcje Inżynierskie 07, 2008, Wydawnistwo Iter, Gdańsk 2008, 14–26.

3. Chlebus E.: Innowacyjne technologie RapidPrototyping – RapidTooling w rozwoju produktu. Oficyna Wydawnicza Politechniki Wrocławskiej, 2003.

4. Chuchro M., Czekaj J., Ruszaj A.: Seminarium: Techniki szybkiego prototypowania w cyklu życia produktu. Mechanik nr 12, 2008, 1063–1070.

5. Czerwiński M., Czerwiński K.: Drukowanie w 3D. Wydawnictwo Infoaudit, Warszawa 2013.

6. Griffin M.: Ultimate 3D Printer Buyer's Guide Make. Wydawnictwo O'Reilly Media, Inc., USA 2012, 38–78.

7. Hopkinson N., Hague R., Dickens P.: Rapid manufacturing: An industrial revolution for the digital age. Wydawnictwo Wiley, 2006, p. 56.

8. Miecielica M.: Techniki szybkiego prototypowania – RapidPrototyping. Przegląd Mechaniczny 02, 2010, 39–45.

9. Wajand J.A, Wajand J.T,: Tłokowe silniki spalinowe średnio- i szybkoobrotowe. Wydanie czwarte. WNT, Warszawa 2005.

10. Wittbrodt B.T., Glover A.G.: Life-cycle economic analysis of distributed manufacturing with opensource 3-D printers. Mechatronics 23, 2013, 713–726.

11. http://www.popsci.com/technology/article/2012-08/researcher-aims-print-3-d-print-entire-houses-out-concrete-20-hours

12. http://domowe2013.pl/ocieplanie-rozwiazanie-ekonomiczne/

13. http://reprap.org/wiki/RepRap/pl

14. http://www.fotoskaner.pl/digitalizacja/category/pracujemy

15. http://www.przyrostowo.pl/artykuly/drukarki-3d-w-edukacji-szkolnej-w-wielkiej-brytanii

16. www.lpfrg.com

2

APPLICATION OF CABRI 3D IN TEACHING STEREOMETRY

Renata Rososzczuk[1]

[1] Department of Applied Mathematics, Lublin University of Technology, Nadbystrzycka 38, 20-618 Lublin, Poland, e-mail: r.rososzczuk@pollub.pl

ABSTRACT

Cabri 3D is a software which connects geometry and algebra to enable measuring length, distance, area, angles, scalar product, volume and use them in calculations or in algebraic expressions. Cabri 3D gives new opportunities for teaching three-dimentional Euclidean geometry. In this work we describe some tools and functions of Cabri 3D. We also give a skech of using this mathematical software to create 2D and 3D figures and explore a figure's properties by manipulating its variable elements.

Keywords: stereometry, dynamic geometry software, Cabri 3D.

INTRODUCTION

Scientific and technical progress gives new opportunities to teach mathematics. One of the best computer programs which make geometry easier to learn is Cabri. Cabri 3D won the 2007 BETT Award in the Digital Content: Secondary (Core Subject) category. Cabri software has been adopted by over 20 ministries of education and is available in more than 25 languages. That program helps students imagine complex objects by manipulating them. Moreover, it also contains the benefits of interactive geometry.

Cabri technology was born in 1985 in the research labs of France's Centre National de la Recherche Scientifique and Joseph Fourier University in Grenoble. At the beinning the main target of that project was to make two-dimensional geometry easier to learn and more enjoyable to teach. Later Cabri philosophy was brought to the world of 3D. Cabri 3D was showed first time during the conference CABRIWORLD in Rome in Semtember in 2004. [1]

The system requirements for installation and activating the program are:

- Microsoft Windows: Windows 8 / 7 / Vista / XP / 2000 / ME / 98 / NT4;
- Apple Macintosh: MacOs X, version 10.3 or higer;
- Minimum configuration for PC: 800 MHz or greater CPU, 256 MB or more RAM, Open GL copatible graphic card with 64 MB or more RAM.

Cabri is not free, but there are evaluation versions available, which offer complete features for 30 days from installation. Once the 30 days period has expired it will operate in a restricted mode (15 min. sessions, save, copy/paste and print unavailable) [2].

BASIC PRINCIPLES

Each object constructed in Cabri 3D is placed in a plane, known as a **based plane**. A grace surface is called **Visible Part** of the based place. Invisible extension of Visible Part is known as the **Non-Visible Part.** Each of these cuboids is placed on the same plane (Figure 1). We can add other planes by choosing three points or two coplanar lines. A new plain can be also defined by an existing polygon or a triangle. Construcion can be viewed from various angles, what may make easier to add new object. The lower objects are darker than the upper ones, which contributes to the effect of depth [2].

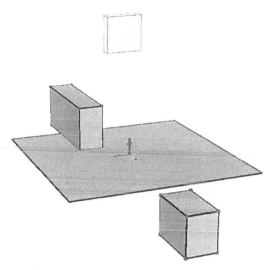

Fig. 1. Cuboids on a based plane

TOOLS AND FUNCTIONS

We can construct 3D fundamental geometric object in Cabri such as points (points on a plane, in a space, on an object, intersection point(s), points in the space defined by its cordinates), curves (lines, rays, segments, vectors, circles, arcs, conics, intersection curves), surfaces (planes, half-planes, sectors, triangles, polygons, cylinders, cones, spheres). Moreover, with just a few clicks a student can construct in Cabri a regular polythedra.

Cabri 3D enables us to open polythedra. We can open polythedra immediately or open a single face. We can print a polythedron net and use it to create a real model. Cabri 3D also enables us to construct the intersection of a polythedron and a plane and view two parts of that polythedron.

Cabri connect geometry and algebra by measuring length, distance, area, angles, scalar product, volume and then attaching these numeric values directly to the figure to use them in calculations or in algebraic expressions.

Cabri 3D allows us to make relative construction such as perperdicular or parallel lines or planes, perpendicular bisector, bisektor plane, midpoint, vector sum, cross product, measurement transfers and transformations (central symetry, half turn, reflection in a plane, translation, enlargement, inversion, rotation).

We can create automatic animations of our objects. By creating a moving point on a circle one can move all objects linked to this point. We can, for example, increase the volume of a sphere, make a triange oscillate. The results can be spectacular.

Moreover, Cabri 3D enables us to insert dynamic and static images in other programs, for example we can export our constructions in HTML and PNG format, insert a dynamic image in a web page and Microsoft Office application, insert a dynamic image in a web browser.

EXAMPLES

We give examples of using Cabri 3D for teaching stereometry at school.

Example 1

Many students have difficulty with immagining tree-dimentional shape. It is not easy for them to open a polythedron in their heads and draw a net. In this example we want to show how we can construct a polythedron, open it in a Cabri 3D and use that program for creating a real model.

First we draw a polygon, for example a regular hexagon. Next, we construct a vector, for instance a vector lying on a perpendicular line. Then we choose the Prism tool and we select a polygon and a vector. We can also construct a segment by connecting two points, change the colour of segment, name points, change the size of the font (Fig. 2).

In order to create a polythedron net we select Open Polythedron tool and click the polythedron. To open the polythedron more completely, we use the Manipulation tool and drag one of the faces with a mouse. We can also open a single face by holding the Shift key. We may hide a plane, a line and vectors (Fig. 3).

In order to print the net, we select the net with the Manipulation tool and choose Document Add Net Page. We can also change the default graphics attributes of net. That net may be used to create a real model (Fig. 4).

Example 2

Very ofen it is difficult to imagine an intersection of a polythedron and a plane or view two parts of the intersected polythedron by a plane. The next example shows how we can find an intersection of a polythedron and a plane.

Exercise

What figure can we get if we intersect a cube by a plane, which is passing through three points: centre of symmetry of a cube and two

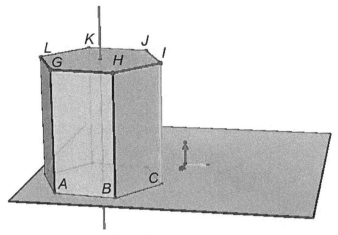

Fig. 2. Prism (defined by a polygon and a vector)

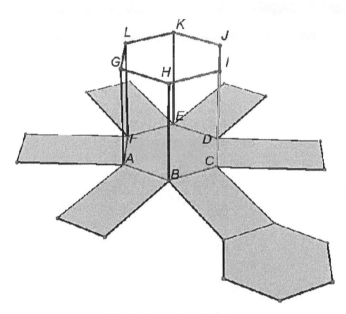

Fig. 3. Opened polythedron

centres of edges having common vertex. Calculate the area of that intersection. Assume, that the edge of cube is *a* [3].

The most difficult part of this exercise for students is to imagine what this intersection of a cube and a plane looks like. If we use Cabri 3D for constructing an appropriate intersection the exercise seems much easier.

We construct a cube. We can also draw segments connecting each two points of that cube. To construct midpoints we use Relative construction tools. We hide a cube (in order to indicate with easily centre of symmetry of a cube) and construct a plain passing through three appropriate points. Next we show a hidden object. To construct the intersection of a polythedron and the half-space deliminated by a plane and hide part of the polthedron we use the Cut Polythedron tool and select cube and intersecting plane.

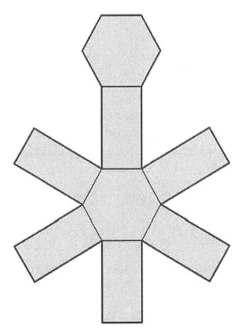

Fig. 4. Polythedron net

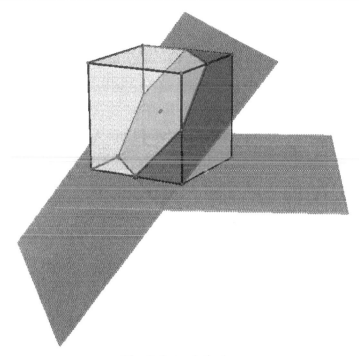

Fig. 5. Cut polythedron

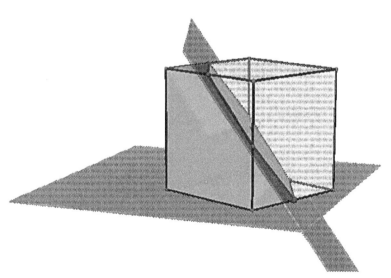

Fig. 6. Another view of cut polythedron

We can also change the default graphics attributes of planes, segments, points, etc. (Fig. 5).

In order to view our construction from various angles, we hold down right mouse button and move the mouse (Fig. 6). Now it is very easy to calculate the area of this intersection.

CONCLUSION

We show new opportunities to teach stereometry, which are given by Cabri 3D. The possibility of creating three-dimensional construction and manipulation objects teaches spatial imagination. Better understanding of three-dimentional shape helps students draw object and solve many mathematical problems. Using that mathematical software increases students' interest in mathematics, information technology and improves their skills.

REFERENCES

1. Cabri: Maths software for students: http://www. cabri.com

2. Sophie and Pierre René de Cotret, Cabri 3D v2.1 Podręcznik użytkownika, Cabrilog S.A.S., 2007.

3. Świda E., Kłaczkow K., Winsztal A., Zdaj maturę: Matematyka, Oficyna Edukacyjna Krzysztof Pazdro, Warszawa 2007.

COMPARISON AODV AND DSDV ROUTING PROTOCOLS WITH USING FUZZY LOGIC IN THE MANET

Hamed Jelodar[1], Javad Aramideh[2]

[1] Department of Computer, Science and Research, Islamic Azad University, Bushehr, Iran, e-mail: JelodarH@ Gmail.com

[2] Department of Computer Engineering, Sari Branch, Islamic Azad University, Sari, Iran, e-mail: Javad_ aram_66@yahoo.com

ABSTRACT

Mobile ad hoc networks have consisted of the nodes which are freely displaced. In other words, this network has dynamic topology. Routing protocols find route of forwarding data packets from the source node to the destination node. A routing protocol plays important role in finding the shortest time and the route path. In this paper, considering significance of the subject, attempt has been made to present a model using fuzzy logic approach to evaluate and compare two routing protocols i.e. AODV DSDV using effective factor of the number of nodes based on 2 outputs of delay and throughput rate (totally fuzzy system with four outputs) in order to select one of these two routing protocols properly under different conditions and based on need and goal. To show efficiency and truth of fuzzy system, two protocols have been evaluated completely equally using NS-2 simulator and attempt has been made to prove efficiency of the designed fuzzy system by comparing results of simulation of fuzzy system and NS-2 software.

Keywords: AODV routing protocol, DSDV routing protocol, fuzzy expert system, MANET.

INTRODUCTION

Mobile ad hoc network is a type of ad hoc wireless networks which has become highly important in wireless communication. This network has composed of a set of wireless nodes and mobile phones and computer can play role of these nodes. Routing in these networks is complex and difficult because there is no fixed topology and nodes are freely displaced. In these networks, each node plays role of a router. Military networks, crime management networks etc. can be among the examples of mobile ad hoc network. One of the most important issues in ad hoc networks is routing. There are different types of routing protocols such as AODV and DSDV routing protocols. This paper analyzes and evaluates these two protocols with fuzzy logic and NS-2 simulator. This paper is organized as follows: previous works, relates to concepts mentioned in this paper, the designed fuzzy system, results of simulation are mentioned with NS-2 software and at the end, result of the research is mentioned.

PREVIOUS WORKS

Good studies have been conducted so far to evaluate and analyze routing protocols in ad hoc networks some of which we describe here. Morshed et al. in their paper compared AODV and DSDV protocols with different parameters. In their test, they showed that AODV protocol was better than DSDV routing protocol for real time applications [1]. Mohapatra et al. in their paper analyzed function of several routing protocols on ad hoc network and studied delay, throughput and packet delivery [2]. Odeh et al. analyzed and compared function of two protocols i.e. DSR and

AODV. Criterion for their comparison was data packet size. They found that DSR protocol had better function for packet of below 7 bytes [3]. Boukerche et al. studied and compared AODV, PAODV, CBRP, DSR, DSDV protocols and found that DSR and CBRP routers had higher power compared with other protocols [4].

STATEMENT OF CONCEPTS

In this Section, we introduce two AODN and DSDV routing protocols in this paper.

A. Routing in mobile ad hoc network

Ad hoc networks are classified into two groups including mobile ad hoc network and intelligent sensor network. Mobile ad hoc network has composed of wireless nodes. Nodes are freely displaced. In other words, this network has dynamic topology. Figure 1 shows an mobile ad hoc network. Routing is difficult in this network. In order to send data soundly and with low delay to destination, routing protocols should be used. DSDV and AODV protocols are of the popular protocols which are evaluated and compared with different nodes size.

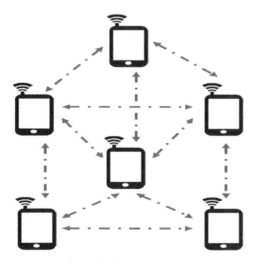

Fig. 1. Ad hoc network

The above figure shows an ad- hoc network and each one of these nodes can be regarded as a router or can have a middle node for routing to send data from the source to the destination.

B. DSDV routing protocol

This protocol performs routing with Bellman–Ford algorithm. Each node has a routing table which is updated continually and periodically. The inputs which are located in routing table include the number of nodes for reaching destination, sequence numbers for reaching destination which is generated by the destination node and is the destination address [2, 5]. Data packets are transferred to nodes with routing table. Preventing creation of loop is one of the features of this protocol.

C. AODV routing protocol

This protocol discovers route with request approach. In other words, this protocol finds routes with RREQ, RREP and RERR messages. When the source node wants to send data to destination, source node first broadcasts messages called RREQ to its neighbor nodes. When the RREQ message reaches destination node, the destination node will send its response to the source node from the same previous path with RREP message and it means that the route has been found from source to destination and the source node can send its data. One of the features of this protocol is that it performs routing action only if necessary. ADOV protocol uses a routing method and acts similarly to DSR [6, 7, 8].

As mentioned above, the source node first broadcasts its route request among neighbors and the node forwards its response message into the source node. Figure 2 shows message broadcasting procedure. This figure has 8 nodes in which node A has role of source and H has role of destination. Node A broadcasts route request among the neighboring nodes and also neighboring nodes route request source node to another node.

When request message reaches node H or destination node is found, the destination node forwards the response message to node A and the source can send its data. Figure 3 shows response of destination node to the source node.

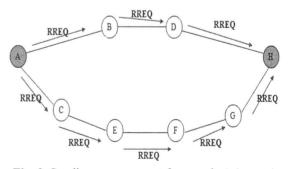

Fig. 2. Sending route request from node A (source)

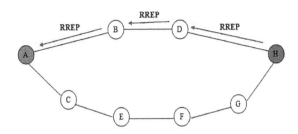

Fig. 3. Sending node H response (destination) to sphere A (source)

FUZZY SYSTEM CONSTRUCTION

In this Section, we introduce the proposed fuzzy system for evaluation of two AODV and DSDV and stages of fuzzy system construction are described as follows:

A. Fuzzy system

Fuzzy systems are able to make decision and control a system with expert systems so that the most applicable case for using them is to model relations in complex medium or anywhere which there is no clear model in the system such that it makes conclusion and decision for the system by relying on some inputs and their results. It is very complex to recognize reasons for efficiency of a test technique. The following Figure shows general diagram of MANET model with fuzzy system. The most important idea in use of fuzzy system which has been shown in Figure 4 is that verbal words are transferred to fuzzy system and the fuzzy system expresses efficiency of the protocols under different conditions considering the signs which have been shown with verbal words.

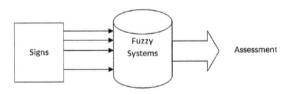

Fig. 4. Function of Fuzzy system

In the fuzzy system, we have used rules as Relation 1 to model the concepts [9].

$$if x_1 is A_1^1,...,x_m is A_m^1 then y = B^1 \qquad (1)$$

Utilized membership functions are triangular, yet they have different number of variables. This difference roots in natural quiddity of parameters such as degree of anemia.

The most paramount reasons justifying use of fuzzy systems are Annabelle Mercier [2005], Kim-Hui Yap [2005]:
- The sophistication of natural world which leads to an approximate description or a fuzzy system for modeling.
- Necessity of providing a pattern to formulate mankindknowledge and applying it to actual systems.

Thus, the following procedure is considered to define expert fuzzy system:
- Defining input-output sets which accept normalized input-output pairs.
- Generating if-else fuzzy rules based on input-output pairs.
- Creating fuzzy rule base.
- Implementing fuzzy system based on fuzzy rules.

In this artical we utilize product inference engine, singleton fuzzifier and center average defuzzifier in order to build fuzzy system. In our inference engine we also used Mamdani product implication and individual-rule based inference combined with algebraic summation and mulitplication for t-norms and max for s-norms. Thus, product inference engine can be written as denoted by equation (2) [9]:

$$\mu_{B'}(y) = \max_{l=1}^{n}[\sup(\mu_{A'}(x)\bigcup_{i=1}^{k}\mu_{A_i^l}(x_i)\mu_{B^l}(y))] \quad (2)$$

In this fuzzy system, singleton fuzzifier and average defuzzifier are utilized. Singleton fuzzifier is widely applied as it simplifies calculation of inference engine. Moreover, center averages defuzzifier is the most popular defuzzifier used in fuzzy systems and fuzzy control systems owing to its simplicity, justifiability and continuity. Center average defuzzifier is calculated as shown in equation (3) [10]:

$$s(A_j \Rightarrow Classh) = \frac{1}{m}\sum_{x_p \in Classh}\mu_{A_j}(x_p) \quad (3)$$

B. Input–output parameters of the fuzzy systems

As mentioned before, 1 factor of the number of nodes has been used in this system for evaluation of two AODV, DSDV routing protocols as input parameter and based on this input factor, effect of the factor on two AODV, DSDV routing protocols is studied but as mentioned above, other factors such as nodes searching speed, number of packets etc. are also effective on evaluation of two AODV and DSDV routing protocols. As a result, it is not possible to determine efficiency of two AODV and DSDV routing protocols under different conditions but attempt has been made to calculate efficiency of two AODV and DSDV routing protocols with a fuzzy system using this single factor for taking suitable measures. Therefore, the above fuzzy system has four outputs which show efficiency of two AODV and DSDV routing protocols based on different input states.

In this research, FIS tools were used in Matlab software to determine efficiency of test technique and its general diagram is shown in Figure 5.

This system has 1 input field which relates to factor affecting evaluation of two AODV and DSDV routing protocols and three classes i.e. low, normal and high verbal words have been assigned to each factor and 4 output fields which show efficiency of two AODV and DSDV routing protocols and the output has been classified

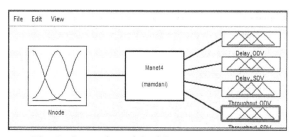

Fig. 5. General model of fuzzy expert system for evaluation of two AODV and DSDV routing protocols

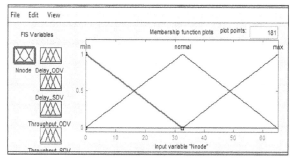

Fig .6. Membership function relating to input of the number of node

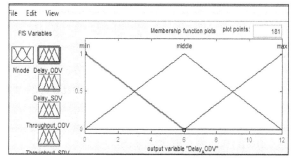

Fig .7. Membership function relating to delay of AODV routing protocol

into three groups and low, normal and high verbal words have been assigned to each factor. In Figures 6 and 7, one of the membership functions of input and output parameters is shown.

C. Construction of rules database

A simple method for generation of fuzzy rules is clustering of input features with specified number of fuzzy membership functions (for example, triangular membership function and assignment of verbal words to each cluster). With the classified space for each model, one way for generation of fuzzy rules is to consider all possible combinations of antecedents (input features) and this method has been also used in this research.

D. Fuzzy if–then rules

With the mentioned facts, we write if-them rules as follows:
1. If (Nnode is normal) then (Delay_AODV is middle) (Delay_DSDV is max) (Throughput_AODV is max) (Throughput_DSDV is max).
2. If (Nnode is max) then (Delay_ AODV is min) (Delay_DSDV is max) (Throughput_AODV is max) (Throughput_DSDV is min).
3. If (Nnode is min) then (Delay_AODV is max) (Delay_DSDV is min) (Throughput_AODV is min) (Throughput_DSDV is min).

E. Simulations and statement of results of fuzzy system

As mentioned above, MATLAB software which is a suitable medium for simulation of such systems has been used. Simulation of two cases of tests with 15 and 35 nodes is given in Figures 8A and 8B we then showed results ob-

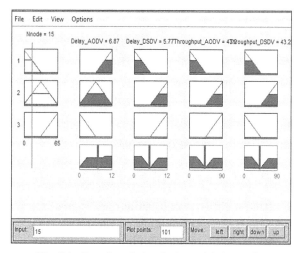

Fig. 8A. Results of simulation with 15 nodes

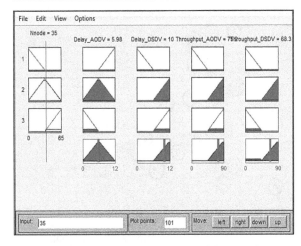

Fig. 8B. Results of simulation with 35 nodes

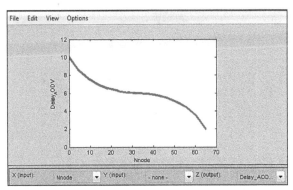

Fig. 9A. Effect of number of node on output of delay in AODV protocol

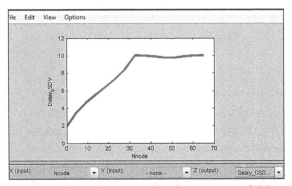

Fig. 9B. Effect of number of node on output of delay in DSDV protocol

tained from effect of the number of node on output as 2D which has been obtained in the simulation model.

F. Results

Results of fuzzy expert system for two outputs of delay and throughput are given in Table 1. The results for two protocols which have been tested with nodes 10, 15, 25, 35, 45, 55 and 65 are shown in Figure 10A and 10B. The obtained results show that AODV protocol has lower delay

Table I. Results of the experiment

Number of nodes	Delay (sec)		Throughput rates (kb)	
	AODV	DSDV	AODV	DSDV
10	7.5	4.79	35.9	35.9
15	6.87	5.77	43.2	43.2
25	6.17	7.75	5S.1	58.1
35	5.98	10	75.2	68.3
45	5.56	9.S2	73.3	50.3
55	4.5	9.S9	74.2	35.9
65	1.96	10	75.3	14.7

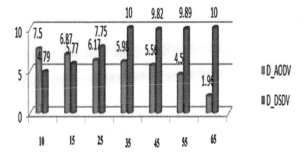

Fig. 10A. Bar chart of delay

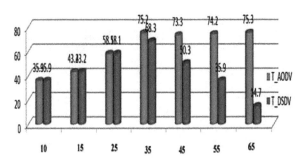

Fig. 10B. Bar chart of Throughput

rate and higher throughput than DSDV protocol with increasing the number of nodes.

Results obtained from execution of the designed fuzzy system for the number of different nodes are exactly mentioned in Table 1. Now, we have evaluated and simulated two AODV and DSDV routing protocols for the number of similar nodes with NS-2 software in order to show performance and reliability of the proposed fuzzy system by comparing results of executing fuzzy system and NS-2 software with each other.

SIMULATION AND STATEMENT OF RESULTS WITH NS-2 SOFTWARE

In this Section, we compare two AODV and DSDV routing protocols by performing test and NS-2 software has been used to simulate the protocols and NS2 Visual Trace Analyzer software has been used to analyze the results. Our evaluation criterion is condition of the sent packets, the maximum delay and maximum forwarded data per second. Each one of them is discussed here. The settings which have been done for analysis of this test are shown in Table 2. Figure 11 shows simulation medium and Figure 12 shows layout of nodes in which number zero is source node and node number 1 is destination node.

Table 2. Parameters used for simulation

Parameter	Values
Channel type	Channel/Wireless channel
Number of nodes	10, 15, 20, 25, 30, 35, 40, 45, 50, 55, 60, 65
Simulation time	150 sec
Area of simulation	500x500
Routing Protocol	AODV, DSDV
Mac Type	802.11
Data Type	TCP/FTP
Interface queue type	QueueIDrop Tail

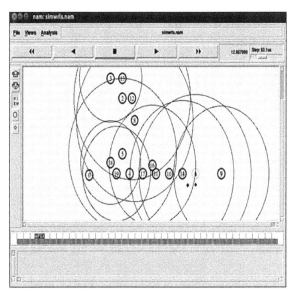

Fig. 11. Simulation medium with NS2 software

A. The forwarded packets

In this Section, condition of the packets which have been generated, dropped and transferred are shown with different nodes with both protocols.

Figure 13 shows the generated packets, dropped packets and transferred packets for AODV protocol with different nodes. For example, a test has been done on 10 nodes in this Figure. There are 4038 TCP packets and 13 packets have been

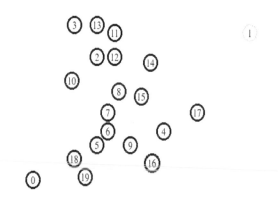

Fig. 12. Layout of nodes with 20 nodes in which node number zero is source and node number 1 is destination

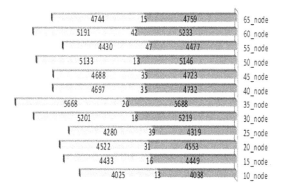

Fig. 13. The forwarded packets with AODV protocol

dropped. The number of packet which has been transferred from source to destination is 4025. Considering this Figure, it can be said that with increasing the number of nodes, the number of packets forwarded from source to destination increases.

Figure 14 shows the generated packets, the dropped packets and transferred packets for DSDV protocol with different nodes. For example, there are 4726 TCP packets in the test which has been performed on 10 nodes and the number of the dropped packet is 41 and also the number of transferred packet from source to destination is 4685.

B. Maximum delay of both protocols

In Figure 15, maximum delay of protocols is shown as line chart for both protocols. Considering the following Figure, it can be mentioned that although we see high delay rate in AODV protocol by analyzing 10 nodes, we see lower delay rate with increasing the number of nodes. Therefore, it can be said that AODV has lower delay rate.

DSDV

■ Generate ■ Drop ■ Transferred

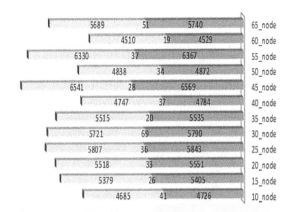

5689	51	5740	65_node
4510	19	4529	60_node
6330	37	6367	55_node
4838	34	4872	50_node
6541	28	6569	45_node
4747	37	4784	40_node
5515	20	5535	35_node
5721	69	5790	30_node
5807	36	5843	25_node
5518	33	5551	20_node
5379	26	5405	15_node
4685	41	4726	10_node

Fig. 14. Number of the forwarded packets with number of different nodes for DSDV protocol

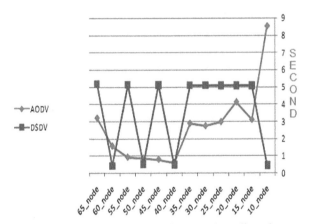

Fig. 15. Maximum delay of protocols as line chart

CONCLUSION

In this paper, fuzzy system has been designed to evaluate two DSDV and AODV protocols in mobile ad hoc network and to prove truth of the fuzzy system, we compare results of comparing two protocols with NS-2 software and the results show that the designed fuzzy system has suitable efficiency for proposing and selecting one of these two routing protocols principally and logically under different conditions and based on different applications. It can be generally said that AODV protocol has better performance than the DSDV protocol in terms of the data transfer rate per second and delay rate with increasing the number of node in the network. Generally, we can say that goal of designing the fuzzy system in this paper is to help ordinary user select type

of the routing protocol only based on information of ordinary user (even if the user has no accurate information about routing protocols of Manet networks) and only based on personal discernment of the user regarding the number of nodes based on application of network as verbal words (high-low-medium).

REFERENCES

1. Morshed Md Monzur, Franz Is Ko, Dongwook Lim, Md Habibur Rahman, Md Rezaur Rahman Mazumder, and Jyotirmoy Ghosh. Performance evaluation of DSDV and AODV routing protocols in mobile ad-hoc networks. In: New Trends in Information Science and Service Science (NISS), 4th IEEE International Conference on, 2010, 399-403.

2. Mohapatra S. and Kanungo. Performance analysis of AODV, DSR, OLSR and DSDV Routing Protocols using NS2 Simulator. Procedia Engineering, 30, 2012, 69-76.

3. Odeh A., Eman A.F. and Muneer A. Performance Evaluation of AODV and DSR Routing Protocols in MANET Networks. International Journal of Distributed and Parallel Systems (IJDPS) Vol. 3, 2012.

4. Boukerche A. Performance evaluation of routing protocols for ad hoc wireless networks. Mobile Networks and Applications 9(4), 2004, 333-342.

5. Ramesh V., Subbaiah P., Koteswar Rao N. and Janardhana Raju M. Performance Comparison and Analysis of DSDV and AODV for MANET. International Journal on Computer Science and Engineering 2(2), 2010, 183-188.

6. Gupta S.K. and Saket R.K. Performance metric comparison of AODV and DSDV routing protocols in manets using ns-2. IJRRAS, Vol. 7(3), 2011, 339-350.

7. Bhosle A.A. and Tushar P.T. International Journal of Computer Science, Engineering and Applications (IJCSEA). Black-Hole and Wormhole Attack in Routing Protocol AODV in MANET, 2(1), 2012, 45-54.

8. Rahman Abdul Hadi Abd, and Zuriati Ahmad Zukarnain. Performance comparison of AODV, DSDV and I-DSDV routing protocols in mobile ad hoc networks. European Journal of Scientific Research.

9. Zadeh LA., Fuzzy Logic, Neural Networks and Soft Computing, Com. of the ACM, vol. 37, 1994, 77-84.

10. Ishibuchi H., Nozaki K., Yamamoto N., Tanaka H., Construction of fuzzy classification systems with rectangular fuzzy rules using genetic algorithm, Fuzzy Sets and Systems, Vol. 65, 1994, 237-253.

4

AN APPROACH TO WEB SERVICE SELECTION BASED ON COMPOSITE QOS PARAMETERS

Mehrnoosh Kheradmand[1], Homayun Motameni[2]

[1] Student, Sari Branch, Islamic Azad University, Sari, Iran, e-mail: m.kheradmand.85@gmail.com
[2] Sari Branch, Islamic Azad University, Sari, Iran, e-mail: motameni@iausari.ac.ir

ABSTRACT

Quality of service (QoS) is an important attribute for selecting a service during the service composition process. Although availability and reliability have been considered as the predominant factors for estimating reputation, two aspects are missing in the literature. First, their use is limited to composite service level and does not count on the atomic level. Second, their combined effect is not evaluated. Better estimation of QoS can be done with both factors considered together, whereas when taken separately for computing reputation, availability will give the probability of a service being up/running and reliability will analyze the change in failure trend of that service. In this research, a mathematical modeling of predominant QoS factors, availability and reliability of atomic services using Markov Chain model and Weibull analysis respectively, are suggested. Also importance of modeling reputation as an aggregation of availability and reliability has been explained. This research concludes two results. First, counting on probability of a service being up/running and its failure trend, together, results in a better estimation of its behavior and helps selecting the most appropriate one. Second, this resulted in selection of a service with higher reputation but lower usage cost, as opposed to using a single factor that resulted in higher reputation with higher cost.

Keywords: web service, web service selection, quality of service, QoS composition, service reputation.

INTRODUCTION

Web services encapsulate operations and intelligence sources, and available them by using standard programming interfaces through the web. With the increasing number of web services that provide similar functions, how to find appropriate web services for user requirements becomes more and more important [5]. User requirements include functional and non-functional requirement. Functional requirements specify the behavioral characteristics and non-functional requirements specify the quantitative characteristics. The selection of an atomic service is based on various quality of service (QoS) parameters. Services are ranked based on their QoS values and selection is done based on rank. One of the QoS ranking criteria is reputation factor. Availability and reliability are considered as predominant factors for computing reputation that analyze the probability of a service being up/running and the change in failure trend of that service respectively. Better estimation of QoS can be done with both factors considered together, whereas when taken separately for computing reputation, may not generate appropriate result. Let us consider the following scenario: Let there be two services S_A, S_B with $A_A = 0.8612$, $A_B = 0.8607$, $R_A = 0.6664$, $R_B = 0.7146$ as availability and reliability of S_A, S_B respectively. Now, if reputation is computed only on availability then service S_A would be the choice for selection and if reputation is computed only by comparing their reliability then service S_B will be selected. So, the study of the behavior of a service in terms of its availability and reliability over a sample space would provide better knowledge about its suitability for selection. In this paper to quantify the predominant factors of QoS, availability and reliability of atomic services use Markov Chain model and Weibull analysis respectively. In continue in section 2 the related work and in section 3 the proposed approach is presented. In section 4 the simulation and in section 5 the result of experiments is explained. Finally, in section 6 the general conclusion and in section 7 future work is presented.

RELATED WORK

Ranking of services and computing QoS is done in two ways: Ranking of atomic services and ranking of composite services. Most researches have focused on ranking composite services and pay less than the atomic services.

In [1] an approach for ranking atomic services using reputation factor for computing QoS is used. This approach suggests a mathematical modeling of factors availability and reliability of atomic services that using Markov Chain model and Weibull analysis respectively. Also reputation is modeled as an aggregation of availability and reliability factors, this composition is done by multiplication operation.

Research in the field of Web service composition based on QoS can be broadly put into two directions. One focuses on how various QoS attributes can be quantified for their effective use and the other focuses on their use at various stages of service selection or composition [1].

In the direction of quantification of QoS attributes a framework to model reputation based on user feedback is proposed. This approach uses past behavior of service providers and uses this knowledge to calculate reputation of a service. One thing that is worth considering here is that there could be a malicious user who could use a biased feedback to alter the reputation of the service, thus there is a need to include automated server side calculated attributes availability and reliability to give a precise estimate of reputation of service [1]. In [16] Feedback Forecasting Model is proposed that considers two major aspects during the rating process: First, to provide an automated feedback for customers who are fearful in giving feedback or do not bother to provide feedback. Second, to check what the feedback of a particular customer's credibility is. Here, user

rating is considered for computing reputation and implicit QoS attributes are not considered. In [28] authors have used both availability and reliability to compute the reputation of the service. However, both attributes are used separately and their combined effect is not studied. Since availability gives the probability of success and reliability gives the change is failure trend, both must be used collectively to compute the reputation of a service. In [29] authors have proposed probabilistic methods to quantify QoS attributes: Cost, Throughput and Time, and studied their aggregated effect on composite service. However, the quantification of QoS attributes Availability, Reliability and their collective effect to compute reputation are not studied.

In the direction of the use of QoS at selection and composition following works are considered. In [17] the Ontology Web Language for Service (OWL-S) is used to perform a functional match among the available services and then these services are rated according to their QoS scores, however, the methodology of calculating the QoS score is not mentioned. A Relaxable QoS-based Service Selection (RQSS) algorithm is proposed in [19] that created a composite service by using heuristic techniques like MMKP (Multi-Dimensional Multi Choice Knapsack). The work studies the composition process for a composite service based on QoS attributes: Execution Time, Reliability, Availability, Reputation and Price. Here, reputation is based on user feedback. Also the combined behavior of availability and reliability to calculate reputation is not considered.

The novelties of this research are first, a probabilistic model for quantifying two different QoS attributes and second, modeling the reputation of a service.

MODELING AND COMPOSITE QOS PARAMETERS TO APPROPRIATE WEB SERVICE SELECTION

To quantify the major factors of QoS availability and reliability of atomic services using Markov Chain model and Weibull analysis respectively and reputation is modeled as an aggregation availability and reliability.

Availability modeling

Markov Chain model is used to study systems that could be represented as discrete states.

Since service availability can have boolean discrete states we used Markov chain to model availability [1].

Service Availability is the probability that a service will be up and running. The main events that reflect status of service availability are the transition of a service from up to down state or down to up state. As an up/running service could fail due to any of these reasons like: server going down, hardware failure, internal logical error etc., these failure conditions are considered to a single down state [1].

Figure 1 depicts the state transitions for a service along with their transition probabilities. Value represents the transition probability of moving from state i to state j [1].

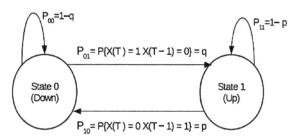

Fig. 1. Markov model for availability [1]

Where p value is the transition probability from state up to state down, means a service is failed because of told reasons and not available, and q value is the transition probability from state down to state up, means the fail service has been repaired and made available. All the transition probabilities could be represented in a form of Transition Probability Matrix (P) as follows [1]:

$$P = \begin{bmatrix} p_{00} & p_{01} \\ p_{10} & p_{11} \end{bmatrix} = \begin{bmatrix} (1-q) & q \\ p & (1-p) \end{bmatrix} \quad (1)$$

Entries of Matrix P (P_{ij}) correspond to the Markov Chain's single-path length transition probabilities. The row elements of matrix P correspond to states that the system currently in and column elements denote the next state. Current transition matrix gives the transition probability of a single-path length. For better estimate of transition probabilities paths of all the possible lengths are considered to obtain P^n matrix [1].

$$P^n = \begin{bmatrix} 1-q & q \\ p & 1-p \end{bmatrix}^n = \frac{1}{p+q}\begin{bmatrix} p & q \\ p & q \end{bmatrix} +$$

$$+ \frac{(1-p-q)^n}{p+q}\begin{bmatrix} q & -q \\ -p & p \end{bmatrix} \quad (2)$$

For sufficiently large values of 'n' the results are interpreted as long run averages or limiting probabilities 'P_i' of system being in state 'i'. In such cases P^n reduces to [1]:

$$\lim_{n \to \infty} P^n = \begin{bmatrix} \frac{p}{p+q} & \frac{q}{p+q} \\ \frac{p}{p+q} & \frac{q}{p+q} \end{bmatrix} \quad (3)$$

From above it is concluded that availability is the probability of moving from state 1 to again state 1 in a path-length n. Thus the availability of the system on the long run can be said as [1]:

$$Availability = P_{11}^n = \frac{q}{p+q} \quad (4)$$

Reliability modeling

Reliability of a service is the rate of change of a service failure under test. Various probabilistic distribution mechanisms are used to study reliability. In a realistic scenario services' failure rate can be increasing, decreasing, or constant. To accommodate all these cases Weibull analysis has been considered. The following assumptions are considered to model reliability: x = threshold for successful samples, n = sample space in a given time frame, $F(x)$ = failure rate and $R(x)$ = reliability [1].

Failure of a service is a rare event as it does not occur as frequently as the success event, thus it is Poisson distributed. In the following failure of an atomic service is modeled. Failure rate $F(x)$ and reliability $R(x)$ can be related by [1]:

$$F(x) = 1 - R(x) \quad (5)$$

where: $\qquad R(x) = e^{-\left[\frac{x}{\alpha}\right]^\beta}$

On simplification equation (5) can be written as:

$$ln\left[ln\left(\frac{1}{1-F(x)}\right)\right] = \beta(ln\,x) - \beta(ln\,\alpha) \quad (6)$$

Comparing parameters in Eq. (6) with that of straight line provides information that used to perform linear regression and this will provide the estimate for α and β for computing the reliability of an atomic service. α parameter is the Weibull Characteristic Life and is a measure of spread in the distribution and β is the Shape Parameter that determine the nature of failure rate. In general failure rate of an atomic service S_i is represented as [1]:

$$FailureRate(S_i) = \begin{cases} increasing, if\ \beta > 1.0 \\ constant, if\ \beta = 1.0 \\ decreasing, if\ \beta < 1.0 \end{cases} \quad (7)$$

Reputation modeling

Reputation is modeled as a composite QoS attribute comprising both availability and reliability.

$$Reputation(S_i) = \min(Availability(S_i), Reliability(S_i)) \quad (8)$$

To composite QoS parameters another method is used, as multiplying availability and reliability parameters. But the reason of using new method of minimum operation is that the availability and reliability values are in range [0, 1] and product of two numbers that smaller than 1, will be very small, so the computed reputation value will be less than the value of minimum parameters means availability or reliability. Thus, it may be an appropriate service but not selected because of low reputation. But by computing reputation by using minimum operation, the obtained reputation value will not be lower than the minimum value of availability and reliability parameters and we have services with more reputation values. So services with more appropriate reputation will be selected.

SIMULATION

CPNTools is used for the simulation. This section is divided into two sub-sections:
1) input data,
2) simulation details.

Input data

In order to compute the QoS parameters, availability, reliability and reputation need to be counted. Failure count signifies the number of samples for which the service is found to be down and not responding. As the event of service going down is a rare event, thus a Poisson distribution is taken to model failure count. In this simulation is considered the acceptable failure count for an atomic service to be 10% of sample space. Such pattern of failure data is Poisson distributed with $mean(\mu)$ = 10% of sample space, such that the distribution generates 75% values in interval of $\mu \pm \delta$. Usage cost, another input data, signifies the cost that a user pays for a service. The usage cost of functionally same services generally lies in a range and thus uniformly distributed over that range.

Simulation details

The nets used in this simulation are depicted in Figures 2 – 4. Figure 2 represents the overall architecture of this approach in form of a hierarchical CPN. All the samples of all the services are taken as input for calculating availability and reliability. On the basis of Eq. (8) the net computes reputation of the selected service which lies in range [0, 1] with the name of *Reputation2*. Also this net computes the reputation of a service based on another type of reputation composite formula that is used for multiplication of parameters with the name of Reputation1 that continues to compare these results.

Figure 3 illustrates the process of computing availability. It takes all the samples of all the services as input and computes availability of one atomic service at a time. Availability for each atomic service is computed by dividing the sum of failure count with the total number of samples. One result token is generated for every atomic service reflecting its availability in the range [0, 1]. A value in this range represents the probability of a service being up/running.

Figure 4 illustrates reliability of computation process. Samples of a selected service forms the input of the subnet. Linear regression is performed on these samples to evaluate regression parameters S_x, S_{xx}, S_y, S_{yy}, S_{xy}. Applying Weibull analysis on regression parameters reliability is computed in the range [0, 1]. Here, the numeric value of reliability signifies the success trend, i.e. higher reliability value is higher success rate. the result also evaluates the Weibull shape parameter

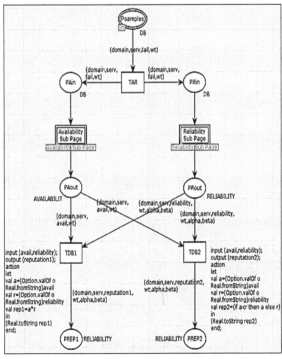

Fig. 2. Reputation modeling

β that represents failure trend. Figure 5 illustrates various colorsets used in creating the CPN nets for availability, reliability and reputation.

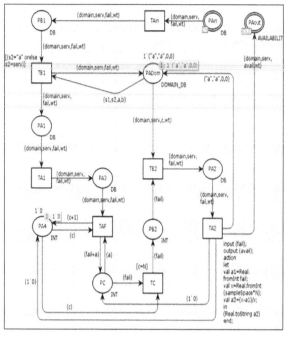

Fig. 3. Availability modeling

EVALUATION RESULTS

A series of experiments is performed to evaluate effectiveness, performance and feasibility of the proposed system. To study the QoS parameters, 20 functionally equivalent services are chosen for our experiment. The usage cost of these services is uniformly distributed in range [10, 40]. The failure count of each service is Poisson distributed with of sample space. QoS parameters of services are studied for these samples.

Figure 6 illustrates modeling reputation based composite QoS. In this figure the reputation value is compared based on computation in several ways: by using availability and reliability parameters individually, by using the first composite formula [1] means multiplication of parameters, and also by using the second composite formula means minimum of parameters. If reputation is taken only on availability then service has highest reputation, and if based only on reliability then service has highest reputation. So, when these parameters are taken individually different estimates of reputation are generated. If reputation computes based on the first composite formula,

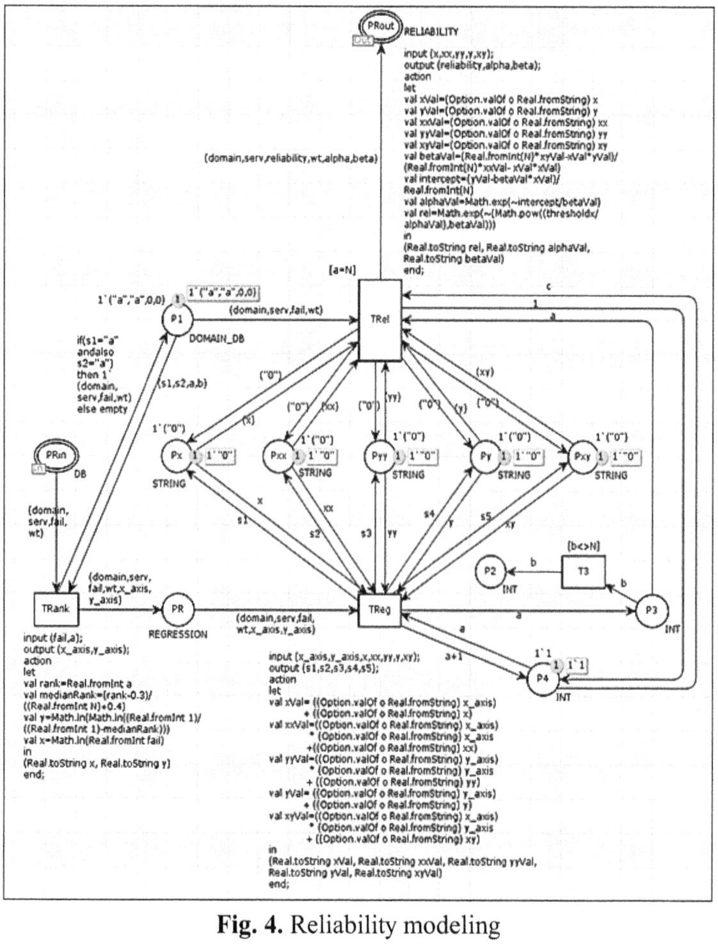

Fig. 4. Reliability modeling

```
▾Declarations
 ▸Standard priorities
 ▾Standard declarations
  ▾colset UNIT = unit;
  ▾colset INT = int;
  ▾colset BOOL = bool;
  ▾colset STRING = string;
  ▾colset SERV_TYPE=product STRING*STRING;
  ▾colset DOMAIN_DB=product STRING*STRING*INT*INT;
  ▾colset DB=product STRING*STRING*INT*INT timed;
  ▾colset AVAILABILIT=product STRING*STRING*
    STRING*INT timed;
  ▾colset REGRESSION=product STRING*STRING*INT*
    INT*STRING*STRING;
  ▾colset RELIABILITY=product STRING*STRING*
    STRING*INT*STRING*STRING timed;
  ▾var count,wt,totalWT,fail,a,b,c,listLen,totalWT1:INT;
  ▾var serv_type:SERV_TYPE;
  ▾var domain,serv,reliability,reputation1,reputation2,alpha,beta,
    s1,s2,s3,s4,s5,avail,x_axis,y_axis,x,xx,yy,y,xy,
    selfFactor,snf,totalRep,snf1,totalRep1:STRING;
  ▾val N=3;
  ▾val fail_count=133.0;
  ▾val sampleSpace=1440;
  ▾val thresholdx=1307.0;
  ▾val hullRep=3;
  ▾val domainCount=6;
```

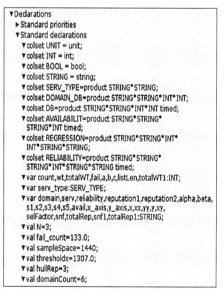

Fig. 5. CPN declarations

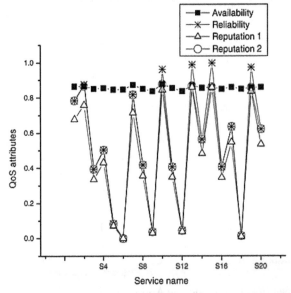

Fig. 6. Reputation based composite QoS

Table 1. Availability, reliability and reputation values

	Cost	Reputation1	Reputation2
S1	11	0.6802	0.7858
S2	15	0.7627	0.8681
S3	17	0.3371	0.3953
S4	34	0.4326	0.5046
S5	22	0.0699	0.0824
S6	12	0.0000	0.0000
S7	32	0.7174	0.8199
S8	37	0.3570	0.4187
S9	36	0.0306	0.0365
S10	31	0.8475	0.8798
S11	14	0.3500	0.4082
S12	13	0.0375	0.0447
S13	28	0.8644	0.8728
S14	19	0.4848	0.5646
S15	26	0.8608	0.8610
S16	21	0.3475	0.4081
S17	20	0.5486	0.6363
S18	33	0.0109	0.0129
S19	24	0.8395	0.8610
S20	30	0.5374	0.6234

service has highest reputation, what that illustrates the combined effect of availability (probability of service being up/running) and reliability (failure trend of service), and gives a precise estimate of service reputation.

Reputation computing based on the second composite formula reputation value is improved in comparison to the first one. Because by computing the reputation based on the first composite formula the availability and reliability values are in the range [0, 1] and product of two numbers that smaller than 1, will be very small, so the computed reputation value will be less than the value of minimum parameters means availability or reliability. Thus it may be an appropriate service but not selected because of low reputation. But by computing reputation by using second composite formula, obtained reputation value will not be less than the minimum value of availability and reliability parameters and we have services with more reputation values. So services with more appropriate reputation will be selected. In this case service will have highest reputation.

Table 1 illustrates the values of availability, reliability, first type of reputation and second type of reputation. By comparing the values of first and second type of reputation, we can realize that the reputation is improved substantially.

Figure 7 illustrates the suitability of this proposed system from business perspective means usage cost than reputation. Generally a high reputation is considered to have high usage cost. But by using this approach there are services with high reputation and lower usage cost. Such a

service with highest reputation has a relatively lower usage cost '31'.

Table 2 illustrates usage cost of each service and its reputation based on first and second type of formula. Thus, with prior usage cost we have services with higher reputation.

CONCLUSION

Web service reputation is an important parameter in QoS based web service selection. Selecting atomic services with high reputation helps creating robust, high performance, and cost ef-

Table 2. Usage cost and Reputation values

	Cost	Reputation1	Reputation2
S1	11	0.6802	0.7858
S2	15	0.7627	0.8681
S3	17	0.3371	0.3953
S4	34	0.4326	0.5046
S5	22	0.0699	0.0824
S6	12	0.0000	0.0000
S7	32	0.7174	0.8199
S8	37	0.3570	0.4187
S9	36	0.0306	0.0365
S10	31	0.8475	0.8798
S11	14	0.3500	0.4082
S12	13	0.0375	0.0447
S13	28	0.8644	0.8728
S14	19	0.4848	0.5646
S15	26	0.8608	0.8610
S16	21	0.3475	0.4081
S17	20	0.5486	0.6363
S18	33	0.0109	0.0129
S19	24	0.8395	0.8610
S20	30	0.5374	0.6234

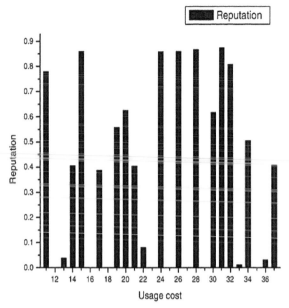

Fig. 7. Usage cost versus reputation

fective composite services. Availability focuses on probability of a service being up/running and reliability computes the failure trend of service. An appropriate composition of both factors, additionally giving a precise estimate of reputation, is resulted in selection of a service with high reputation and lower usage cost. Using these factors individually or inappropriate composition generates high reputation and high usage cost.

REFERENCES

1. Singh R.P., Pattanaik K.K. An approach to composite QoS parameter based web service selection. The 4th International Conference on Ambient Systems, Networks and Technologies ANT 2013. Procedia Computer Science 19, 2013, 470–477.

2. Rajeswari M., Sambasivam G., Balaji N., Basha M.S.S., Vengattaraman T., Dhavachelvan P. Appraisal and analysis on various web service composition approaches based on QoS factors. Journal of King Saud University – Computer and Information Sciences 26, 2014, 143–152.

3. Rostami M., Mohamadi M., Yaghoubi F., Nikrouz M. A proposed model for the standardization of web services discovery results using static and dynamic parameters. First National Conference on Electrical and Computer South of Iran, Khurmuj, 2013.

4. Mohammadi N., Mohsenzadeh M., Dezful M.A. Service discovery based on QoS parameters and service reputation. 3rd Iranian Conference on Electrical and Electronics Engineering, ICEEE 2011.

5. Parsa S., Aqdasinia H. An extensible quantitative model for the dynamic web services discovery. 16th Iranian Conference on Electrical and Electronics Engineering, ICEEE 2008.

6. Khoshtarash A., Kheirkhah I., Jahan M.V. Evaluation and comparison of web service discovery and selection methods by syntactic and semantic procedures. 1st National Conference on Applications of Intelligent Systems (Soft Computing) in Science and Technology, Islamic Azad Univercity of Quchan Branch, 4-5 March, 2013.

7. Rostami M., Malazizi L., Dejdar S. Provide a protocol to ensure reliable messaging between web services. 2nd Conference on Computer, IT, Electrical and Electronic Engineering 2012.

8. Khoshtarash A., Mahmoudzadeh M., Abedini T., Mohammadzadeh J., Rahmanian S. An efficient ranking model based on qos for web service selection with consideration of user requirements. 1st National Conference on Applications of Intelligent Systems (Soft Computing) in Science and Technology, Islamic Azad Univercity of Quchan Branch, 4-5 March, 2013.

9. Nayerifard T., Jobbehdari S., Modiri N. Web services security, review the latest guidelines. The First National Conference on New Approaches in Computer Engineering and Information Retrieval, Iran, 2013.

10. Khoshtarash A., Kheirkhah I., Jahan M.V. Evaluation of ranking methods for discovery and selection of optimum web service. 1st National Conference on Applications of Intelligent Systems (Soft Computing) in Science and Technology, Islamic Azad Univercity of Quchan Branch, 4-5, March, 2013.

11. Banks J., Carson J., Discrete event simulation systems. Sharif University.

12. Law A.M., Kelton W.D. Simulation modeling and analysis. McGraw Hill, 2000.

13. Abernethy R.B. The weibull analysis handbook. 5nd ed., Robert B. Abernethy, Florida 2006.

14. Scholz F. Weibull reliability analysis. FWS 5, 2002, 21-23.

15. Coles S. An introduction to statistical modeling of extreme values. Springer Verlag, 2001.

16. Al-Sharawneh J., Williams M.A., Goldbaum D. Web service reputation prediction based on customer feedback forecasting model. 14th IEEE International Enterprise Distributed Object Computing Conference Workshops 2010, 33–40.

17. Benaboud R., Maamri R., Sahnoun Z.. Towards scalability of reputation and qos based web services discovery using agents and ontologies. Proceedings of the 13th International Conference on Information Integration and Web-based Applications and Services, ACM, 2011, 262–269.

18. Martin D., Burstein M., Hobbs J., Lassila O., McDermott D., McIlraithm S. OWL-S: semantic markup for web services. Aug 6, 2011.

19. Chia-Feng Lin, Ruey-Kai Sheu, Yue-Shan Chang, Shyan-Ming Yuan. A relaxable service selection algorithm for QoS-based web service composition. Information and Software Technology 53(12), 2011, 1370–1381.

20. Esfahani P.M., Broumandnia A. Clustering web services based on the qualitative features. The First National Conference on New Approaches in Computer Engineering and Information Retrieval, Iran, 2013.

21. Giallonardo E., Zimeo E. More semantics in QoS matching. Proceedings of the IEEE International Conference on Service-Oriented Computing and Applications, Newport Beach, CA, 2007, 163–171.

22. Sha L., A QoS based Web service selection model. Proceedings of the International Forum on Information Technology and Applications, Chengdu, 2009, 353–356.

23. Yan J., Piao J., Towards QoS-based web service discovery. Proceedings of the International Conference on Service Oriented Computing, Sydney, 2009, 200–210.

24. Chifu V.R., Salomie I., Dinsoreanu M., David T., Acretoaie V. Ant-inspired technique for automatic web service composition and selection. 12th International Symposium on Symbolic and Numeric Algorithms for Scientific Computing, 2010.

25. Kossmann D., Borzsony S., Stocker K. The skyline operator. Proceedings of the 17th International Conference on Data Engineering, Heidelberg, 2001, 421–430.

26. Skoutas D., Sacharidis D., Simitsis A., Sellis T. Ranking and clustering web services using multicriteria dominance relationships. IEEE Transactions on Services Computing, 3(3), 2012, 163–177.

27. Mahdavi F., Motameni H., Momeni H. Automatic generation of web services based on genetic-fuzzy approach. First National Innovation Conference on Computer Engineering and Information Technology, Tonekabon, Iran, 2013.

28. Janardhan D.B., Devane S.R.. Web service reputation-based search agent. IEEE Student Conference on Research and Development (SCOReD) 2009, 184–187.

29. Zheng H., Yang J., Zhao W. Probability distribution-based QoS analysis for web service composition. [In:] Dickson Chiu et al. (eds.) Web Information Systems Engineering WISE 2010 Workshops, Lecture Notes in Computer Science, 6724, 98111, 2011.

5

MEMBRAIN NEURAL NETWORK FOR VISUAL PATTERN RECOGNITION

Artur Popko[1], Marek Jakubowski[2], Rafał Wawer[3]

[1] Fundamentals of Technology Faculty, Lublin University of Technology, ul. Nadbystrzycka 38, 20-618 Lublin, Poland, e-mail: a.popko@pollub.pl

[2] Management Faculty, Lublin University of Technology, ul. Nadbystrzycka 38, 20-618 Lublin, Poland, e-mail: m.jakubowski@pollub.pl

[3] University of Maria Curie Sklodowska, Multimedia Communications Lab. 20-011 Lublin ul. Narutowicza 12, Poland, e-mail: rafal.wawer@poczta.umcs.lublin.pl

ABSTRACT

Recognition of visual patterns is one of significant applications of Artificial Neural Networks, which partially emulate human thinking in the domain of artificial intelligence. In the paper, a simplified neural approach to recognition of visual patterns is portrayed and discussed. This paper is dedicated for investigators in visual patterns recognition, Artificial Neural Networking and related disciplines. The document describes also MemBrain application environment as a powerful and easy to use neural networks' editor and simulator supporting ANN.

Keywords: Neural Network, pattern recognition, neuron model.

INTRODUCTION

Artificial Neural Networks (ANN) have been successfully employed in many applications of visual pattern recognition. Application areas include system identification and control (vehicle control, process control, natural resources management), quantum chemistry [1], game-playing and decision making (backgammon, chess, poker), pattern recognition (radar systems, face identification, object recognition and more), sequence recognition (gesture, speech, handwritten text recognition), medical diagnosis, financial applications (automated trading systems), data mining (or Knowledge Discovery in Databases – KDD), visualization and e-mail spam filtering.

ANN deals with recognition and classification of characters from an image, especially in Optical Character Recognition. For the recognition to be accurate, certain topological and geometrical properties are calculated, based on which a character is classified and recognized [2].

A given pattern, its recognition/classification may consist of one of the following two tasks:

1) supervised classification (e.g., discriminant analysis) in which the input pattern is identified as a member of a predefined class,
2) unsupervised classification (e.g., clustering) in which the pattern is assigned to a hitherto unknown class [3, 4].

MemBrain is a neural network editor and simulator supporting neural networks of arbitrary size and architecture [5].

MEMBRAIN ARTIFICIAL NEURON NETWORK

The neuron and link model of MemBrain is very flexible: everything from simple time invariant Feed-Forward Networks to Nets with spiking neurons, arbitrary loopback connections and signal runtime delays on the links can be simulated. It is even possible to connect directly the output of a neuron to its own input. In principle, every net in MemBrain is a valid net. Through the consequent object-oriented approach every neuron and also every link in MemBrain can have different properties. Links can have user-defined logical lengths, so that real runtime behaviour can be simulated and visualized. The following learning algorithms are implemented in MemBrain. Supervised learning: Standard Backpropagation (only forward links are trained), Standard Backpropagation with momentum (only forward links are trained), Backpropagation with support for loopback links, Backpropagation with support for loopback links and with momentum, RPROP (Resilient Backpropagation) with support for loopback links, Cascade Correlation with support for loopback links (using Backpropagation with momentum), Cascade Correlation with support for loopback links (using RPROP), Trial and Error with support for loopback links. Unsupervised learning: Winner Takes it All for SOMs (Self Organizing Maps)

The aim of this paper was to determine and optimize the structure of neural network built to recognize six visual patterns (O, X, −, |, /, \). A required structure of Artificial Neural Network (Figure 1) was created in MemBrain application

environment. Vectors of input and output data were generated with help of "lesson editor" tool (Figure 2). A sample of one pattern visualization was presented in Figure 3. Training algorithm - Standard Back Propagation was enabled and Target Net Error was established for value equal 0.01 (Figure 4). In order to achieve proper results during teaching the net has to be randomized before undergoing the first teaching process. Randomizing a net means that all the link weights and the neuron activation thresholds are initialized with small random values (unless the corresponding link or neuron properties are locked). The next stage of the research was to test the networks with the amount of 3–14 neurons in the hidden layer. The results are shown in Figures 5–16. Better result are obtained when the neural network requires less training.

Hidden layer neurons are the neurons that are between the input layer and the output layer. These neurons are typically hidden from view, and their number and organization can typically be treated

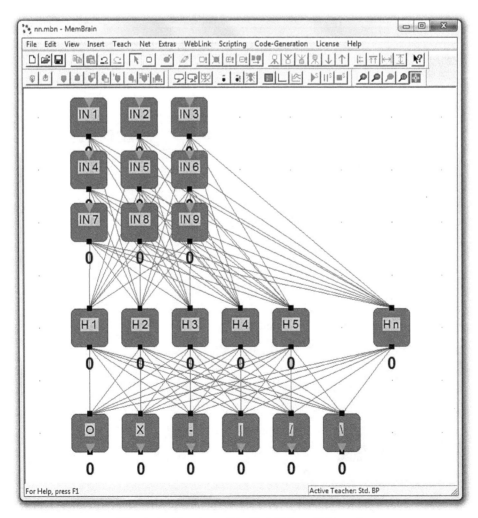

Fig. 1. Architecture of Artificial Neural Network

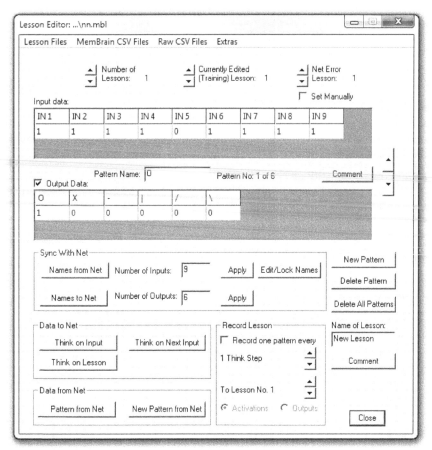

Fig. 2. View of "Lesson Editor" tool

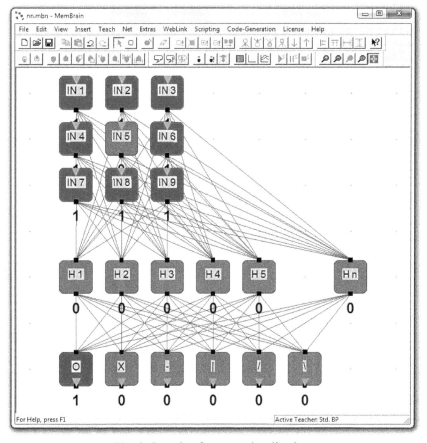

Fig. 3. Sample of pattern visualization

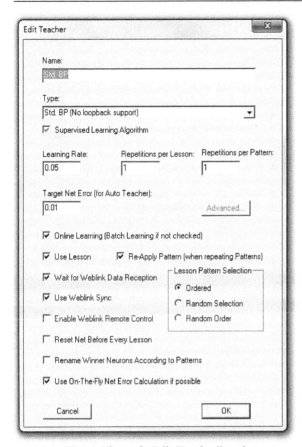

Fig. 4. View of "Edit Teacher" tool

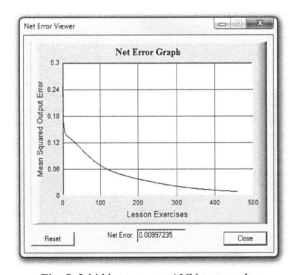

Fig. 5. 3-hidden neurons ANN test results

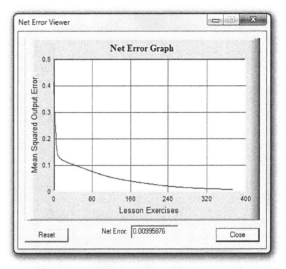

Fig. 6. 4-hidden neurons ANN test results

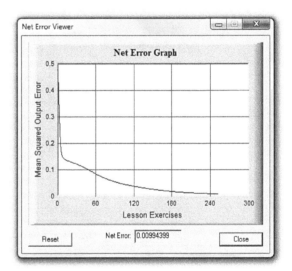

Fig. 7. 5-hidden neurons ANN test results

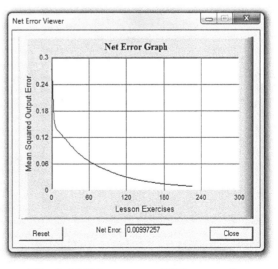

Fig. 8. 6-hidden neurons ANN test results

as a "black box". Using additional layers of hidden neurons enables greater processing power and system flexibility. This additional flexibility comes at the cost of additional complexity in the training algorithm. Having too few hidden neurons can prevent the system from properly fitting the input data, and reduces the robustness of the system. Having too many hidden neurons, the system is over specified, and is incapable of generalization.

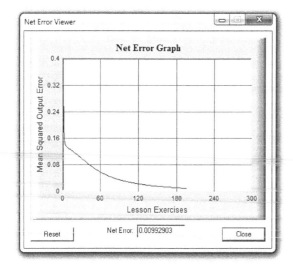

Fig. 9. 7-hidden neurons ANN test results

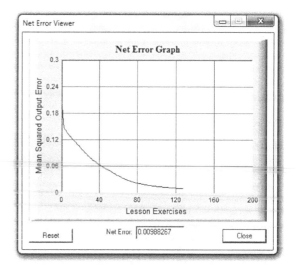

Fig. 12. 10-hidden neurons ANN test results

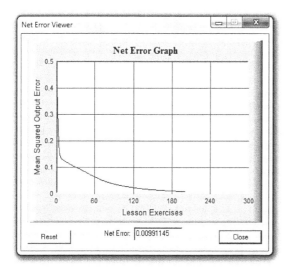

Fig. 10. 8-hidden neurons ANN test results

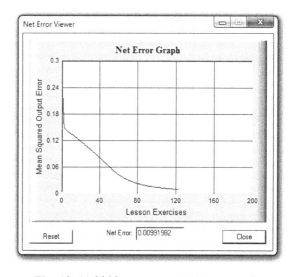

Fig. 13. 11-hidden neurons ANN test results

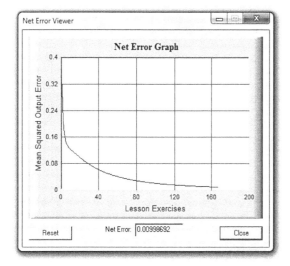

Fig. 11. 9-hidden neurons ANN test results

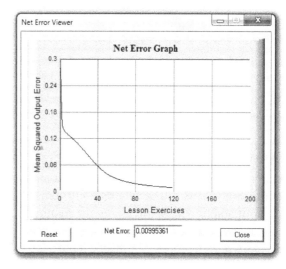

Fig. 14. 12-hidden neurons ANN test results

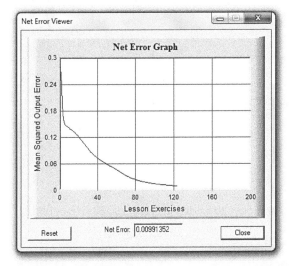

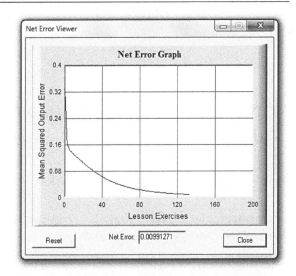

Fig. 15. 13-hidden neurons ANN test results   **Fig. 16.** 14-hidden neurons ANN test results

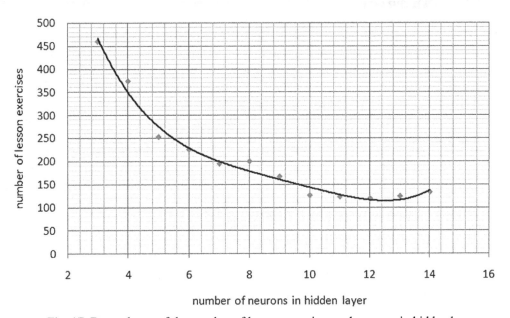

Fig. 17. Dependence of the number of lesson exercises and neurons in hidden layer

The final resulting dependence of number of lesson exercises and number of neurons in hidden layer is shown in Figure 17.

CONCLUSIONS

Most effective architecture of tested ANN consist of 12 neurons in a hidden layer. The number of lesson exercises in this case was smallest and was equal 119. The constructed and tested neural network recognizes visual patterns without errors. MemBrain is a powerful and easy to use neural network editor and simulator supporting neural networks of arbitrary size and architecture, it can be also very helpful in teaching in Artificial Neural Networks.

REFERENCES

1. Balabin R.M., Lomakina E.I.: Neural network approach to quantum-chemistry data: Accurate prediction of density functional theory energies. J. Chem. Phys., 131(7), 2009: 74-104.
2. Shrivastava V., Sharma N.: Artificial Neural Network Based Optical Character Recognition. Signal & Image Processing. An International Journal (SIPIJ), 3(5), 2012.
3. Basu J. K., Bhattacharyya D., Kim T.: Use of Artificial Neural Network in Pattern Recognition. International Journal of Software Engineering and Its Applications, 4(2), 2010.
4. Dung L., Mizukawa M.: Designing a Pattern Recognition Neural Network with a Reject Output and Many Sets of Weights and Biases. Pattern Recognition Techniques, Technology and Applications, 2008.
5. http://www.membrain-nn.de/english/details_en.htm (May 2013).

6

FUNCTIONS OF THE IMAGE IN SHAPING THE TECHNICAL THINKING OF STUDENTS

Mariusz Śniadkowski[1], Agnieszka Jankowska[2]

[1] Fundamentals of Technology Faculty, Lublin University of Technology, 38 Nadbystrzycka Str., 20-618 Lublin, Poland, e-mail: m.sniadkowski@pollub.pl

[2] Student of Lublin University of Technology, e-mail: aga.jankowska89@wp.pl

ABSTRACT

The world of technology can be a tool to support development processes, primarily cognitive, emotional and motivational. Adoption issues shaping the image function in the technical thinking of students is justified in many ways: a – impact on the development of human image; b – multidimensional image and diversity of its media resources; c – the influence of the image on shaping the attitudes and behaviors of education; d – state of research on the evolution of technical thinking of youth. Development of the technical thinking is one of the objectives in the process of technical education. A picture taking part in it by building concepts and technical imagination fulfilling a significant role in the illustration and understanding of issues and technical products and the specific technical action. Technical education requires from teachers to enter a wide range of activities in the teaching process in the direction of the effective application and the use of image in the development of technical thinking and imagination of students. Pictures have a prominent role here.

Keywords: education, technical thinking, technical training.

"SPEECH" OF THE IMAGE

Direct sensory experience consists of abstract sensations, for each visible image. A human is the only being who perpetuates things visually and has a meaning for them. When any of these items is restrict or even completely eliminate, it brings to the impoverishment of communication. Metaphorical image and essence consist in putting a particular subject in a particular material using a mold, which not only serves as a measure of representation, but also retains some value independently and is subject to its own laws.

An image, according to its genus and species, comprises a layer of sensory experience, which appears on the background layer of meaning. If it has some content it may appear in the ideas that are usually carried of particular momentous of human values. We mean a `layer of appearance, sensory perceptions, and meanings. In terms of aesthetics, there are three systems of representation because of the perception: representation of the iconic, symbolic and enactive. The first representation arises as a result of "selective organization insights and perceptions in terms of time and space", and creates a "pictorial equivalent of things and events". Symbolic representation subordinates these images' representation of the world through a linguistic code. Language code is a "way of creating experiences and transform it". The result of this translation is an enactive representation, which allows you to define events through patterns of actions that cause it, other owls is a bridge that transition from knowledge to action [11].

Psychology refers to aesthetic experiences as those reflecting feelings and attitude to objects, situations and processes, which primary feature the beauty and property. The aesthetic emotions are triggered by the beauty of nature, architecture, man, but also for many everyday objects that "suddenly and unexpectedly reveal its beauty"

[10]. The aesthetic experience according to this definition is associated with a spontaneous reaction, which is not due to the competence of the object as experienced, is the emotional expression of admiration for its unique beauty.

For specific feature of the aesthetic experiences are considered portraying things unique, concealed, unknown or unusual experienced in special emotional stress. Particularly active in the sense of illumination is a sight. Floodlights survival has a physical basis, occurring with the beauty of nature, the beauty of man or works of such, for example art or technique. In the experience caused by illumination comes to the perception of new properties of things and seeing them in a new light. Novelty of these observations makes the vision continues for some time even after the resignation of incentives that stimulate the senses. This is the time in which the entity caused the need to understand their meanings, intensely guess rediscovered meanings in reflective activity [7].

Pedagogy contrast uses the aesthetic experiences in implementing many of its educational goals. The effect of parental or educational image is dependent on the intensity of personal experience, energized by a certain type of experience or action. This experience is not limited to a passive perception, it must be an expression of a deeper, include the contents of human experience [14].

In the process of image perception the aesthetic experience is very important having the character of personal experience. The fact that each image can interact aesthetically, is due to human imagination. If something has to work it must be made knowingly, with the intent to act in a certain way to imagination and guided people in a new direction [7].

A characteristic feature of the image is a kind of speech quality, under which the entire contents of the work fully and explicitly included in a specially shaped mold. Picture, although shows us a known world , it affects the recipient differently than in real life. Its qualitative expression forces reflection and makes us see previously invisible relevant aspects.

For the picture to be clear and have an educational need, it is important to be accessible accessible. Generally speaking, the sharing of works can be reduced to three methods. The first consists in communicating their own experience and aesthetic judgment to others on the unwitting recipient of a joint analysis of the structure

of the work, the administration of its explanations of the history of art and the exchange of feelings and sensations associated with the reception of the image. The second method is to create people who have this passion and predisposition conditions to create their own forms of imaging techniques (drawing, painting, video, etc...), which is exploring the nature and shape of the pieces by their own artistic activity. And the third method is to study the development of contemporary visual culture, participating in exhibitions, events or performance, the subject and object is the body of the performer in a specific context of time, space and their own limitations. Educational activities undertaken within making accessible arts are essential to the effectiveness of education through art image.

Modern man is different than a man of previous eras. Mass media and the development of new technologies have blurred the difference between the natural world and the world of illusion,; men lives among the images they created , at least at this stage, what in the world of nature. This entails the danger of moving into the world of images without checking whether or not we can understand that world which is created just for the recipient. Therefore, the duty of the educator is to adapt the process of education according to the principle of gradation of difficulty with the help of images. At the very beginning there were feelings of affirming the established order of the world, in all aesthetic, moral, and cognitive terms. Only when the recipient is mature enough to understand more complex representations of reality, we can turn on the educational process work harder in perception, images that raise questions, express concerns, and show the drama of human life [15].

THE IMAGE AS AN EDUCATIONAL TOOL

Culture of the image especially in today's media suggests that we live in a world dominated by the transfer of information through images. The image plays an increasingly important role in the transmission of a variety of content; it is an integral part of telegrams with layers of linguistic and nonlinguistic, which implies acceptance of it as a very important means of communication [13]. The image is one of the most natural remedies which we refer to when we experience difficulties in receiving, understanding and assimilation of verbal information. The easiness of transition from one code to another, and their complementarily demonstrates the positive role of the image in learning verbal material.

The image in education is part of a set of tools for supporting teaching and education, and improves work efficiency. The role of technology in the education process and the challenges around us actually cause the need for more dynamic processes of adapting the education system to the needs posed especially by civilization and modern information society. Thanks to information technology, an image became the main carrier of information and communication as well as a tool for learning and student's intellectual work. Hence, the formation of the information age implies a change in the teaching and implementation of the educational process [5].

Various technical means and technologies are used to optimize educational processes. Computer-aided teaching, which is in fact based on images, has become a reality. Computer and the Internet are two basic passwords and directions of the contemporary use of information technology in education. We should pay attention to the infrastructure supporting science and the potential of information technology for use in the modern school. Materials and visual texts can be regarded as an important part of the education process, as they provide both existing communication standards, shaping attitudes towards the objects of the social world and the physical, aesthetic sensitivity affect consumers and become the basis for constructing collective representations of reality and their naturalization as the only and validated by knowledge of the world [9].

Information technology, information, communication and media used in education consist of educational technology. Largely based on the image, they create conditions for learners to build knowledge and provide a set of cognitive tools. Illustration arouses feelings of aesthetic, curious, easily introduces the topic, and makes learning more enjoyable [1]. The aim of education should be creating a model of education that will allow the young receiver function iconosphere. The inclusion in the model complex relationships between word and image in the communications of various functions, various images and discourses is essential.

Because of its common receiving widespread superficial attention to reading the information,

without having to be in the relationship between the objects placed on the transmission of pictorial, without taking into account the structure of the verbal acceptance – imaging, without reflection on the deeper meaning of speech.

THE ESSENCE OF THE TECHNICAL THINKING

The technical thinking as an intellectual process is conceptually-imaginative [3]. Thinking is a process integrated conceptually, based on the material-pictorial, and not only pictorial or conceptual layer, although the conceptual component and the imaginary component is involved in the thought process, and sometimes emphasizes one or the other aspect that sets the tone for the whole thinking or phase [6]. The role of the imagination in the process of understanding in terms of technical products used in those rights and principles is significant. Comprehension is an aspect of the technical thinking and the guarantor of success in technical action [3]. Technical action creates a large number of situations that modify the course and structure of thinking while solving specific tasks. We can also indicate the variety and types of thought process: theoretical and practical thinking, concrete and abstract, reconstructive and creative.

The technical thinking, due to the particularity of the object of thought allows extracting typical types:

- practical thinking, in which mental operations take place in the course of action on the real object;
- graphic thinking (drawing- technical) in which mental operations take place on the basis of a graphic image of the technical structure;
- imaginative thinking, in which mental operations take place entirely in the plane of imagination and rely on imaginative representation of technical structures;
- conceptual thinking, in which the base for mental operations are primarily words and descriptions [3].

These types of the technical thinking are merely intellectual diversity of operations when solving specific technical tasks. They are characterized by a hierarchy of abstractness. The first step is the drawing and the related graphical thinking, the second stage is based on imaginative thinking patterns, and third grade is conceptual thinking imaginatively based on models – conceptual. All of them are intertwined when thinking in terms of technical precision in the creative process. Components of thinking include: knowledge, experience and aptitude, and these are associated with specific person.

Thus, the development of technical thinking in the first place needs to be personalities to shape the student. In the process of personality formation, it is essential to pay attention to:

- shaping research attitudes – seeking qualities of things, activities, and events, while waking interests of the society, nature and technology;
- shaping diagnostic attitudes – identifying the causes of the effects observed, and analyze properties and values of things, actions and phenomena;
- shaping organization attitudes – self-organization of the executive work;
- development of creative attitude – to show creativity in solving problems in the operation;
- shaping the moral and social attitude – an element of the whole, which is the collective

Students learn to behave responsibly in action;

- shaping the aesthetic attitude – it develops when students keep order in the workplace, respect the order of behavioral operations, care about the figment aesthetics.

These tasks and tasks of the technical thinking draw attention to the functions of the image in the educational process. Pilot studies among students of Lublin Technology University indicate the importance of image in the educational process, especially the media materials (and visuals).

IMAGE FUNCTIONS IN THE LEARNING PROCESS

From the literature we know that visuals and especially the media have a variety of impacts on students [2, 12]. Preliminary studies conducted among the students of the Technical University of Lublin suggests that in the process of the technical thinking students can indicate cognitive function, activating information and practical visual materials.

Cognitive function

It is to bring the learner to the analyzed reality. It occurs during the process of learning and memorizing the learning material for synthetic imaging and sound representation of the subject matter. The use of an appropriate image, which forces to think and search for solutions, improves the quality, speed and accuracy of remembering the contents. It helps to extract and organize messages more accurately and effectively apply them in practice.

The information function

This feature is reflected in the rapid and accurate transmission of messages through images. Information which is provided in a multi sensory manner is easier and more durably adopted by the students. Showing the application of laws and theories in practice, patterns, implementation of technical activities is expected by students.

The activating function

This function is activating learning through curiosity and interest. Moreover, it has an influence on the development of perception, imagination and triggers thought processes. The use of the device and media content at the right time of the learning process gives a keen interest in the subject of knowledge, implies a positive motives and curiosity and the desire and willingness to learn about technical issues.

The practical

Many types of teaching materials used in the educational process of students affect opinion and encourage the search for practical solutions and applications, and the ability to think creatively. The use of images makes it easy to reference and comment on the specific technical situation, it is helpful during observations and exercises conducted in the studios, performed work and professional practice.

Isolated above features are essential for the respondents. Preliminary studies indicate the use of the image in the learning process is highly required. In the process of forming an image meets the technical thinking – a basic function, an open issue is the practical use and teaching implications.

CONCLUSIONS

Shaping the technical thinking is a complex issue. In the process the image takes part in building concepts and ideas.. In students' opinions images play primarily the following functions: cognitive, information, activating and practical. Theoretical and practical approach requires their use in the learning process, so as to assist the student in technical thinking.

An important issue is the development of the use of the image projected achievements in shaping the technical thinking and methods of measurement. One of the tasks is to prepare teachers towards effective application and the use of image. Therefore, the task of the University is to provide necessary materials, aids and equipment. Adoption of the above tasks will allow teachers to have more effective educational work.

The undertaken research does not close the research field. It opens the possibility of testing for, barriers and effects of shaping technical thinking of students and the use of video as a teaching oriented towards post conventional level.

REFERENCES

1. Arnheim R.: Sztuka i percepcja wzrokowa. Słowo-Obraz-Terytoria, Gdańsk 2005.

2. Berezowski E., Długoszowa J.: Techniczne środki nauczania. Warszawa 1973.

3. Franus E.: Myślenie techniczne. Wrocław-Warszawa-Kraków-Gdańsk 1978.

4. Furmanek W.: Jutro edukacji technicznej. Rzeszów 2007.

5. Gejdoš M.: Kultura szkoły jako wartość szkolnej wspólnoty. [W:] Zborník materiálov z medzinárodnej vedeckej konferencie. Češrnivci. Zelena Bukovina 2008.

6. Gejdoš M.: Vplyv prostredia výchovy na integrálny rozvoj dieťaťa. [In:] Dialog Europa XXI, 16 (3-4), 2006.

7. Lach-Rosocha: Pedagogika przeżycia estetycznego. Wychowanie człowieka jako osoby. Kraków 2003, 88–89.

8. Nazar J.: Kształtowanie zainteresowań technicznych dzieci i młodzieży. Warszawa 1975.

9. Ogonowska A.: Przemoc ikoniczna. Kraków 2004.

10. Przetacznikowa M., Makiełło-Jarża G.: Psychologia ogólna. Warszawa 1975.

11. Siuta J. (red.): Słownik psychologii. Kraków 2005.

12. Strykowski W.: Audiowizualne materiały dydaktyczne. Warszawa 1984.

13. Tomaszkiewicz T.: Przekład audiowizualny, Warszawa 2006.

14. Wojnar I.: Sztuka i wychowanie. [W:] W. Szewczuk (red.), Encyklopedia psychologii. Warszawa 1998, p. 806.

15. Wojnar I.: Teoria przeżycia estetycznego. Zarys problematyki. Warszawa 1995.

7

DESIGN OF CAMERA MOUNT AND ITS APPLICATION FOR MONITORING MACHINING PROCESS

Nadežda Čuboňová[1], Miroslav Císar[1]

[1] Department of Automation and Production Systems, University of Zilina, SK-010 01 Zilina, Slovak Republic, e-mail: nadezda.cubonova@fstroj.uniza.sk; miroslav.cisar@fstroj.uniza.sk

ABSTRACT

The article deals with the solution to the problem of holding a scanning device – GoPro camera in the vicinity of milling machine EMCO Concept MILL 105, practical part solves the design and production of the fixture. The proposal of the fixture includes the best placing of the fixture within the milling area. On this basis individual variants of this solution are elaborated. The best variant for holding of the camera was selected and fixture production was experimentally performed on a 3D printer – Easy 3D Maker. Fixture functionality was verified on the milling machine.

Keywords: camera mount, machine tool, GoPro, turret.

INTRODUCTION

Continuous development and application of technical and research devices constantly affect our lives, whether it is the area of work, entertainment or education. Implementation of progressive modern technologies to education process is essential for sustaining competitiveness of graduates and educational institutions. Modern technical facilities should aim to promote activity and creativity of students. The article deals with the application of such resources to support teaching which deals with CNC manufacturing technology. The proposed solution includes the design and production of a mount for GoPro HD HERO 3 camera in the interior of educational machine tool EMCO Concept MILL (CM) 105. The need for such a device from high level of implemented safeguards that prevent machine operates with open door. The device does not enable making recordings of machining process in acceptable quality.

The proposed solution includes design, construction and placement of a special camera mount in machine tool interior. The functionality of the selected solution was tested on a prototype created on a 3D printer – Easy 3D Maker.

DESCRIPTION OF EQUIPMENT

Camera

We selected a so-called action camera because of its waterproofness that allows us to use a coolant during machining process without the risk of camera damage and also because of its size, weight, durability and mounting possibilities. Such cameras can usually produce slow motion videos, what is an interesting feature to have for analyzing of the machining process.

The proposed solution uses GoPro HD HERO 3 (Fig. 1). The camera is features video resolutions up to 1080p30, 5 MP photos up to 3 frames per second, an ultra-wide angle lens and built-in Wi-Fi. The camera can be equipped with a wide scale of stands and mounts usually connected together with forks forming angle joints. One of these forks is fitted with M5 closed cap nut and joints are fastened with a knob screw.

Machine Tool

EMCO CM 105 (Fig. 2) is a compact machine tool designed mainly for education purposes. Tools are stored in ten station turret. Slides and load-bearing elements are made of

Fig. 1. GoPro HD HERO 3 with standard accessories

Fig. 2. MCO Concept MILL 105
(www.emco-world.com)

Safety glass window provides high level of protection against chips and prevents coolant leakage, but at same time it makes high quality video recording virtually impossible because of reflections. The control for the CM 105 is connected via PC with interchangeable WinNC control from EMCO.

Workspace (Fig. 3) provides a capability of clamping workpiece with dimensions 200×150 mm and its maximum size in Z axis depends on the length of used tool. Effective length of Z axis is 150 mm. Inner space of machine tool is significantly larger than effective workspace, therefore there is more than enough space for a placement of small action camera mentioned above.

DESIGN OF CAMERA MOUNT

Combination of specific selected camera and machine tool provides several possible places for mounting (Fig. 4), each of which provides different type of view:

gray cast iron. This machine is equipped with infinitely variable main drive and 10-station turret tool changer. Compact table format is ideal for teaching manufacturing technologies.

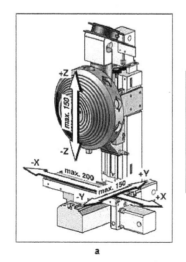

a

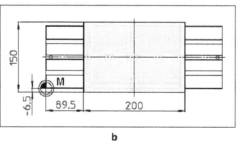

b

Fig. 3. Size of EMCO CM 105 workspace

Fig. 4. Spots for camera placement at workspace of EMCO CM 105

1) mounting on turret – tool POV,
2) mounting on worktable – workpiece POV,
3) mounting on machine tool frame – static video.

This proposal deals only with mounting on turret, which provides a tool point of view what eliminates possible problems with changing focusing distance. Turret have ten positions, therefore, the mount had to allow recording individual tools in their specific positions. The camera and mount components should not affect production capability of the machine tool in any negative way and operation of machine should not affect the camera and its stability. There were two basic designs of mounting on turret. First one (Fig. 5 – left) uses several mounting places – one for each tool and camera have to be remounted after each tool exchange – usually several times during machining one part. This design uses standard GoPro mounts glued on turret. A problem with this design is that flat part of turret is too small to place ten of them, therefore, we had to use only five mounts placed equidistantly around the turret.

Second design (Fig. 5 – right) uses a pendulum-like construction mounted in the center of the turret. This design removes necessity for manual manipulation with camera during each tool exchange. As turret spins during tool exchange, the camera keeps facing downwards because it is oriented by gravity. This way, the camera is constantly facing the tool which is currently active. Below is a further elaboration of this design.

The comparison of these two variants resulted to further development and implement the second mentioned variant. The decisive advantage was lack of necessity for manual handling of camera during machine tool operation.

DESIGN OF PENDULUM-LIKE VARIANT

Principle of pendulum requires at least parts which move relatively to each other. One part has to be fixed on a turret as close to its center of rotation as possible, in order to reduce unwanted movement of the camera during tool exchange.

First, we planned to use only the parts printed on 3D printer (Fig. 6 – left). The biggest disadvantage of this design is relatively high friction between moving components, which can affect fluency of movement and cause vibration during tool exchange, but on the other hand, it is easy to produce.

Fig. 5. Variants of camera mounting on turret

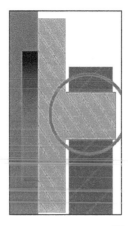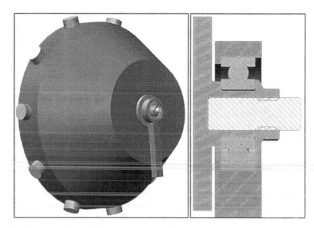

Fig. 6. Variants of pendulum construction

An improved variant (Fig. 6 – right) includes a ball bearing and other standardized parts in order to make movement more fluent and prevent jams and vibrations. We decided to make the mount demountable, therefore, the pivot was designed with loose fit. The bearing is fixed and aligned in place with a nut and rod with thread on the end glued in the center of pivot. Placing the camera and assembling the whole mount can be done without tools, just by bare hand.

Another task was to allow positioning the camera in space. This can be done either by using standard camera accessories or by modifying current design of our mount. We decided to use several simple parts to form a mount compatible with standard camera accessories. The designed construction allows simple positioning of camera in workspace in order to precisely aim the camera to an active tool at the angle suitable for recording.

The final construction (Fig. 7) consists of rotary joint described above, angle joint connecting rotary section with carrier rod with attached clamp with standard fork that allows connection of camera or its equipment.

Carrier rod is made of long Allen screw, screwed into a nut glued in hexagonal hole in one part of the angle joint. Using standard size thread allows us to easily replace carrier rod by another screw with different length if necessary. Screw head serve as stopper that prevents a slip-off and fall of the camera.

Clamp (Fig. 8) consists of two plastic parts printed on 3D printer and fastened with two standard M5 nuts glued in hexagonal holes and two wing screws. Camera case can be connected to clamp via simplified version of fork that together with its counterpart forms angle joint. We expect just small vibrations, negligible forces and acceleration and generally small forces. Therefor we were able to use simplified fork with just two tines. Such a solution provides less friction and higher stiffness of the fastened joint but it is suffi-

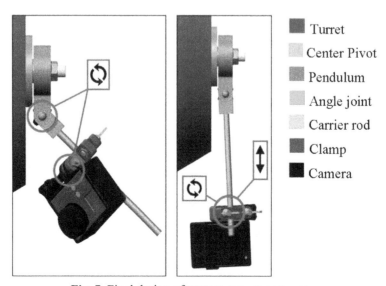

Turret
Center Pivot
Pendulum
Angle joint
Carrier rod
Clamp
Camera

Fig. 7. Final design of camera mount on turret

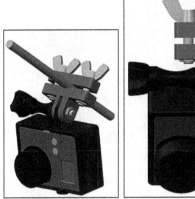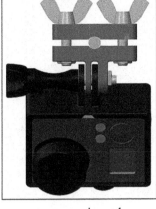

Fig. 8. Mounting camera on carrier rod

cient for the described application and at the same time, it is less demanding on accuracy of parts printed on a 3D printer.

DESIGN VERIFICATION

All parts were designed in Autodesk Inventor 2013. Models were printed on 3D printer Easy 3D Maker from PLA material. Industrial double sided tape was used for mounting central part to turret. Epoxy was used to fix nuts into hexagonal holes and bearing into pendulum.

Field of view provided by used camera (GoPro HERO 3 Silver edition) is wide more than enough for purposes of capture of machining process.

FURTHER IMPROVEMENTS

The fact that mount places camera too close to the active tool to focus on it properly was discovered after a short period of usage. Such a problem can be solved in several ways. We decided to use so called close up filter. There are several commercial solutions for used camera, but we used material that was virtually laying around - 58mm close up filter ×2 and step up ring 37 to 58 mm. A rectangle of the same size as the front part of the camera case was milled into the stepped ring, which was glued on a 3D printed adaptor designed to fit on front element of the camera lens. The inner surface of 3D printed part was covered by rubber tape in order to increase friction between camera case and filter mount.

Such a big diameter of close up filter was selected in order to reduce the risk of picture vignetting. Figure 10 shows parts of described accessory and its mounting on camera case. A test confirmed that, with a close-up filter attached, the camera is able to focus on tool properly and quality of recorded video increased dramatically.

A disadvantage of this solution is that it reduces possibility of usage camera and described mount in machine working with coolant because of non-waterproofness of the ring adaptor.

The laboratory where the described machine tool is placed is equipped with an interactive whiteboard. Therefore, we decided to use

Fig. 9. Camera mounted in machine tool

Fig. 10. Close up filter and its mounting

the function of streaming video from the camera through a wireless network. Wi-Fi dongle was attached to a computer in order to connect it to the camera. We used VLC player to open video stream from camera on the computer. Normally, such a function can be used just with mobile device, but address of video stream is stored in camera and it can be obtained with web browser from camera IP address on port 8080 (usually http://10.5.5.9:8080/). This webpage contains a tree structure, folder "live" should contain file "amba.m3u8" URL address of this file is the address for network stream that can be opened as a network stream in VLC player.

In this way the device can be used not only for recording video of machining but also for supervising of long processes or as teaching aid. Usually it is impossible to observe machining process for more than a few people simultaneously, but with this device we are able to show almost real time image from machine tool in an interactive whiteboard or even in multiple screens.

The above-mentioned machine tool is usually used for machining aluminum. There is a small, but not negligible risk of damaging surface of camera, case, lens or close up filter by flying sharp and hot chips produced in machining. In order to reduce possible damage we first used 58mm clear glass filter but it was too thick and it caused vignetting. Better results were obtained by covering the close-up filter with clear kitchen foil. It is soft and it can be easily damaged but it protects front element well enough; it is cheap and easy to replace. There is almost none visible decrease of video quality caused by foil application if it is straightened properly and all bubbles are removed.

Even with the front element protected it is better to set the camera position high where it is not in a path of flying chips, in order to reduce a risk of video quality reduction during machining process and necessity for replacement of protecting filter. It is relatively easy to find a damaged spot on the foil and therefore it can be used to verify the position where is safe to place the camera without protection.

CONCLUSION

Implementation of multimedia devices, such as cameras, become an essential part of modern teaching practices, therefore, it is important to utilize available technology and to develop new ways to use it to further improve.

The proposed solution of mounting a camera in a machine tool workspace allows to freely set up the height and angle of the camera. Moreover, height setup is not limited to standard heights, as it would be with standard accessories, construction with a carrier rod and clamp allows to set up the position to any necessary height.

There are several possible variations of camera placement in machine tool workspace, such as mounting on a worktable, machine tool frame, etc. This article deals with just one of them. Design of other mounting systems can be solved as a part of future development.

Acknowledgements

This article was made under support projects KEGA 037ŽU-4/2014 "The Development of Complex Interactive Educational Portal for Support the Teaching of CNC Production Machines Programming".

REFERENCES

1. Náprstková N., Hricová J.: Přípravky a nástroje: programování výrobných strojů. Ústi nad Labem: Fakulta Výrobných Technológií a Manažmentu, 2012, pp. 206.

2. Machine Description EMCO CM 105, EMCO Maier Ges. M. b. H., Edition A2003-02, 70 s. Red. No. EN2105 EMCO GROUP. 2013. Concept Mill 105. [online]. Online: <http://www.emco-world.com/en/products/industrialtraining/machines/milling/cat/26/d/2/p/1000045%2C26/pr/concept-mill-105/view/11.html>

3. Didactic Martin, s. r. o. 2007. Technický popis Concept MILL 105: Stolné CNC obrábacie centrum pre frézovanie vŕtanie a rezanie závitov s vymeniteľným riadiacim systémom. 2013, Online: <http://www.didactic.sk/Data/802/UserFiles/emco_tech_popisy/spec_cm105-sk.pdf>

4. GoPro, Inc. 2013. GoPro HERO 3 Silver edition. 2013, Online: <http://gopro.com/cameras/hd-hero3-silver-edition#technical-specs>

5. Martinka L.: Proposal and production of sensing device clamping (in Slovak). MSc. thesis, University of Zilina, 2014.

8

COMPUTER SUPPORT IN NON-VERBAL COMMUNICATION SYSTEMS WITH USING GRAPHIC SINGS IN EDUCATION OF PEOPLE WITH INTELLECTUAL DISABILITIES

Konrad Gauda[1], Monika Nowosad[2]

[1] Fundamentals of Technology Faculty, Lublin University of Technology, Nadbystrzycka 38, 20-618 Lublin, Poland, e-mail: k.gauda@pollub.pl

[2] Special Educational Centre, Kozice Dolne 33, 21-050 Piaski, Poland

ABSTRACT

The article presents the possibility of using a computer with specialized software to support education of students with communication disorders. It also presents the results of preliminary tests based on the original program developed for students with intellectual disabilities in moderate and significant degree of disability in the field of alternative communication with using pictograms and pcs.

Keywords: alternative communication, pictograms, intellectual disability.

INTRODUCTION

A large part of the population is not able to fully communicate with the speech. These are people wholly devoid of the ability to speak, or those whose speech does not meet all the features of communication functions. Therefore, they may need non-verbal means of communication, which would be complementary to or substitute for speech. The problems of people in need of alternative communication are very diverse. For many children whose speech develops over time fades away the necessity of using alternative communication. In the case of people who use this type of communication throughout their lives the understanding of language comprehension and motor skills may willed their entire existence. Speech disorders are very common among students with intellectual disability. This causes significant difficulties in communication, and gives as well as a negative impact on development in all spheres of life, including their ability to acquire knowledge in the educational process. The use of alternative communication gives students the opportunity to expand to a process of communicating, and facilitates the understanding of their statements by others. The particular importances in both the public alternative and complementary systems of communication have different graphics. These systems consist of more or less stylized drawings, which show mostly pictorial similarity to counterparts in reality [8]. An important factor in the selection of appropriate graphics system is primarily the degree of understanding of the language by the child and the ability of its perception of visual sensations. In practice, however, there are brought together different systems but nevertheless using them is closely related to the use of communication support starting from ordinary arrays, and ending with tools based on PC technology. Access to aid communication is particularly important for people with autism, with movement disorders or intellectual disabilities [4].

OVERVIEW OF SELECTED SYSTEMS OF GRAPHIC CHARACTERS

The first graphic signs which a person with a disability learns are particularly important because they form the basis of the understanding how you can use the characters in the educational process. Teaching them is most difficult and takes a lot of time. Making a distinguished selection can greatly facilitate the subsequent process of education. It is very rare that a disabled person is not communicating in a certain way at the start of the study. This is why; when choosing a system of signs we must take into account already existing communication skills. In the world, particularly in the United States, the United Kingdom and the Nordic countries to the most popular systems of graphic characters include: pictograms, PCS symbols, the system Rebus, leksigrams, and Bliss symbols [8]. In Poland, we widely utilize the pictograms, PCS and additionally Makaton system, which is connected to the Rebus system. Although the Bliss system is the most advanced graphic system accessible to persons with nonverbal. However, it is a relatively difficult way of communication and requires special teaching methods. Differences between the symbols are small and difficult to grasp, especially by people with mental disabilities. The system is most fully benefitial for intellectually disabled people with speech and reading difficulties [6].

There is no reason why we could not combine different systems. A limited number of pictograms can sometimes be complemented with the signs coming from the PCS. When the same user predefined the system the choice is not a big problem. In general, PCS and PIC become too limited for many people, and only then Bliss symbols are introduced [5].

Pictograms

Pictograms (Pictogram Ideogram Communication - PIC) consist of identikit drawings of white silhouettes against black background. Each pictogram contains a verbal description of one word above the figure (Figure 1). Currently, there are 1400 characters PIC [1]. The system comprises several classes of words. The focus is on nouns and verbs, but the system also contains pronouns, adjectives, numerals, conjunctions, prepositions, interjections and adverbs. Pictograms are not a complete system of language (as for example in Polish), but are support in science and communication, both verbal and non-verbal.

Pictograms are considered a sign system friendly and easy to learn. They can be used for lying of whole sentences, but due to the limited number of them is not always a simple task. When the user needs more meanings than those offered by the system are often introduced graphic signs of a more general nature with other systems.

PCS

PCS (Picture Communication Symbols) is a collection of simple drawings in identifying basic words necessary for daily communication (Figure 2). The system consists of 3500 characters – simple black and white (recently introduced a color) line drawings with slogans scrawled above or below the symbols. Symbols are arranged in categories: social, people, verbs, descriptive, food, leisure, and other nouns. Some elements such as articles and prepositions are presented using traditional orthography without the linear image. A characteristic feature of these characters is that they are easily drawn.

Fig. 2. Example of PCS [2]

PCS is the most common graphic system in the world. Many of the symbols submitted comes in two versions: a fewer and more abstract one, which provides utility system for people who are at different levels of understanding [9].

Polish library of PCS symbols (symbols are labeled with Polish names) contains a com-

Fig. 1. Example pictogram [1]

puter Boardmaker program. The library of the program is enriched with new, typically Polish PCS symbols, namely: Polish cuisine, images of famous people, poems and rhymes, holidays, popular sports games, money, etc. Another advantage of this system compared with the PIC is greater than the number of characters [3].

Makaton Symbols

In Makaton symbols each concept has its corresponding symbol (graphic symbol). The program (Basic) consists of approximately 450 basic symbols and about 7000 symbols supplementing additional. Symbols are always accompanied by correct grammar question (depending on the capabilities of the child / adult). The characters were created (adaptation consists in changing of the image of the certain symbols and creating new ones) in Poland in the years 2001–2003 by Bogusława Kaczmarek. Makaton symbols are black-and-white (black figure, white background) drawings, covering the importance of concepts that they represent (Figure 3). They are characterized by transparency and simplicity, which allows them manually (without having to use a printer) to draw. In addition in Makaton symbols manual sings are also used. These characters are mainly used by children whose parents wish to communicate with them in the pre-verbal stage, when they do not speak yet and the child's natural communication system is gestures.

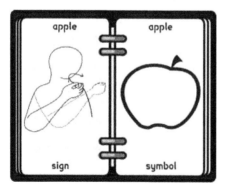

Fig. 3. Example of Makaton graphic symbol with a corresponding sign manual [10]

COMPUTER AIDED PROCESS OF NON-VERBAL COMMUNICATION

As communication aids we use all kinds of measures that support the expression of the user. Access to them is particularly important for peo-

ple with impaired mobility, people with autism who have problems with language and mental disabilities. Most frequently, they are different kinds of plaques, indicators and books with logos or pictures. However, in the era of developing computer technology they are made with modern computer aids both hardware (such as touch screens, switches, keyboard, instant messaging) and pro-speech (e.g. games, speech synthesizers, etc.) (Figure 4) [7].

Fig. 4. Examples of hardware supporting communication process [11]: a) AbleNet buttons; b) portable communicator GoTalk – allows you to record up to 45 messages; c) touch screen monitor 17"

In the case of people using graphic signs is necessary to introduce a computer program with an appropriate system of signs. On the market today there are several programs that use systems Bliss, PIC, or PCS. An example of this type of program is Boardmaker & Speaking Dynamically Pro which supports the alternative communication by creating interactive charts, educational materials: sticks, work cards, plans for the day, and task boards with the ability to print and use them directly using a computer. The application works with a speech synthesizer, so that messages can be read aloud. In turn, software SymWord is a talking text editor that allows writing the sings by using the supplied program symbols, full of words or letters. SymWord is a tool both for people using buttons or other devices of this type (e.g. de-vice responsive to the blowing and suction), people who do not know letters and communicate with symbols, as well as for people with learning difficulties - for example, dyslexia (Figure 5) [11].

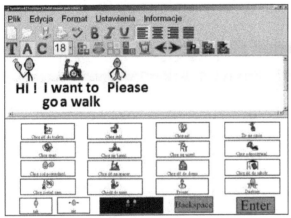

Fig. 5. The SymWord program interface

Other common applications of this type are: Altik, Happy Duck, Puzzle Tile, This pictorial fun with Makaton (Figure 6)

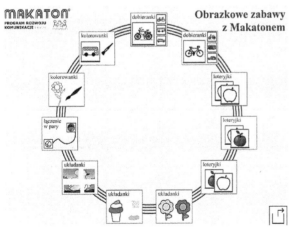

Fig. 6. The program interface this pictorial fun with Makaton

In Poland, in many centers Makaton program is used which uses the PECS strategies (Picture Exchange Communication System – The system of communication through the Picture Exchange) for enhancing the effectiveness of teaching graphic symbols.

EXPLORATORY RESEARCH

Purpose and organization of research

The aim of the study was to determine the role of specialized classes with the use of computers in teaching alternative communication using pictograms and PCS. The research was conducted at the Special Education Centre in Kozice Dolne. A proprietary curriculum, which was completed within 45 hours individually with each of the three students involved in the study was used (Table 1).

Table 1. Characteristics of examined pupils

Pupil	Age	The degree of mental disability
Mateusz	5 lat	moderate
Karol	7 lat	substantial
Kacper	7 lat	substantial

Introducing the symbols and pictograms pcs we retained a sequence, namely:
- used pictograms and pcs to express "yes" and "no",
- shaped in the concept of "I",
- built the dictionary of the child by placing symbols of things from the nearest surroundings, symbols, names of people, symbols defining characteristics of objects, phenomena,
- the corresponding terms used symbols steps.

Familiarizing the pupils with the words (symbols) was done by performing the following exercise:
- matching, or combining a pictogram or pcs of the concrete,
- matching, or combining a pictogram or pcs of illustration,
- combining two of the same pictograms or pcs,
- joining of two identical or pcs pictograms, but of different sizes,
- choosing from two or more pictograms or pcs specific-noted by the teacher,
- exercising of understanding the meanings of the symbols through the creation of pictograms or pcs the straight assortment associative (matching objects that match each other with the function, purpose, sorting objects by groups)
- conducting interviews with children on a specific topic; selecting the "words" of pictograms or pcs on the subject.

There were used when the computer aids such as: Tile Puzzle, pictorial fun with Makaton, Altik, Boardmaker with Speaking Dynamically Pro, SymWord database PCS symbols.

The study began with an initial diagnostic whose aim was to assess up-to-student communication skills, establish contact with students and guarantee them a sense of security. Then we developed the ability to recognize the symbol and receptive communication (recipient) and expressive (sender). The final stage of the research was to perform a final diagnosis, the purpose of which was to check the progress of students after the program implementation and effectiveness of the acquisition of communication skills.

For individual learning outcomes we adopted 7 step scales, where 0 meant you lack of verbal communication skills, and 6 points is a normal development of non-verbal communication. In order to assess the variation in the size of the respondents was introduced K-factor, which was the percentage ratio of the number of points obtained after the implementation of the program of non-verbal communication (final diagnosis Dk) to the number of points obtained after the initial diagnosis (Dw) described in equation (1):

$$K = Dk / Dw \cdot 100\% \qquad (1)$$

This factor allows the assessment of the degree of changes in the student's communication skills in relation to their competence prior to testing.

Analysis of test results

The results of testing are shown in three tables (Table 2–4) and a radar chart (Figures 7–9).

For the second test student – Karol, we also found an increase in communication skills (K = 194%). However, this increase is more than twice lower compared to Mateusz. This is due to the fact that these students have ordered different degrees of intellectual disability. Hence, despite the

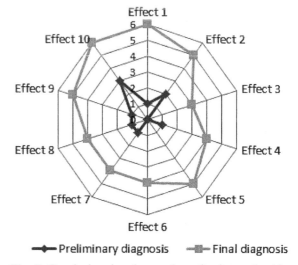

Fig. 7. Graph showing the number of points gained by the student after the initial and final diagnosis, taking into account the different learning outcomes (Mateusz) in the first test student (Mateusz) it can be concluded that the activities of non-verbal communication using computer programs significantly influenced its competences in communication. For all the assumed effects of education can be seen a marked increase in skills (K factor = 460%).

Table 2. The results of the initial diagnosis after implementation of the program of activities of non-verbal communication (Mateusz)

Effect number	Learning outcomes for pupils	Mark	
		preliminary diagnosis	final diagnosis
1.	Attempts to communicate non-verbal	1	6
2.	Has a passive dictionary	2	5
3.	Has an active vocabulary	0	3
4.	Understands the situation, gestures, few words, colloquial language	1	4
5.	Responds to his name	0	5
6.	Understands the commands and prohibitions	0	4
7.	Can choose one of the two elements	1	4
8.	Can adequately and consistently indicate YES	1	4
9.	Can adequately and consistently indicate NO	1	5
10.	Has a perceptual capabilities sufficient for the use of graphic symbols	3	6

The rating scale from 0 to 6, wherein:

0 – the total absence of non-verbal communication skills,

6 – the normal development of non-verbal communication.

Table 3. The results of the initial diagnosis after implementation of the program of activities of non-verbal communication (Karol)

Effect number	Learning outcomes for pupils	Mark	
		preliminary diagnosis	final diagnosis
1.	Attempts to communicate non-verbal	3	5
2.	Has a passive dictionary	2	4
3.	Has an active vocabulary	0	0
4.	Understands the situation, gestures, few words, colloquial language	2	4
5.	Responds to his name	3	5
6.	Understands the commands and prohibitions	2	4
7.	Can choose one of the two elements	2	4
8.	Can adequately and consistently indicate YES	0	2
9.	Can adequately and consistently indicate NO	0	3
10.	Has a perceptual capabilities sufficient for the use of graphic symbols	4	4

The rating scale from 0 to 6, wherein:
0 – the total absence of non-verbal communication skills,
6 – the normal development of non-verbal communication

Table 4. The results of the initial diagnosis after implementation of the program of activities of non-verbal communication (Kacper)

Effect number	Learning outcomes for pupils	Mark	
		preliminary diagnosis	final diagnosis
1.	Attempts to communicate non-verbal	1	2
2.	Has a passive dictionary	1	2
3.	Has an active vocabulary	0	0
4.	Understands the situation, gestures, few words, colloquial language	2	3
5.	Responds to his name	2	3
6.	Understands the commands and prohibitions	1	2
7.	Can choose one of the two elements	0	1
8.	Can adequately and consistently indicate YES	0	1
9.	Can adequately and consistently indicate NO	0	1
10.	Has a perceptual capabilities sufficient for the use of graphic symbols	2	2

The rating scale from 0 to 6, wherein:
0 – the total absence of non-verbal communication skills,
6 – the normal development of non-verbal communication.

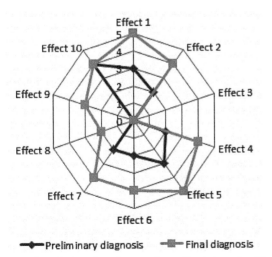

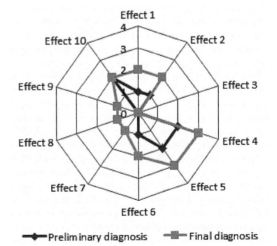

Fig. 8. Graph showing the number of points gained by the student after the initial and final diagnosis taking into account the different learning outcomes (Karol)

Fig. 9. Graph showing the number of points gained by the student after the diagnosis of the initial and final taking into account the different learning outcomes (Kacper)

fact that Karol is older two years from Mateusz achieved lower scores. He needs more time and attention on it to have full communication skills, in particular, to have a dictionary open.

The last of the tested students, Kacper, has the least-developed communication skills, in his case, although there was a slight increase in skills (K = 188%).

The reason may be the fact that his perceptual capabilities are at their lowest level among all the surveyed students (a score of 2 points). Through the use of specialized computer programs can be noted that Kacper is more motivated to work longer, he is able to keep focus on the task and take a greater extent to try to agreement with the teacher.

CONCLUSIONS

Communication is the basis of the knowledge about yourself and the surrounding world by naming objects, phenomena, events, determining their characteristics and relationships between them. Ability to communication is a source of discovering and trying out own skills to influence the environment. It is also one of the main determinants of psychosocial development. When a child does not speak, it does not mean that he does not have anything to say. He sometimes does not know an effective way to engage in dialogue. The need to communicate with the environment is undoubtedly the most important psychological need of every human being. When speech is severely impaired we should help the child to use adequate support or alternative ways of communication.

The results clearly indicate that the main objective of the curriculum realized where students had to provide a means of communication enriching their communication with the environment is achieved. Learning to use pictograms or pcs according to the rules and recommendations of content based on the preferences of child registry. A teacher must create a plan to work with the child. The number of symbols placed in the students is based on their skills, the needs and requirements. The word that fit best child's needs are included in the dictionary. The most appropriate test of students' understanding of the meanings of the pictograms or pcs is their use in natural situations of everyday life at school and at home, even for determining the tasks to be performed, or to obtain

from answers to questions. It is also important that parents are involved in the process.

An important place in the educational process of communication skills is occupid bys specialized computer programs. Currently, they are indispensable aids so that the teacher can easily create a variety of communication boards, plates, cards work or plans of the day. High interactivity applications of this type make the student does not feel the hardships arduous process of education or rehabilitation and eager to participate in the classes. These programs implement the principle of ludic which is extremely important for the youngest pupils. With the creative use of computer programs significantly increases the efficiency of education – developing thinking cause-and-effect relationships and communication skills. The results are achieved in less time than in case when using traditional methods.

REFERENCES

1. Brzegowa A.: Metody komunikacji alternatywnej i wspomagającej AAC – piktogramy. (www.edukacja.edux.pl – 15.05.2014).
2. Glennen S. (ed.): The handbook of augmentative and alternative communication. Singular Pub. Group, San Diego 1997.
3. Grycman M., Kaniecka K., Szczwiński P.: PCS. Stowarzyszenie *Mówić bez słów*, Kraków 2001.
4. Morris D.: Dictionary of Communication Disorders. Chichester Wiley 2013.
5. Orkan-Łęcka M.: Wczesne wspomaganie rozwoju komunikacji u dzieci niewidomych i słabo widzących ze złożoną niepełnosprawnością – model programu edukacyjnego. Rewalidacja nr 2, 1999.
6. Posner R., Burkhardt A., Ungeheuer G., Wiegand H., Steger H.: Handbücher zur Sprach und Kommunikationswissenschaft. Walter de Gruyter, Berlin 2004.
7. Quist R., Lloyd L.: Principles and use of technology. [In:] Lloyd L., Fuller D., Arvidson H.: Augmentative and alternative communication. A handbook of principles and practices. Allyn and Bacon, Boston 1997.
8. Tetzchner S., Martinsen H.: Introduction to augmentative and alternative communication. 2nd edition, Wiley 2000.
9. Warrick A.: Porozumiewanie się bez słów, Stowarzyszenie *Mówić bez słów*, Warszawa 1999.
10. www.makaton.pl (17.05.20014)
11. www.harpo.com.pl (25.05.2014)

MODELING OF HIGH STORAGE SHEET DEPOT WITH PLANT SIMULATION

Andrzej Jardzioch[1], Jędrzej Jaskowski[2]

[1] Department of Mechanical Engineering and Mechatronics, West Pomeranian Technical University of Szczecin, al. Piastów 19, 72-300 Szczecin, Poland, e-mail: andrzej.jardzioch@zut.edu.pl

[2] Department of Mechanical Engineering and Mechatronics, West Pomeranian Technical University of Szczecin, al. Piastów 19, 72-300 Szczecin, Poland, e-mail: jjaskowski@zut.edu.pl

ABSTRACT

Manufacturing processes are becoming increasingly automated. Introduction of innovative solutions often necessitate processing very large number of signals from various devices. Correctness tests of the components configuration becomes a compiled operation requiring vast expenditure of time and knowledge. The models may be a mathematical reflection of the actual object. Many actions can be computer-assisted to varying degree. One example is construction of simulation models. These can also be simulation models developed in advanced software. The stages of creating a model may be purely random. This paper aims at a closer analysis of the simulation model based on the high storage sheet depot modeling using Plant Simulation software. The results of analysis can be used for optimization, but this stage is a separate issue.

Keywords: Plant Simulation, simulation, model, warehouse, sheet depot.

INTRODUCTION

Nowadays, simulation is one of the most important techniques supporting production management [1]. Market economy forces companies to solve increasingly complex problems in the shortest possible time. Modeling of manufacturing systems is aimed at understanding the structure and operation of constructed facilities. Models can be material (physical) and abstract (e.g. a computer model). They are necessary because the industrial equipment, and even consumer products, are becoming increasingly complex. In most cases, multiple models are created to presentdifferent approaches towards the same or different parts of the system [2]. Modeling and simulation are widely used in many industries. Due to strong competition in global markets, manufacturing companies cannot afford even the slightest error or delay in production. Such errors can result in increased production costs, as well as significant losses. It is vital to strive to improve the technological and economic conditions of the enterprise. This can be achieved by modeling and simulation.

A large number of variants of possible solutions are often developed in the process of design and analysis of automated manufacturing systems. The number of variants and their complexity often make a simple and clear selection of an appropriate solution impossible. The problem can also be a quick reaction to change in production by modifying the schedule currently carried out. In this case we can speak of a dynamic production scheduling [19]. The results of simulation studies prove useful in such a case.

A characteristic feature of the simulation experiments is a comprehensive examination of the manufacturing system configuration, i.e. analyzing not only the throughput of the system itself, but also the impact of other resources, such as, for example, interoperable buffers and transport system [3].

Measures aiming at building the simulation model and performing the test using a simulator usually have a cyclic multifaceted nature. They require many iterations and modifications to obtain a model that resolves the issue and achieves the goal. Unambiguous separation of these activities into independent sequences is a matter not possible to be solved explicitly [4-13, 17]. The proposed methodology distinguishes three sets of activities:

- Identification of research tasks,
- Identification and modeling of the system,
- Experimental research implementation.

The paper presents the problem of developing a simulation model of automated high storage sheet depot. Attempts have also been made to determine the effect of the depot working time on the whole production system. Section 2 of the paper presents definition of depots and describes automated high storage sheet depot. Section 3 presents the stages of depot modeling. Efforts have also been made to analyze the various tools offered by Plant Simulation. Section 4 contains verification of simulation model operation. Section 5 summarizes the works carried out and plans for model development and subsequent research.

PROCESSES IN AUTOMATED HIGH STORAGE SHEET DEPOT

According to the definition provided in [14] the term "depot" can be used to describe the structure designed specifically for the purposes of receiving, storage, shipment and preparation for shipment of materials intended for shipping or further processing. Another definition used by the author of the publication [15] denotes it as an organizational – functional facility, having separate space, equipped with technical devices, registration devices and trained personnel to operate them. The last definition found in the literature [16] defines it as planned organizational – functional space for efficient storage and movement of materials.

Storage units are generally arranged in two different ways, occupying storage space in the block or in-line system [16]. Block layout is a free arrangement of units where repeated stacking of units can be observed. It is one of the ways to save space. The disadvantage of this approach is difficult organization and computerization of depot works. Movement of units located deeper inside the storage space forces the movement of the outside units. It should be remembered that each operation costs, so the total cost involves movements that do not add any value. The in-line system of arrangement means storing units in rows, allowing free access to each packaging

unit [16]. The disadvantage of this solution is the large number of transport routes and worse rate of space utilization. The advantages include better access to the packaging unit which, simultaneously, facilitates better use in terms of organization and information technology. Both the block and the in-line arrangements have the third dimension - the height of storage. The number of storage levels depends on the type of component part and storage facility. A specific type of in-line storage is a high storage sheet depot where load units are stored in racks arranged in rows so that each level is limited by the height of storage shelf slot. From the perspective of the depot organization and standardization of depot operations, high storage sheet depot is the best solution [16].

Analysis of the storage processes in high storage sheet depot

The analysis of the processes occurring in the high storage sheet depot will be conducted on the example of Europe's Product Systems shown in Figure 1. This depot is used for storing the material in a form of sheets or plates. The raw material is placed on separate shelves. Number of shelves depends on customer requirements. Shelves capacity depends on the type of stored material. To collect a specific shelf, the carry unit is equipped with a chain which removes the shelf from its space in the rack. Then both (shelf and carry unit) lowers it to the bottom of the depot. Then, using the roller conveyor and another chain, the shelf is moved underneath and goes to the right side of the unload station.

Six types of material shelf-storage can be distinguished. A typical solution is storing only the new sheets. In this case, you can define two storage options. In the first option, a separate shelf for each type of material is designed; in the second case, the material is stored on the shelves in random order. The first solution makes it easy

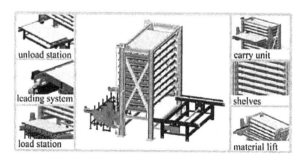

Fig. 1. Inside the depot [20]

to manage your inventory, however, it strongly limits the number of material types. In the latter case, the management is more complicated. It is necessary to regularly update the current inventory list. The vital information is the location of the material - which container and position in the particular container stack it is in. This solution greatly increases the number of different materials. However, there may be the case of production unit where, after excision from the sheet, a large piece of unused material still remains.

The problem of determining when to classify the residue as waste, and when to allocate it for further use, is a task that cannot be unambiguously resolved. To simplify, a minimum number of conditions, depending on the length of the surface and edges of the remaining material, can be assumed. For example, to qualify the material for re-use, the surface residues must fulfill the minimum requirements. This assumption is not good because if the residues have a form of a web, the area can meet the above requirement, but it will be impossible to lay any minimum cut-out on it. A better requirement will be the possibility to enter the circle in the remaining area. The diameter of this circle is the diameter of the circle circumscribed on the minimal object possible to manufacture. The minimum size of the object can be determined on the basis of many categories. The form of a table cutter where the sheet will be processed is important here, as well as the availability and the capability of fastening, mounting and handling tools that will be used to hold the sheet and retrieve the finished product. After determining the minimum dimension of the object, the conditions can be formulated in terms of defining the boundaries for classifying the remaining as material or waste. In the case of classifying the sheet as material, it returns to the depot, while in the latter case it goes to the waste storage.

There are two storage options worth considering for partially used material. The first case assumes that the depot has provided separate empty shelves for both returned material and unused material. In this variant, storage capacity is considerably limited by the necessity to plan the empty shelves for returned material. This makes it easier, however, to conduct inventory of the depot, identify the material and implement IT processes. In order to save space separate shelves can be planned for particular types of new material. Common shelves can be planned for material that is not fully utilized. Such solution would complicate inventory management processes to a great degree. It can lead to a situation where many manipulative operations would have to be performed in order to access the required sheet and each operation costs, as mentioned in the introduction. Another option is to store each type of new and returned material in a separate container. This solution is the most transparent from the point of view of management, IT processes and inventory.

It is also the least possible solution of using different types of material. In the cases where we deal with returned material, it is hard to unambiguously determine the use of storage space. The number of returned sheet is strongly correlated with the specific character of particular enterprise. Depot works options have been shown schematically in Figure 2.

The following section of the paper presents the analysis of the modeled magazine where the material is stored according to the first variant.

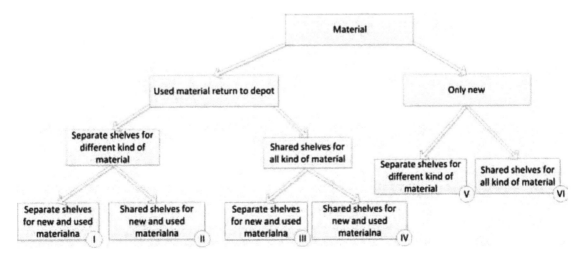

Fig. 2. Options for storing the material in the depot

It was assumed that at the beginning of works that there is only new material on the shelves. The computer transmits signal specifying the number of shelf where the specific sheet is retrieved from. The cart moves horizontally to the appropriate container, and then chain system is activated, which removes the container from the shelf. After collecting the container, the cart is pulled down. Afterwards, using another chain system, the container is pulled to the unloading station and then material is used for processing. Should there be unused material left after processing, the management system sends the information in which container the returned sheet is to be stored in. The procedure of container collection is repeated. If the depot is to work in accordance with the adopted variant 1, empty shelves must be provided from the beginning. The assumption has been adopted, that the depot will have 10 shelves, 5 for the new and returned material respectively. The amount of material stored on the shelf depends on its type. Shelf capacity and the amount of space between the shelves is the limit. There will be more material that is light and thin at the same time, than the one that is thick or heavy. In order to simplify the planned study, it has been assumed that each container holds 10 sheets.

Depot possible working cycle is shown in Figure 3, indicating the most important operations. It has been divided into two parts: the first part is related to the logical operations of the management system; the second part shows the control system operations. The essential element worth noticing is the fact that the work of the depot is strictly dependent on information regarding the status of the sheet after excision.

SIMULATION MODEL

Stages of simulation model construction, possible tools and common features of the program have been presented below.

Plant Simulation Program has a readymade "Store" type object which was presented in Figure 4. This is equivalent to the pallet yard. Its parameters include the X, Y dimension. Defining the dimension enables changes in the storage capacity. All moving objects available in the software can be stored.

Using „store" object is justified when we are not interested in processes taking place directly in the depot. With advanced parameters, the time necessary to collect the item can be defined. „Failure" tool has an interesting feature: it is used to generate the object failure in a wide range of ways provided by software manufacturer.

The next step was projecting the assumption that storage capacity is 10 containers of 10 sheets each. The container can be modeled in several

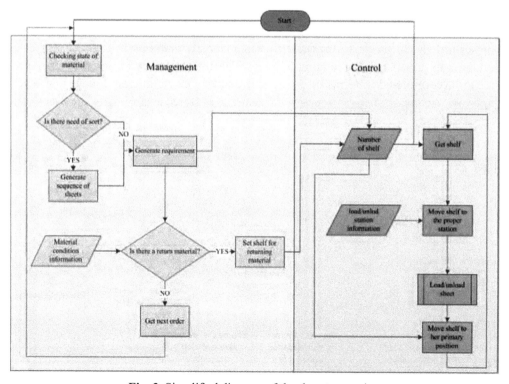

Fig. 3. Simplified diagram of the depot operation

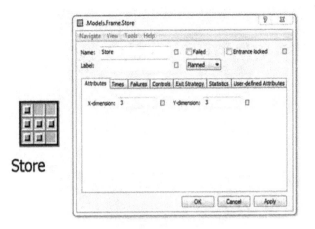

Fig. 4. „Store" object

ways. It may be symbolized by a moving „Container" type object. It is an object that literally corresponds to the actual pallet type object. As far as the parameters are concerned, the dimension that has been set to suit the capacity can be changed. This is not the only object within Plant Simulation. Another object that can be used for container simulation is „Transporter". It symbolizes the cart. As in the previous facility, dimension responsible for capacity can be changed, or random failures set. Additional advantage is the ability to change the speed of the conveyor movement.

It has been defined that for the correct simulation it is necessary to create a model responsible for the movement of the cart. According to the construction of the actual object, the cart is responsible for moving containers to the loading or unloading station. The easiest way to replace the cart is a conveyor. Plant Simulation has a „Line" type object shown in Figure 5. It is exact projection of the conveyor belt.

The parameters describing the object are length, velocity and acceleration. It is the method

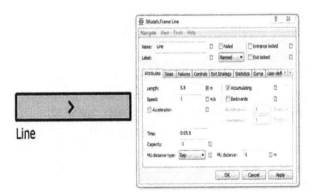

Fig. 5. Line object and its parameters

to reproduce the properties of the actual object. Additionally, sensors can be set in a line at certain distances. After activating the sensor, a program corresponding to a particular sensor is triggered. This way an object can be stopped on a particular position in the line.

The problem occurs when the line is to work in both directions. It is possible to move backwards, by selecting the "backwards" option in the parameters. At this point, the direction of motion is reversed. However, the location of the entry does not change, which by default is left. To easiest solution to this problem is using the second line, as shown in Figure 6.

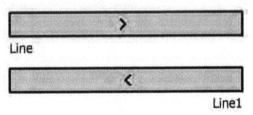

Fig. 6. Using the second line for object return

This solution is good but not the best. The line serves its purpose when the item is moved from the beginning to the end of the line. Otherwise, the object cannot be placed at random segment of the line. This problem can be avoided by using line segments as presented in Figure 7.

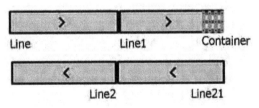

Fig. 7. Use of line segments

Each section corresponds to the route between depot floors. If you want to change the direction of object movement to the opposite when it gets to the end of the line, it should be moved to the line corresponding to inverse direction, as shown in Figure 8.

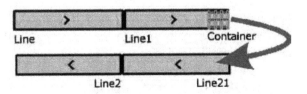

Fig. 8. Moving the object to return line

Another solution designed to simulate the route is to use "Track" object, particularly "TwoLaneTrack", as shown in Figure 9.

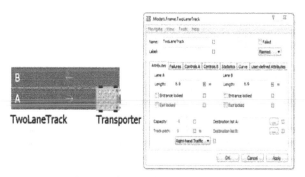

Fig. 9. TwoLineTrack and its parameters

This object represents the vehicle route. In contrast to "Line", the container cannot move directly along it. Instead, it has an opportunity to move in 2 ways. This movement is carried out similarly to the use of two "Line" objects side by side, but in this case a single object is implemented. This simplifies the procedure for setting the sensors. Unfortunately, in this case you also cannot put the vehicle on a random segment of the route.

In the next step of model creating it was necessary to specify the time of the cart passage between the respective stations while sorting containers. This can be achieved using the aforementioned "TwoLaneTrack" and the transporter. The values can be determined based on the transporter speed and the length of the passage. Additional advantages of this solution are: possibility of independent failure simulation for the passage and the transporter, placement of sensors symbolizing the limit switches, inclusion of acceleration and deceleration of the cart.

The last stage was to create a combination of the aforementioned objects into a coherent whole, reflecting the depot operations. The model is shown in Figure 10. Horizontal paths symbolize collection and deposition of containers. The vertical path is responsible for the simulation of cart movement between floors. "Store" objects have been used to model the containers. In the course of work the cart moves to the appropriate container, then moves horizontally, what symbolizes the process of container collection. In the next stage a sheet of material is loaded and the cart is moved back to the vertical line and moves down along it, symbolizing the movement of the container to the bottom of the storage.

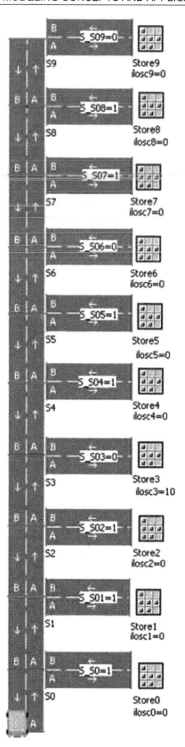

Fig. 10. Depot – final form

Such storage model requires control logics. Plant Simulation allows saving complex algorithms using Sim-Talk language. Each object has built-in parameters, which offer many useful features. If the model requires more detail, or very different properties, they must be programmed. Programming with the aforementioned language requires the use of a 'Method " type object shown in Figure 11.

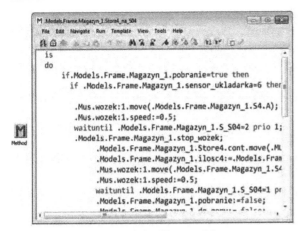

Fig. 11. „Method" type object

Each method has the following structure:

[parameters]
[data type of the return value]
is
[local variables]
do
[source code]
end;

Parameters – The structure begins with the declaration of parameters. If you do not need any parameters, you do not have to declare any.

Data Type of the Return Value – Enter the data type of the return value next if the Method is going to return a result (see Result of Function Value of a Method).

Is – The keyword is separates the declaration of parameters from the declaration of local variables.

Local Variables – Declare a local variable by entering its name and its data type (see Local Variables). If you do not need any local variables, you do not have to declare any.

do – The keyword do designates the start of the source code proper.

Source Code – Enter the source code, which the Method executes. You can enter built-in methods, assignments, control structures, method calls, branches, and loops.

end – The keyword end, followed by a semicolon, designates the end of the source code. After end you can only enter a comment. When Plant Simulation issues a syntax error in this line it is likely that you did not enter the closing end followed by a semicolon of a loop or branch [18].

Using the appropriate functions, commands were created. They are responsible for: the work of sensors, the direction of cart movement, movement to appropriate containers, collection and

deposition of sheets. Five methods were created for each container, responsible for: signals from sensors on vertical route, sensors on horizontal route, horizontal direction, vertical direction, collection and deposition of the sheet. In addition, a separate algorithm identifies the status of containers. This algorithm uses a table stored in "Table" object. It is a structure of embedded tables, what means that the cell may correspond to the next table. Such embedding is used until grade ‚3 as shown in Figure 12.

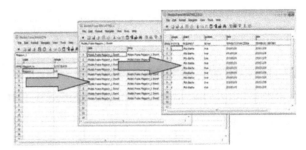

Fig. 12. Tables embedding representing the stock

MODEL VERIFICATION

Data

In order to verify the correctness of the model simple tests were carried out. It was examined how the speed of the cart affects the time of carrying out a sample set of manufacturing orders. The speeds of cart movement is the following: 1, 0.5, 0.1 [m / s]. It was assumed that distance between shelves is 0.4 m. The parameters and their order are shown the Table 1. A and B.

Sheets are transported to a cutting machine. Then, each shear is collected separately and transported for further processing. Another sheet is delivered after the last shear has been collected and residues removed from the working space of the shearing machine.

Results

System working time was longer than the total time of production of orders. It is due to a number of factors, including the depot working time. Table 2 shows the total working time of the system and the differences obtained for each cart speed, comparing each time with the best result.

Times differences in Table 2A show that for orders with long processing time and large number of items, the impact of the depot working time is minimal. The difference in time is no longer

Table 1. Orders used to carry out research

A

Thickness	Workpieces	Sheets	Cutting time [h:min:s]
2	100	10	01:40:00
3	10	1	00:15:00
4	1	1	01:00:00
3	28	1	00:13:00
5	100	4	01:00:00
4	40	1	00:17:00
4	10	1	01:00:00
2	5	1	00:05:00
2	2	1	00:02:00
2	75	3	00:15:00
5	66	3	00:30:00
5	100	5	01:40:00
3	10	1	00:05:00
3	77	1	01:17:00
2	128	2	02:08:00
3	256	4	02:08:00
5	15	3	00:30:00
4	40	1	00:40:00
4	32	1	00:50:00
2	11	1	00:33:00
Total:		46	16:08:00

B

Thickness	Workpieces	Sheets	Cutting time [h:min:s]
2	10	1	00:05:00
3	10	1	00:15:00
4	33	1	00:10:00
3	28	1	00:37:00
5	100	4	00:25:00
4	40	1	00:17:00
4	10	1	00:25:00
2	5	1	00:05:00
2	2	1	00:02:00
2	75	3	00:15:00
5	66	3	00:30:00
5	10	5	00:50:00
3	10	1	00:05:00
3	17	1	00:17:00
2	28	4	00:28:00
3	56	4	01:00:00
5	15	3	00:30:00
4	40	1	00:40:00
4	32	1	00:50:00
2	11	1	00:33:00
Total:		39	08:19:00

Table 2. Summary of results

A

Speed [m/s]	Working time [d:h:min]	Difference [min]
1	01:17:16	0
0,5	01:17:18	-2
0,1	01:17:39	-23

B

Speed [m/s]	Working time [d:h:min]	Difference [min]
1	00:12:19	0
0,5	00:12:21	-2
0,1	00:12:38	-19

generate increased costs of renovation and maintenance, and achieving such results would often be impossible for technical reasons. Table 2B shows the results for the second set of orders. Set B was designed for single and non-mas production. In this case more attention should be paid to transport operations and less to the processing times itself, which are much shorter due to smaller number of elements. Here, although the time difference is not great, it starts to be more important when equated to ca. 12 hours of work. Another important conclusion is that increasing the speed 5 times (from 0.1 to 0.5 m / s) can improve the times by respectively 21 and 17 minutes. This result is just 2 minutes worse from the best obtained for the velocity 1 m / s.

SUMMARY

Modeling methodology presented here shows different solutions for various stages of creating a model offered by modern software. Depot example illustrates how precisely object work can be projected. Each step of building the model shows at least two possible methods of achieving the goal. In developing the model, it is possible to grasp the enormity of tasks, which the actual operator often performs automatically, without even paying any attention. Creating a fully automated system, or its model, requires saving all these activities. This often involves dealing with a large compilation of "if ... then ..." conditions. Additional verification of the model proves correctness of its construction. There is a certain doubt, however, concerning the control algorithm and only comparing it with other algorithms – such as FIFO, SJF, EDF – will provide unambiguous results.

than 23 minutes. Comparing it to over 41 hours of the total time, it turns out that increasing the speed of the material lift has virtually no effect on the working time of the system. In fact, increasing the speed 10 times (from 0.1 to 1 m / s) would

During the research, the depot overflow phenomenon occurred. It took place at longer work interval, after several stages of adding new sheets. The amount of returned material exceeded the capacity of containers provided. Determining the suitability of the material used and the appropriate scheduling and combining orders are the issues requiring separate studies. Another question is the justification for the disposal of material if there is no prospect for its use in the near future and depot work is at risk. Further analysis of the depot work requires planning and conducting additional research. In subsequent studies, additional elements of manufacturing system, management control system algorithms and algorithms using artificial intelligence methods will be developed. Certain steps will also be taken towards validation of simulation model with a miniature actual model.

Acknowledgment

The work was financed from the Resources for National Science Centre as a research project no. N N503 193237.

REFERENCES

1. Świder J., A. Baier, P. Ociepka, K. Herbuś. 2005. Zastosowanie metod obiektowych w procesie projektowo – ponstrukcyjno – wytwórczym. Inżynieria Maszyn.

2. Mrozek. Z. 2003. Modelowanie fizyczne Pomiary Automatyka Robotyka 4/200.

3. Zdanowicz. R. 2007. Modelowanie i symulacja procesów wytwarzania. Silesian University of Technology Press.

4. Barton R.F. 1977. Wprowadzenie do symulacji i gier. WNT, Warsaw.

5. Fishman G.S. 1981. Symulacja komputerowa. Pojęcia i metody. PWE, Warsaw.

6. Gordon G. 1974. Symulacja systemów. WNT, Warsaw.

7. Jaźwiński J., Pabis S., Wieremiejczyk W. 1975. Zasady symulacji systemów technicznych. OPT, Katowice.

8. Koleśnik K., Huzar Z., Fryźlewicz Z. 1976. Symulacja komputerowa. Warsaw University of Technology Press, Warsaw.

9. Kondratowicz L. 1978. Modelowanie symulacyjne systemów. WNT, Warsaw.

10. Martin F.F. 1976. Wstęp do modelowania cyfrowego. PWN, Warsaw.

11. Naylor T.H. 1975. Modelowanie cyfrowe systemów ekonomicznych. PWN, Warsaw.

12. Rajski J., Tyszer J. 1986. Modelowanie i symulacja cyfrowa. Poznan Universyty of Technology.

13. Zeigler B. 1984. Teoria modelowania i symulacji. PWN, Warsaw.

14. Polish Standard: PN-ISO-6707-1.

15. Kaczmarek A., Korzeniowski A., Skowroński Z., Weselik A. 1997. Zarządzanie gospodarką magazynową. PWE, Warsaw.

16. Majewski J. 2006. Informatyka w magazynie. Institute of Logistics and warehousing. Poznan.

17. Ruta R., Mazurkiewicz A. 1991. Modelowanie symulacyjne systemów eksploatacji. Radom.

18. Bangsow S. 2010. Manufacturing Simulation with Plant Simulation and Simtalk. Springer-Verlag Gmbh.

19. Jardzioch A., Honczarenko J. 2004. The Application of eM-Plant Software for Constructing Virtual Manufacturing System. I[st] International Conference "Virtual Design and Automation". Poznan 3-4 June 2004.

20. http://www.europasystems.pl

10

INTERNET TOOLS IN EDUCATION AT DIFFERENT LEVELS OF TEACHING

Dorota Wójcicka-Migasiuk[1], Arkadiusz Urzędowski[1]

[1] Faculty of Fundamentals of Technology, Lublin University of Technology, Nadbystrzycka 38, 20-618 Lublin, Poland, e-mail: d.wojcicka-migasiuk@pollub.pl

ABSTRACT

Modern education opens up broad prospects for the use of the Internet and its applications. Global computer network helps us to cross all limits allowed for the development and transfer of knowledge and to stimulate and create personal skills. Time and distance are no longer an obstacle. Recently, it has also been popularized in the use of online tools for professional work and intellectual and to the education at all levels of education. In this way, teachers are able to adapt teaching tools to the students' individual needs. Moreover, the aspects of graphical visualization can be more efficient and interesting for students from previously used resources. This paper presents various methods of the Internet in education, and in particular the use of software to solve advanced problems in the art, for example, to calculate transient states. These tools are not only used for training skills or to solve specific tasks but also to shape attitudes and social behavior.

Keywords: modern education, training software, e-learning, research software.

INTRODUCTION

Modern information technology, which is based on computers, has a huge impact on students, teachers and on the whole process of education. The era of ubiquitous access to mobile devices absorbs standard teaching techniques. Increasingly, traditional student's books and handbooks are less popular nowadays as they are replaced by e-books, tablets and smartphones. The methodology of teaching must keep up with the rapidly changing environment. Teachers at all levels, starting from primary school, through middle school, high school and ending at universities should adapt to the needs of their pupils. Nowadays when, even a four-year deals well with a tablet type toy or an interactive pen, the Internet aided education might be more understandable, interesting and above all more fruitful. The consequence of this situation is a continuous need to improve skills of teachers. They can not close themselves or ignore increasing technological progress. They should make use of the vast resources of information and opportunities that the internet brings. And on the other hand the teaching processes with the use of software and their applications should be modern and necessarily valid. The role of the teacher is not only to explore innovations of taught subjects but also the corresponding transmission of information which is a message to the students. It is a huge challenge for the teachers because they need to keep up with technological advances and sometimes learn the programs or applications from a scratch. What sense for students would be to transfer knowledge about the "archaic" technology - not usable to the world today. In order to effectively and interestingly convey messages many methods and means are used during teaching process but the best of them turned out to be the use of information technology.

AIDED EDUCATION AT DIFFERENT LEVELS IN RELATION TO THE REFERENCE

Lublin University of Technology actively participated in numerous tests in computer network applications in education. The Faculty of

Technology is leading in the research on applied computer science. The tests show that internet mainly provides educational material for 90% in higher primary schools, for 55% in secondary schools and 25% at higher levels – academic, for example. That is because we can find especially some basic information in the internet. The process to find high-technology (specialized) information is a much more sophisticated task and thus more complex.

Internal research carried out at the Faculty (in different research, groups reached about 100 students) show that during daytime activity, described by most of the stationary students as 18 hrs, even 90% of them are connected continuously to any of computer systems for all the time (including mobile phones) but more than 50% time i.e. 9 hrs. and more, systems are actively used (including different types of entertainment and communication).

Recent studies on the use of the Internet conducted by the Public Opinion Research Center in 2014 showed that within 10 years the number of people using the Internet at least once a week has increased more than double (from 26% to 63%). Studies have also shown that the accessibility of the Internet very much influences education. Most people who use the network has a university degree (93%) or lower secondary school degree (94%), although in the second case it is due to their young age. The lowest use of the Internet is among people with primary education (20%), the reason for this is that many of them are people who are over 60 years. Age group that is most likely to use the Internet and its applications are those between 18 and 24 years old (they represented 96% of the study group). The research show that it is almost impossible to live without internet nowadays. If we are not at home we use smartphones or tablets to surf in internet, it is almost like a life style or can be an addiction. The research was carried out in June 2014 on a population of 1028 people [1].

APPLIED METHODS

Problem solving processes in many areas of research in all fields of technology take advantages form simulation tools of different access possibilities. Researchers use typical software available in the whole world and particular dedicated software installed on personal computers or in local networks but also use online software (not only popularly recognized as freeware) which is very advanced and often requires special license. It is omitted in this consideration if it is permitted free or by payment.

The paper is focused on the methods enabling the researchers on different level of fluency use Internet as a tool for serious and advanced investigations, to solve deep scientific problems and to generate reliable results.

The first area where such methods can be applied, and that is considered in the paper, concentrates in the broad thematic field of energy and environment which is in the focus of interest in the regional policy of research, education and commerce. The examples that can be used for the description of this method are TRNSYS [2], CICUITLAB [3], ANSYS Fluent [4], WUFI+ FLUX [5], etc. These are quite well known tools, for specialists, to investigate transient states in energy supply systems for either renewable or conventional systems and, in general, heat and humidity transfer problems.

The first group of problems that can be solved this way, are based on the needs to design concepts, then if user's skills allow, one can introduce local environment conditions and engineering parameters, and on the top level of advancement, mathematical calculations according to relevant energy flow formulae and their modifications if they are available. The solving processes, at different levels of visibility, are based on numerical methods, usually represented by Finite Element Method, Circuit Theory methods, Elementary Balance Method, which are the most popular in technology but of course more advanced mathematical tools are also available and used in e.g. neural network problems and nanotechnology. All types of simulations e.g. forecasts, behavior in different circumstances, application of varied parameters and time changes in transient states form different approaches towards solutions in this group.

Some other methods are used in teaching of Software Engineering. Software Engineering is one of the most important areas of modern science and is included in the curriculum provided by the Department of Technology Fundamentals, Lublin University of Technology. It trains students for careers in business involved in the generation, adaptation, implementation or administration of the variety of software.

There are some increasingly important areas in the design of information systems. These are design systems that allow recognition of this process as a whole, in all aspects of the system and at all stages of its creation. The main importance is the language i.e.: the notation of the technology integrated, UML software design and project management, which is recognized both from the theoretical side as well as through independent performance system designs. The students form a software specification, i.e.: they establish a theoretical internet enterprise and determine the requirements that the software must comply with [6].

The next step is to design and thus to determine the overall system architecture and requirements for each of its components. Students work out use case and suitable scenarios and diagrams. Usually it is sufficient to formulate use case diagrams, class and object diagrams, action and state diagrams and time sequence diagrams. The selected part of the class diagram is shown in Figure 1a. It contains information about the statistical relationships between elements – classes. The drawing shows, according to UML rules, classes (as rectangles divided into names, attributes and operations) and also established links between them (association, aggregation, conjunction). This interpretation of the system allows to formalize the specification of data and methods. Figure 1b presents a diagram of objects that visualizes hypothetical actions of the system at the time. Object diagram notation uses simpler notation than the class diagram, showing objects that are instances of the classes. There is a diagram in Figure 2 that shows operations that are used to model the dynamic aspects of the system. It visualizes a gradual course of action. Thanks to the work in Star UML^R it is possible to design the system architecture and any modification before putting into implementation and system integration [7].

The aim of teaching in this course is not only to provide knowledge and skills in the program. The process of design and creation of diagrams is only the end result made thanks to the creative activity of students, preceded by a thorough analysis of the issues, reading the projects already functioning in the market, often proposing innovative approaches and preparation of use cases scenarios. Among others, students develop projects for the retail and service systems, fault diagnosis systems, reservation and even electronic banking systems. They are encouraged and stimulated to think independently how project will operate, what mechanisms will guide him and they are suggested to recognize and describe the relationships between employees and beneficiaries. The last aspect is not the least and it is even very important because it helps student to recognize the service and commercial relations that prevail in companies and institutions. This way, the students acquire the skills of individual and group creative work, instead of frequent copying and pasting information searched over the network. Usage of own ideas based on previously analyzed independent ventures makes that the systems become less virtual and more strongly associated with life and reality. In the process of teaching many mechanisms are being developed which are necessary for conscious functioning in the information society and some creative skills are trained to engage further graduates in the process of modeling. Surprisingly to the learners, computer classes character is based on knowledge of psychology and sociology much more than it could be expected and this way additionally shows the importance of these non technical areas to the students.

The other group for the consideration is the one with the possibility to create and use an interactive simulation on a selected platform. This group examples the main focus of interest in the paper because, thanks to these tools, advanced

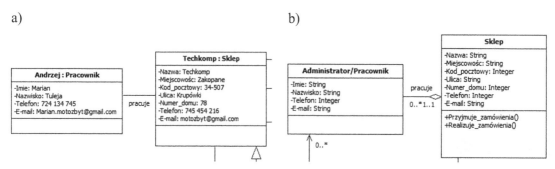

Fig. 1. The application of the UML Star visualization system architecture in computer sales online: a) a selection from the class diagram, b) a part of the object diagram

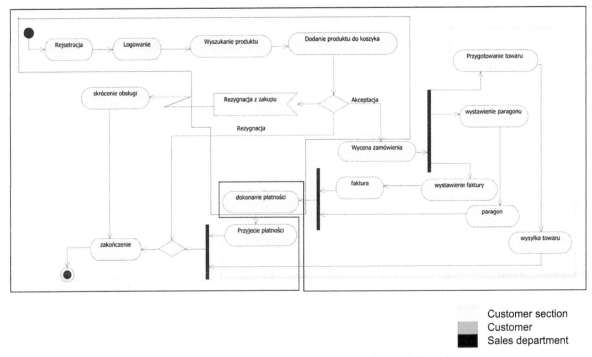

Fig. 2. Visualization of dynamic sequence of steps in the modeled sales system, shown in diagram steps by means of UML Star

students, still remaining in their process of education, can show their creative and discursive abilities and develop them into deep scientific research.

The first task of young academic researchers is usually connected with didactic process and that is why it is suggested to stimulate these abilities through the course creation and its development processes. The configuration of a course starts this process and it is presented in the paper by means of an example of a course entitled "Training service in the area of renewable energy sources on the basis of theses elaborated in the Department of Technology Fundamentals". The configuration procedures make that creators take the position of a decisive person and make possible for new users to set up their account on their own through a confirming e-mail to activate the account and to enable the enrollment.

For the purpose of the particular course three course subcategories have been developed, i.e.: photovoltaics, solar thermal and biofuels. Activity modules that should be available for an efficient course are: Registration, Tasks/Problems, Forum, Reply information, Questionnaire, Survey, Lesson, Quiz, Workshop. These modules make that courses are not only delivered but also their effectiveness can be checked, students can be evaluated and the system can evaluate different levels of usage and give the information to an administrator who at the

same time serves the role of a remote teacher. All such surveys are necessary even currently in real time when e-learning is used.

It is also worth to remember that graphic visualization aspects can be adjusted and they are especially important if higher perception need is considered. If engineers are evolved it can be assumed that they represent good imaginative skills but the wide range of future teachers can benefit from standard graphic styles which are also available but need additional download, unpack and installation. Afterwards, personal skills in HTML, CSS, PHP and optional use of software such as for instance as Gimp[8] and Notepad++[9] are trained.

Because e-learnig procedures allow for the diversification of time boundaries, the character of courses can be adjusted to educational effects that should be achieved. One can decide whether one of the following approaches is advantageous:

• Weekday – administrators can define exact time boundaries when a course is to be carried out.

• Social – courses are carried as the exchange of knowledge on established problems.

• Thematic – subsequent lessons are available as long as administrator decides.

Another methodological aspect is the decision if all sections of a course should be hidden or visible, as for example marks or activity reports. It is dependent not only on privacy aspects but on the course content. Let's take the example of a lesson named "Characteristics of operation of photovoltaic cells" in Photovoltaic course. This is the introductory and fundamental lesson in this course but not the simplest. The administration of further material depends on proper considerations and memorizing of this lesson and it is understandable that successful test after this lesson enabling the entrance to the next one does not guarantee that a student will remember its content all along the whole course. The possibility to return to the content of the previous lesson should be available but should not be visible or a subject to control, to let the students use it freely for their benefit but their activity during the lesson before the successful evaluation should be under control (including time control). It is important to activate a section for lesson flow control which stimulate students to increase their self-control.

It is justified that lessons created in this course are linear. Students can go back to the previous lesson and enter the next one if the test is successful. Wrong answers can be corrected but the number of corrections is registered and can cause relevant reaction from the course or its administrator remotely. Lessons consist of text, graphics, voice and video. The introduction of these elements is possible thanks to HTML graphic editor or YouTube imports. Tests can be diversified in their forms as the following:

- multiple choice questions,
- true/false decisions,
- short answers,
- numerical answers,
- select-and-drop the right answer type,
- text answers with no possibility of copy/paste function.

Another method, which can serve as an example of usage either in research or in didactics, is a mutimedial course. This can be used to explore and test students' creativeness and to train others. Although the effectiveness testing is typical then, the creativeness exploration is worth mentioning and can be different in the variety of science and even art fields.

Let's maintain the focus of Faculty of Technology Fundamentals practice. New educational string has been developed related to labor safety and thus new courses appear continuously. Regional safety inspection practice is of course of long history and students can frequently benefit from, but also can add quite stantial values to

it. This is possible in a kind of synergy system when regional bodies cooperate well with research and educational centers. This process can be traced on the example of the below presented course for the work at height, its problems and requirements.

Such comparatively typical course requires and should be elaborated in a kind of discursive way, let's say just at the level of Master's thesis. At this level, students acquires the knowledge but also become co-creators of multimedia content adaptation and thus training not only technical skills but also psychological methods and tools to adapt the course of safe behavior in the workplace, to their colleagues and potential learners using available tools. The use of animation and slide transitions is a good practice to add expression and influence students' skills in the hidden way under the course content. It is particularly important when safety intuitive behavior is trained and at the same time content appreciation, understanding and also professional layout matters. *Articulate storyline* software product are flexible with the library of animation ins and outs, available for images, motion pictures etc.[10].

It is also useful if *Record Screen* tool can be used to add multimedia to the course without necessity to engage additional software. Creativeness resulting from own production of motion pictures cannot be overestimated and the possibility to insert a motion file or record a movie is helpful.

Typical course units should have average content comparative to one full lecture if the general purpose of e-learning is to be maintained. In the series of trial the author has established this within the following frame: 40 multimedial slides + 80 layers composing the whole content, 4 quizzes to memorize the knowledge, 10 problems to be solved in the final test [11].

CONCLUSIONS

The elaborated tool was tested in two target groups: students in the regular curriculum and employees of regional inspection office who are regularly involved with their activity with client enterprises. The student group consisted of equal proportion between men and women and the level of knowledge assimilation after 1 hour trial was 60%, the employee group (consisting of 60% women and 40% men) showed 95% assimilation [12].

Both groups had earlier knowledge in the subject but students did not treat this activity as an opportunity to extend their knowledge. This was in the contrary to the employees who, however not involved in this field of professional life (not engineers), showed much more responsible attitude to their obligations. Majority of students reported that the course was boring but the majority of employees were pleased with this form of education.

This research, however estimative only, can be indicative that the appreciation of e-learning is very strongly vulnerable to personal motivation. The previous research conclusions published by many authors and presented in the introduction of this paper are very dependent on general conditions usually not envisaged by such simple questionnaires as they report. The general acceptation of e-learning by academic environment is somehow not justified when only brought up aspects matter, partially justified when educational aspects are important and well justified only when economical aspects are leading in front of personal brought up and high quality processes. Personal motivations can be comprehensively raised when proper brought up processes extend far beyond school and high school education.

Universities train not only employees, but also, often, not their own researchers and thus, academic institutions should not limit their high quality methods only to the target group of their further most promising individuals. The other aspect of conclusions refers to the applicability of software tools in training of research skills and this is positive.

Moreover, the aspect of researcher's personal responsibility is again a problem to be solved not by means of computer software. The continuous positive feedback between e-learning and personal tutor's relation towards students is impossible to overestimate.

REFERENCES

1. Feliksiak M.: Internauci 2014. Fundacja Centrum Badania Opinii Społecznych, Warsaw 2014, http://www.cbos.pl/SPISKOM.POL/2014/K_082_14.PDF, June 2014.

2. http://www.trnsys.com, July 2014.

3. https://www.circuitlab.com, July 2014.

4. http://www.ansys.com/, July 2014.

5. http://www.wufi-pro.com, July 2014.

6. Socha K.: Inżynieria oprogramowania. Wydawnictwo Naukowe PWN, Warsaw 2010.

7. Hnatkowska B., Huzar Z.: Inżynieria oprogramowania – metody wytwarzania i wybrane zastosowania, Wydawnictwo Naukowe PWN, Warsaw 2008.

8. http://www.gimp.org, May 2014.

9. http://notepad-plus-plus.org, May 2014.

10. http://www.articulate.com, June 2014.

11. Wójcicka-Migasiuk D.: Regional research on Internet aided educational processes at different levels. Issues of Global Education, Vol. 7, Lublin 2013, 53–65.

12. Wójcicka-Migasiuk D.: Regionale Forschung über Internet gestützte Bildungsprozesse auf verschiedenen Ebenen. Angewandte Philosophie, Lublin 2014, 54–69.

11

COMBINING FUZZY AND CELLULAR LEARNING AUTOMATA METHODS FOR CLUSTERING WIRELESS SENSOR NETWORK TO INCREASE LIFE OF THE NETWORK

Javad Aramideh[1], Hamed Jelodar[2]

[1] Department of Computer Engineering, Sari Branch, Islamic Azad University, Sari, Iran, e-mail: Aramideh.javad@gmail.com
[2] Department of Computer Engineering, Bushehr Branch, Islamic Azad University, Bushehr, Iran, e-mail: JelodarH@gmail.com

ABSTRACT

Wireless sensor networks have attracted attention of researchers considering their abundant applications. One of the important issues in this network is limitation of energy consumption which is directly related to life of the network. One of the main works which have been done recently to confront with this problem is clustering. In this paper, an attempt has been made to present clustering method which performs clustering in two stages. In the first stage, it specifies candidate nodes for being head cluster with fuzzy method and in the next stage, the node of the head cluster is determined among the candidate nodes with cellular learning automata. Advantage of the clustering method is that clustering has been done based on three main parameters of the number of neighbors, energy level of nodes and distance between each node and sink node which results in selection of the best nodes as a candidate head of cluster nodes. Connectivity of network is also evaluated in the second part of head cluster determination. Therefore, more energy will be stored by determining suitable head clusters and creating balanced clusters in the network and consequently, life of the network increases.

Keywords: wireless sensor network, clustering, fuzzy logic, cellular learning automata.

INTRODUCTION

Wireless sensor networks which are used to collect information and study an environment multilaterally are composed of cheap sensors which have been dispersed in an environment and information collected with sensors should be transferred to a basic station. Since the sensor nodes have limited weight, size and cost which have direct effect on access to sources and considering that nodes have batteries, processing capability and limited communication and it is not proper to replace batteries in many applications, low power consumption is one of the essential needs in these networks and life of each sensor can be effectively increased by optimizing energy consumption. In this paper, an attempt has been made to present a combined strategy for clustering of dispersed sensors in the environment to lead to effective and efficient storage resulting in reduction of the consumed energy and increase the life of the network. In this paper, we present some performed works and the proposed method and results of simulation.

RELATED WORKS

Application of clusters for transmission of information to a base station increases advantages of short transmission to most nodes by requiring only limited number of nodes for remote transmission to base station. Clustering concerns dividing the network into some independent clusters, each with one head cluster which collects all the information from nodes inside its cluster. This head cluster sends information to the base center after data compression and Single-hop Communication directly or in Multi-hop Communication with lower number of hob and only with head cluster nodes. Clustering can reduce communication cost of most nodes considerably because they should only send information to the nearest head cluster instead of sending it directly to the base center which may be very far [Fahmy 2004].

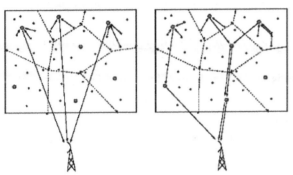

Fig. 1. Single-hop Communication and Multi-hop Communication with clustering

SOME WORKS WHICH HAVE BEEN DONE IN THE FIELD OF CLUSTERING

Xu et al. [2005] and Rosemark et al. [2005] have presented methods based on search. In these methods, a query has been created in a sink node and broadcasted in the network. Each node processes query by receiving it and sends it to its neighbors. After complete query was processed, the result will be returned to the sink node. In this scenario, some nodes process only queries and others broadcast them and obtain partial results. They aggregate results and return them to sink node.

In some works by Bontempi et al. [2005], Virrankoski et al. [2005] and Soro et al. [2005], network is first clustered and then head clusters aggregate the data received from each cluster separately.

Lotfi Nejad et al., [2004] tried to study effect of relatively dependent data on efficiency of the clustering methods in aggregation of data. They showed that dependence of data had a considerable effect on efficiency of clustering. It means that lower dependency of data lowers efficiency of clustering. They also showed that energy spent in a node is highly dependent on location

of that node in the network and the node which has longer distance from sink node consumes more energy and they also showed that life of the network had reverse relationship with energy consumption rate.

Other methods have been suggested for aggregation of data in the sensor network and Guestrin et al., tried to estimate data of a node in a time interval with a cubic function and send polynomial coefficients to sink node instead of sending data [Guestrin et al. 2004].

PROPOSED METHOD

As mentioned above, clustering is one of the considered methods for reduction of energy consumption in the wireless sensor networks. Therefore, in this paper, we decide to present a method for clustering of sensor network by combining two fuzzy method and cellular learning automata method to increase life of the network by reducing energy of the network. The proposed method has composed of several sections which are mentioned as follows.

Specifying candidate nodes for being head cluster

At the beginning of the proposed method, we will specify a candidate sensor nodes for being head cluster and for this purpose, we use fuzzy method. In this case, we use 3 factors effective on candidacy of a node for being head cluster in a network as input of fuzzy system. These factors include:
1) number of neighbor node (the nodes which are in communication range of each sensor),
2) remaining energy of sensor node,
3) distance between node and sink node.

Therefore, the used fuzzy system is composed of 3 inputs and 1 output and each of the inputs and also output of the system are divided into classes and we assign verbal words to each class and verbal words are classified and assigned to each input and output.

Two inputs of the number of neighboring node and distance to sink node were divided into 3 classes with low, medium and high verbal words.

The third input i.e. remaining energy of the sensor node was divided into 4 low, medium, high and very high classes.

Only output of the fuzzy system which specifies probability of candidacy of the sensor node for becoming head cluster was also divided into five very low, low, medium, high and very high classes.

In the above fuzzy system for AND and OR, Min and Max operators and Center of gravity defuzzifier. General scheme of fuzzy system, membership functions for input of energy level, output, fuzzy laws and a sample of test for determination of candidature of a sensor is shown and simulation of all of them has been done in the MATLAB software.

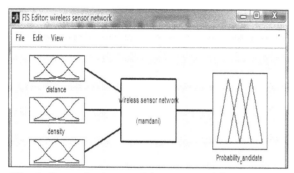

Fig. 2. General scheme of the presented fuzzy system

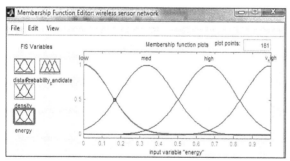

Fig. 3. Membership function relating to energy level

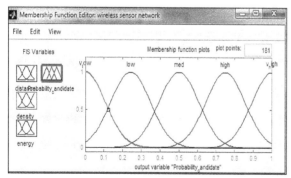

Fig. 4. Membership function relating to output

Set of the fuzzy laws applied in the discussed fuzzy system is as follows:

If (distance is low) and (density is low) and (energy is low) then (Probability_candidate is v_low)

If (distance is low) and (density is low) and (energy is med) then (Probability_candidate is med)

If (distance is low) and (density is low) and (energy is high) then (Probability_candidate is med)

If (distance is low) and (density is low) and (energy is v_high) then (Probability_candidate is high)

If (distance is low) and (density is med) and (energy is low) then (Probability_candidate is low)

If (distance is low) and (density is med) and (energy is med) then (Probability_candidate is med)

If (distance is low) and (density is med) and (energy is v_high) then (Probability_candidate is v_high)

If (distance is low) and (density is med) and (energy is high) then (Probability_candidate is high)

If (distance is low) and (density is high) and (energy is low) then (Probability_candidate is low)

If (distance is low) and (density is high) and (energy is med) then (Probability_candidate is high)

If (distance is low) and (density is high) and (energy is high) then (Probability_candidate is v_high)

If (distance is low) and (density is high) and (energy is v_high) then (Probability_candidate is v_high)

If (distance is med) and (density is low) and (energy is low) then (Probability_candidate is v_low)

If (distance is med) and (density is low) and (energy is high) then (Probability_candidate is med)

If (distance is med) and (density is low) and (energy is v_high) then (Probability_candidate is high)

If (distance is med) and (density is med) and (energy is low) then (Probability_candidate is v_low)

If (distance is med) and (density is med) and (energy is med) then (Probability_candidate is low)

If (distance is med) and (density is med) and (energy is high) then (Probability_candidate is med)

If (distance is med) and (density is med) and (energy is v_high) then (Probability_candidate is high)

If (distance is med) and (density is low) and (energy is med) then (Probability_candidate is v_low)

If (distance is med) and (density is high) and (energy is low) then (Probability_candidate is low)

If (distance is med) and (density is high) and (energy is med) then (Probability_candidate is med)

If (distance is med) and (density is high) and (energy is high) then (Probability_candidate is high)

If (distance is med) and (density is high) and (energy is v_high) then (Probability_candidate is v_high)

If (distance is high) and (density is low) and (energy is low) then (Probability_candidate is v_low)

If (distance is high) and (density is low) and (energy is med) then (Probability_candidate is low)

If (distance is high) and (density is low) and (energy is high) then (Probability_candidate is med)

If (distance is high) and (density is low) and (energy is v_high) then (Probability_candidate is high)

If (distance is high) and (density is med) and (energy is low) then (Probability_candidate is low)

If (distance is high) and (density is med) and (energy is med) then (Probability_candidate is med)

If (distance is high) and (density is med) and (energy is high) then (Probability_candidate is high)

If (distance is high) and (density is med) and (energy is v_high) then (Probability_candidate is v_high)

If (distance is high) and (density is high) and (energy is low) then (Probability_candidate is low)

If (distance is high) and (density is high) and (energy is med) then (Probability_candidate is high)

If (distance is high) and (density is high) and (energy is high) then (Probability_candidate is v_high)

If (distance is high) and (density is high) and (energy is v_high) then (Probability_candidate is v_high)

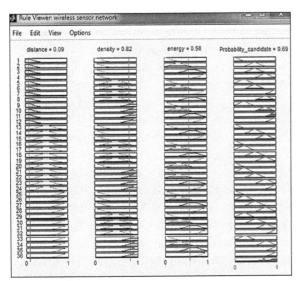

Fig. 5. A sample of a performed test for determination of candidate probability of a sensor\

It is necessary to note that the nodes are introduced as candidate node when the calculated probability in output of the fuzzy system is higher than the average rate.

Selection of head clusters among the candidate nodes

In this stage, we use cellular learning automata for determination of the certain condition (becoming or not becoming head cluster) of the nodes which have introduced them as node of its

candidate head cluster in the previous stage. Since each node of the sensor has two conditions, then each one of the candidate nodes can select one of two states of cluster head and common node. For this work, we consider a learning automata corresponding to each one of the candidate sensors and the corresponding automata can select one of two states of CH and CN based on their probability vector where CH indicates cluster head and CN indicates common node and probability of selecting each one of two actions is equal to 0.5. Probability of being cluster head based on different parameters decreases or increases based on different parameters with each selection. The parameters which we use for determination of cluster head among the candidate nodes include:

- **Energy rate.** Since cluster head node should collect information and send it to the sink node, it consumes more energy than other nodes. Therefore, attempt is made to select a node which has more energy than its neighbors. For this purpose, we use a difference between node energy and mean energy of its neighbors.

- **Number of neighbor nodes.** Since the energy consumption rate in cluster head node is high, an attempt should be made to select the lowest number of cluster head among the candidate nodes, therefore, the candidate nodes which should be selected for becoming a cluster head when the number of its neighbors is higher than the mean number of its neighbor nodes, otherwise, the selected candidate node is found for becoming cluster head.

- **Number of neighbor cluster head nodes.** One of the important criteria for clustering is connectivity. It means that each node should be able to send its information to sink node. Therefore, either each node should have a cluster head node or one of its neighbors should be cluster head. Hence, in case a candidate node is selected as common node so no cluster head node is its neighbor, it will be finally fined. Another important point is that since the number of cluster heads of the network should not be high, in case the candidate node which is selected as cluster head had neighbor cluster head node should be fined.

- **Capacity of cluster.** One of the connectivity criteria is maximum size of cluster. If the number of nodes of a cluster is high, the consumed energy of cluster head will be high for receiving and sending data and information may be lost on the other hand. Therefore, considering the capacity of the cluster, more balanced clusters will be created. Then, in case one of the candidate nodes is selected as common node and ratio of the number of its common neighbors to the number of its cluster head neighbors is higher than the capacity of cluster, it will be fined and we consider the capacity of cluster equal to 1.13N, based on some performed works.

Considering the above-mentioned parameters, probability of performing that action will change by selecting each action with node automata. For rewarding and penalty, we use Relations (1) and (2), where a is a reward coefficient and b is a penalty coefficient.

$$p_i(n+1) = p_i(n) + a[1 - p_i(n)] \quad (1)$$
$$p_i(n+1) = 1 - p_i(n+1)$$

$$p_i(n+1) = (1-b)\, p_i(n) \quad (2)$$
$$p_i(n+1) = 1 - p_i(n-1)$$

In each round of node, reinforcement signal i_β is calculated after selecting an action based on Relations (3) and (7). If i_β is equal to 1, the selective action is fined with Relation (2) and if it is equal to 0, it will be rewarded in Relation (1). If the selective action is head clustering, value of i_β is obtained from Relation (3):

$$\beta_i(n) = \begin{cases} 0 & : \quad w_i \psi_i(n) + w_u(\lambda_i/2 + \tau_i(n)/2) > 0 \\ 1 & : \quad otherwise \end{cases} \quad (3)$$

So that:

$$\psi_i(n) = \frac{\left| e_i(n) - e_\mu(n) \right|}{e_i(n) - e_\mu(n)}$$

where: $e(n)$ is the remaining energy in the n-th round and $e_\mu(n)$ is mean energy of node.

$$\lambda_i = \frac{\left| N_i - N_\mu \right|}{N_i - N_\mu} \quad (4)$$

where: N_i is the number of neighbor node and N_μ is the mean number of neighbors in the neighbor nodes.

$$\tau_i(n) = \begin{cases} 1 & : \quad \sum_{j=0}^{N_i} \alpha_j(n) > 0 \\ -1 & : \quad otherwise \end{cases} \quad (5)$$

where: $\alpha_j(n)$ is the selective action of node j.

Constant coefficient of w_e is the weight given parameters of energy in the clustering algorithm.

Constant coefficient of w_u is the weight given to parameters relating to quality of clustering infrastructure and these two coefficients are between 0 and 1 so that sum of coefficients becomes equal to 1. If the selective action is a selection of node as a common node, value of β_i will be obtained from Relation (6):

$$\beta_i(n) = \begin{cases} 0 & -w_e \psi_i(n) + w_u(-\lambda_i/2 + \gamma_i(n)/2) > 0 \\ 1 & otherwise \end{cases} \quad (6)$$

So that:

$$\gamma_i(n) = \begin{cases} 1 & \sum_{j=0}^{N_i} \alpha_j(n) > 0 \quad and \quad \dfrac{N_i}{\sum_{j=0}^{N_i} \alpha_j(n)} < MCS \\ -1 & otherwise \end{cases} \quad (7)$$

This stage is performed in several rounds. In each round, each sensor node selects one of the conditions of becoming or not becoming cluster head based on its probability vector and broadcasts a message to all of its neighbors and the message which contains node selective action, remaining energy and the number of its neighbors. After the specified time which all nodes received message of their neighbors, each node is rewarded or fined based on its selective action based on Relations (1) and (2) and increases or decreases probability of becoming or not becoming cluster head. In the next round, nodes select new state based on new probability and repeat operations.

Each node of which probability of becoming head cluster reaches zero or one selects a state based on probability vector and reaches stable condition. This algorithm continues until a clear percent of candidate nodes (95% in the performed tests) reach stable conditions. At this time, all nodes select their state and this stage ends. The status of the major part of the candidate nodes has been determined while status of few candidate nodes may not be determined. There are statuses where some nodes of which status has been determined as a common node are not in neighborhood of any cluster head node. Here, we add some candidate nodes to the cluster head nodes due to coverage of such common nodes and they are selected as cluster head node based on having abundant neighbors, compared with the adjacent nodes.

Formation of cluster

After specifying the status of the candidate nodes and determining cluster heads in the previous stages, it is time to create clusters. In this stage, the cluster head nodes broadcast a message based on their geographical position to the adjacent nodes and then common nodes select the nearest node as cluster head among cluster head neighbors. To create cluster, each common node sends a packet to its cluster head and identifies members of the cluster by collecting these packets and form cluster and then broadcasts them to all nodes of the cluster based on time schedule. Time for submission of packet is specified by each one of the members.

Data transmission

In this stage, common nodes send their data to cluster head nodes alternatively and with specified time intervals and node of the cluster head aggregates packets and sends it as a single packet to the sink node after all nodes in a cluster have sent their data to cluster head. In this stage, each common node of which data was sent is activated based on time schedule and is inactivated after sending the packet to the sink node. The cluster head node will not be active in all time periods and is activated only when it wants to receive data of the member nodes.

Change of cluster head

It is evident that energy of cluster head nodes is consumed faster than other member nodes due to higher activity and the network is disrupted. Under such condition, we use change of cluster head node to prevent this problem such that the member nodes send some of their remaining energy to the cluster head node in each data submission period and after the cluster head node sent the aggregated packet to the sink node, the cluster head node would calculate mean energy of the member nodes and if this energy rate is higher than the threshold limit, the node which has more energy will become cluster head and in the new time period, each node which sends data to it responds with message of chang_clustering and introduces the new cluster head node [Saeedian at al. 2011].

Calculating energy consumption rate

In this paper, to calculate energy consumption rate of the sensors, it has been assumed that all sensors will send K bit data in each round. To calculate energy consumption of each sensor in each round, Relation (4) which was known as Hizelman's Relation will be used and this Relation is mentioned as follows:

$$TX = \varepsilon_{elec} \cdot K + \varepsilon_{amp} \cdot d^2 \cdot K \qquad (8)$$

where: K – is the number of the transmitted bit in each round which is sent from each sensor node. K value is constant for all sensor nodes.

d – is distance between common sensor node and cluster head node. For the cluster head node, there is a distance between cluster head node and sink node.

Parameters ε_{amp} and ε_{elec} are regarded as energy which internal circuit of each sensor consumes at time of data transmission and is equal to constant values. ε_{amp} is equal to 100 Pj/bit·m² which is equivalent to $100 \cdot 10^{-12}$ j and ε_{elec} is equal to value of 50 nj/bit which is equivalent to value of $50 \cdot 10^{-9}$ j.

The point is that the cluster head nodes consume energy for receiving data and there are different methods to calculate energy of the cluster head at time of receiving data from member sensors. In the method which has been used in this paper, the cluster head node receives n-bit packets based on the number of member nodes and converts them into n-bit packet and sends them. The difference is that we consider the consumed energy for this conversion. This consumed energy is known as E_{DA} and its value is considered as $5 \cdot 10^{-9}$ which is added to the consumed energy value for submission of data to sink node [Al-Obaidy et al. 2008].

SIMULATION

In this paper, we evaluate the proposed method with 2 different scenarios and compare the above method with Leach's algorithm to show efficiency. In this research, attempt has been made to continue evaluation until the network has real value. For this reason, the network continues working until the number of the live nodes in the network is such that they create acceptable cover in the environment [Heinzelman et al. 2000].

In this paper, MATLAB software which is a suitable environment for simulation has been used for simulation and the constant parameters used in simulation are mentioned as follows:

- The sensor nodes are dispersed in the environment randomly and each node has range of sensor Rs and sensor environment of each node is a circle with radius of Rs.
- Base station (sink) is located in the middle of the environment.

- All nodes have equal energy and power at the beginning.
- Identification number of all nodes was recognized for sink node.
- The initial energy of all nodes is first 0.1 joules.
- In the performed tests, the network continues its activity until it has effective cover in the environment and when a node dies, its energy reaches below 0.05 joules.
- To determine effective cover of the entire plate as set of points that is we produce points $0 \cdot 0$ to $L \cdot L$ for a environment with dimensions of $L \cdot L$. at the end of each round, we check data submission and some points are present in sensor range of the active nodes.

First scenario – studying death time of 10%, 20% and 30% of sensors. 100 sensors have been broadcasted in the environment with dimensions of $500 \cdot 500$ and sensor range of each sensor is equal to 20 and the diagram of number of live node relative to the number of executive round for the proposed method compared with LEACH algorithm (Figure 6, Table 1).

Second scenario – studying the number of effective executive round of the network. In this test, 30 sensors have been broadcasted in an environment with dimensions of $100 \cdot 100$ and the number of the executive round of the network has been compared with Leach algorithm until it creates effective cover in the network (here, we considered effective cover equal to cover above 59%).

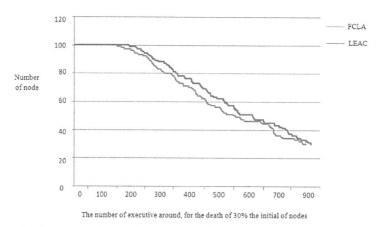

The number of executive around, for the death of 30% the initial of nodes

Fig. 6. Diagram of the number of live node relative to the first scenario time

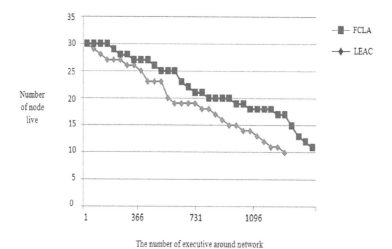

The number of executive around network

Fig. 7. Diagram of the number of executive round

Table 1. Comparing results of two algorithms in the first scenario

Method	Death time of the first node	Death time of the first 10%	Death time of the first 20%	Death time of the first 30%
FCLA	224	317	436	523
LEACH	172	275	363	457

CONCLUSION

Clustering is one of the main works for reduction of energy consumption and increase of life in the wireless sensor networks. For this reason, in this paper, attempt has been made to present a new method of clustering which is based on energy with combination of fuzzy and cellular learning automata (FCLA) and results of simulation prove that FCLA method shows clear preference over LEACH protocol in terms of increase of useful life of the network (suspension of the death time of the first node and initial death percent of nodes) and also the number of executive rounds.

REFERENCES

1. Fahmy Y.S.: Distributed clustering in ad-hoc sensor networks: A hybrid, energy-efficient approach. In: Proceedings of IEEE INFOCOM, Vol. 1, 2004, 629–640.

2. Xu Y., Lee W.C., Xu J., Mitchell G.: Processing window queries in wireless sensor networks. IEEE International Conference on Data Engineeing, GA, April 2005.

3. Rosemark R., Lee W.C.: Decentralizing query processing in sensor networks. The Second International Conference on Mobile and Ubiquitous Systems. Netmarking and Service, CA, 2005, 270–280.

4. Bontempi G., Le Borgne Y.: An adaptive modular approach to the mining of sensor network data. Proceedings of the Workshop on Data Mining in Sensor Network, SLAM, SDM, CA, USA, April 2005.

5. Virrankoski R., Savvides A.: TASC: topology adaptive spatial clustering for sensor networks. In: IEEE International Conference on Mobile Adhoc and Sensor systems. DS, November, 2005.

6. Soro S., Heinzelman W.: Prolongingthe lifetime of wireless sensor networks via Uneven clustering. Proceedings of the 5th International Workshop on Algorithms for Wirelees, Mobile, April 2005.

7. Lotfi Nezhad M., Liang B.: Effect of partially correlated data on clustering in wireless sensor networks. Proc. First IEEE Int'l Conf. Sensor and Ad Hoc Communications and Network, Santa Clara, California, October 2004.

8. Guestrin C., Bodik P., Thibaux R., Paskin M., Madden S.: Distributed regression: an efficient framework for modeling sensor network data. Intel corporation, 2004.

9. Al-Obaidy M., Ayesh A., Sheta A.F.: Optimizing the communication distance of an ad hoc wireless sensor networks by genetic algorithms. Artif. Intell. Rev. 29, 2008, 183–194.

10. Heinzelman W.R., Chandrakasan A., Balakrishnan H.: Energy-efficient communication protocol for wireless microsensor networks. IEEE, Proceedings of the 33rd Hawaii International Conference on System Sciences, 2000.

11. Saeedian E., Jalali M., Tajari M.M., Torshiz M.N., Tadayon G.H.: CFGA: Clustering wireless sensor network using fuzzy logic and genetic algorithm. IEEE, 7th International Conference, Wireless Communications, Networking and Mobile Computing (WiCOM), 2011, 1–4.

12

THE USE OF OPTICAL SCANNER IN MEASUREMENTS OF COMPLEX SHAPE OBJECTS

Barbara Juras[1], Danuta Szewczyk[1], Jerzy Sładek[1]

[1] Laboratory of Coordinate Metrology, Mechanical Department, Cracow University of Technology, 24 Warszawska Str., 31-155 Kraków, Poland, e-mail: juras@mech.pk.edu.pl; dszewczyk@mech.pk.edu.pl; sladek@mech.pk.edu.pl

ABSTRACT

The paper presents the topic of measurements of simple and complex shaped objects. Optical measurement method with the use of laser scanner was presented, as well as the issues of geometry measurements and shape assessment by the use of the strategy of fitting to standard elements. The construction of a reference model for given elements by measuring of malformed elements was shown. The given examples confirmed the usefulness of presented optical method in the assessment of shape compatibility of real element with nominal one, as well as in the assessment of objects' deformation.

Keywords: optical scanner, complex shape elements, reference model, shape compatibility assessment.

INTRODUCTION

Measurements of dimensions and shape of elements are often the basis for assessment of possible objects loadings and elements using up. The analysis of the possibility of using different measurement techniques in measurements of complex shape objects is discussed by many authors [1, 6].

Among issues considered, special attention is paid to the problems of accuracy assessment of used measurement systems in relation to given tasks [3, 4, 7, 10, 11].

A special place in this field is taken by a coordinate measuring technique, where for the geometry description coordinates of points located on the object of researches are used. Typical coordinate systems include, among others, in contact techniques: coordinate measuring machines, measuring arms with contact probes or laser trackers and in contactless systems: optical scanners or computed tomography.

ELEMENTS SHAPE ASSESSMENT BY FITTING THEM TO STANDARD ELEMENTS

In coordinate metrology the analyzed shapes are often compared with simple elements, including the shapes, such as point, line, plane, circle, cylinder, cone, sphere and torus. For elements with a more complex shape the fitting is done using CAD models. In the paper various ways of elements assessment depending on their geometry were presented. First, the elements with a relatively simple construction were considered, then plates with complex spatial geometry, and as a third example elements consisting of many connected profiles were used.

The shape assesment of simple elements

The element, whose shape was assessed, were fusion plates made in a form of simple bars with holes used for bone fusion. Among the considered shapes there are elements presented in Figure 1.

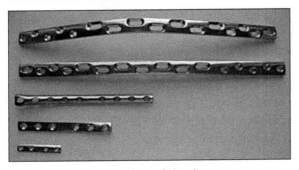

Fig. 1. Fusion plates of simple geometry

In this case, new plates are simple elements with oval or round holes. These holes have chamfers for better fitting of mounting screws; the chamfers are visible in the pictures. Transfer of large forces and bending moments through the whole elements and fitting of plates to bones shape causes significant changes in their geometry. Changes in plates' shapes related to bones' fusion and with loads transferring in case of longest plates is most commonly associated with their curvature. The assessment of the above mentioned deformation is relatively simple. It is harder to change the object geometry spatially. Such a deformation has the element shown in Figure 2.

To assess the plate deformation was used the R-Scan RX2 optical measurement system cooperating with Omega 2025 arm (Fig. 3).

Fig. 2. Spatial deformation of fusion plate

Fig. 3. OMEGA measuring arm of Romer company with R-Scan scanning probe

This system allows to collect point cloud mapping the tested shape with use of a laser scanning probe. Data cleaning and filtering operations allow obtaining information on the size and shape of the measured object. The accuracy of used system and its usefulness in assessment of elements shape was analyzed in works [2, 3, 8, 9]. The tested object is shown in a form of point cloud in Figure 4.

3DReshaper software used for data processing allows, among other, to fit obtained points to certain basic geometric shapes such as: planes, cylinders or spheres. As a result of fitting, the assessment of the actual shape of measured surface can be done (Fig. 5).

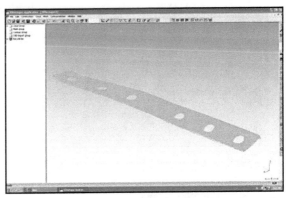

Fig. 4. Point cloud mapping the geometry of tested object

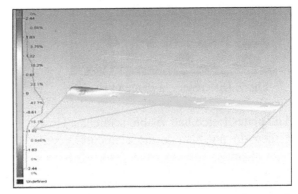

Fig. 5. The shape element assessment with the use of best fit plane according to the least squares method

Deformation values in certain points are presented in a form of a map. Distance values of measurement points and their distribution on the whole object can be read using the scale shown in a form of a graph in the left side of the diagram.

The shape assesment of complex geometry elements

Aside from objects of relatively simple shapes, there is also a separate group of elements of complex spatial geometry. Examples of spatially shaped elements taken into consideration are presented in Figure 6.

The considered elements have smooth holes, threaded with different diameters and different angles of hole axis in relation to the face plane.

Particular plates of similar geometry may differ in small details, such as additional undercuts in the concave part (Fig. 7).

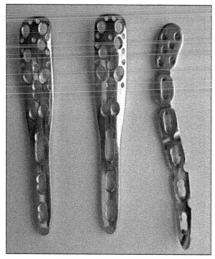

Fig. 6. Complex geometry elements

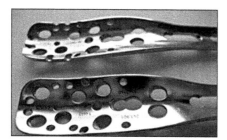

Fig. 7. Differences in elements shape

The plates tested had visible scratches. However, they do not change the elements' geometry significantly. To assess the shape change of such complex surfaces the optical scanner with 3DResaper software was used, as in the case dis-

cussed previously. The measuring system used allows for tested shape assessment in relation to the reference model. The standard shape can be obtained from the CAD model of the element or by measuring of the under-formed element. The way of model building based on the measurement and the element shape assessment is presented in the following part of this paper.

Building of a reference model

The first phase of the element shape assessment is to obtain the reference model. Because of the absence of the source CAD model, the model built on the basis of standard part measurements was adopted as a standard. Point cloud scanned on the plate is shown in Figure 8.

Due to the high reflectivity of the measured surface, during measurement appears some scatter of measurement points that requires their cleaning from noises. Points cleaned from noises allow to construct the model by applying appropriate triangle mesh on them (Fig. 9).

Models built in accordance with the presented method can be used not only to the element geometry assessment, but also as a basis for strength calculations carried out for example by finite elements method. Different software use various ways to build a mesh based on the point cloud [5].

The shape assessment by comparison with a model

The element, whose shape we compare with the standard is scanned also in the first step, then the data are filtered and in the next step the elements are fitted to each other (Fig. 10).

Elements fitting according to the Gaussian procedure are the basis for the plate surface shape assessment. The visualization of shape change is

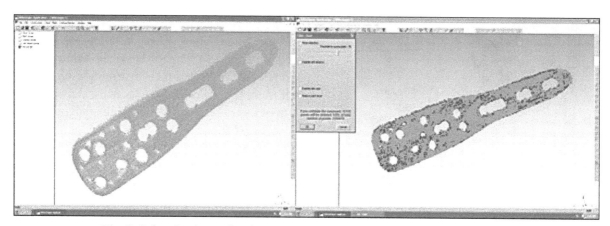

Fig. 8. Point cloud mapping the standard element and the process of its filtering

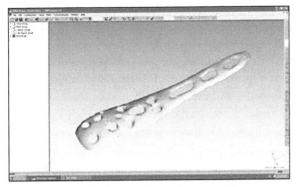

Fig. 9. Element face plane model

THE GEOMETRY ASSESSMENT OF MULTI CELLS ELEMENT

As an example of an element with a complex geometry we may take the window profile which has a form of two to eight cells, which differ in wall thicknesses. Such a construction guarantees good thermal insulation, and therefore low heat transfer coefficient. Plastic profiles have also an excellent acoustic insulation. Since the PVC profiles usually have low stiffness, the most suitable method to measure their geometry is to use optical methods. The high complexity of the shape of concerned element makes it very difficult to measure it as a whole body, due to the lack of possibility to map inner cell surfaces over the whole object length. Figure 12 shows the tested object and the effect of its digitization with visible fitting of the cylinder to one of the external open cells with the use of 3DReshaper software.

possible, as in the case of a simple geometry element, in the form of a map. Values of deviations in certain points can be presented in a form of labels, in which are given points coordinates (x, y, z), components of shape deviation in given directions and its value.

For compared elements obtained from measurements differences between shape of face planes in the area out of holes were up to 0.16 mm, which was the accuracy limit value of used measurement system. This allows to conclude that there are no significant differences in the geometry of assessed complex shape elements.

An alternative method for body measurements is performance of measurements and comparisons in cross-section.

It is possible here to use the comparison with the CAD model (Fig. 12) or performance of dis-

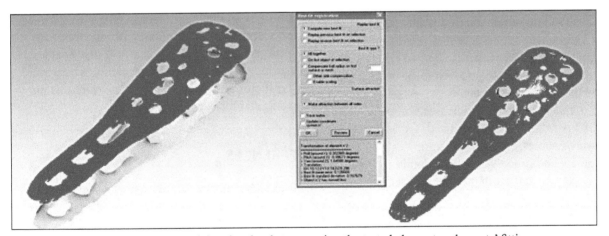

Fig. 10. Reference model and a cloud representing the tested element – elements' fitting

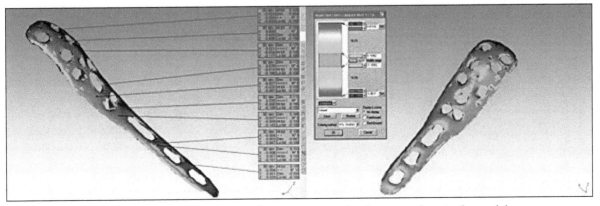

Fig. 11. Results of the element shape assessment by the comparison to the model

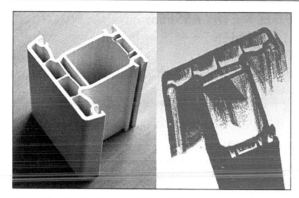

Fig. 12. T window profile and the point cloud representing thereof

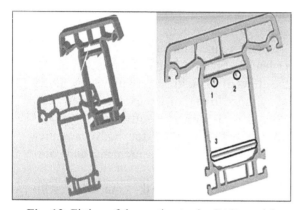

Fig. 13. Fitting of the section to the CAD model

tance measurements of selected points. A preliminary assessment lets to note differences in shape (fragments marked with no. 1, 2, 3) and wall thicknesses of the measured element in relation to the model (3DReshaper).

To measure wall thicknesses for each cell GOM Inspect software was used. GOM Inspect software enables, among others, to:

- review and process 3D point clouds,
- 3D control and mesh process realization.

The data processed in the system can be derived from white light scanners, laser scanners, computed tomography and coordinate machines.

Elements fitting in the front and side view realized in GOM system are shown in Figure 14.

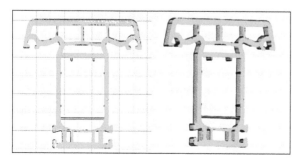

Fig. 14. Elements fitting in GOM system

Measurement of cell wall thicknesses

Measurements of wall thicknesses will be referenced to the nominal geometry as shown in Figure 15. Figure 16 presents exemplary measurements results and their visualization in relation to the external dimension of the profile.

In Figure 15 the nominal dimensions are marked with numbers 1–12. The obtained measurement results of certain characteristics are summarized in Table 1 and 2.

All the obtained wall thicknesses are larger than nominal values what results in greater rigidity of the profile.

CONCLUSION

The optical measurement method using laser scanner presented in the paper has proven to be an effective tool in measurements of objects of different shape complexity. The presented examples have proven its high usefulness in both the assessment of conformity of a real element shape with nominal element and the assessment of objects deformation caused by wear and tear. The use of different programs to results assessment expands possibilities of the used measurement systems. Laser scanner in connection with an appropriate data processing system is a tool that enables measuring variable curvature elements, which are very difficult or impossible to be measured using conventional measurement systems.

REFERENCES

1. Gąska A., Olszewska M.: Porównanie różnych urządzeń metrologicznych wykorzystywanych w zastosowaniach biomedycznych, Postępy Nauki i Techniki, 06, 2011, 155-163.

2. Juras B., Sładek J., Szewczyk D.: Możliwość identyfikacji błędów kształtu przy wykorzystaniu skanera optycznego, czasopismo Pomiary Automatyka Kontrola, 01, 2012, 112-114.

3. Juras B., Szewczyk D.: Dokładność pomiarów realizowanych skanerem optycznym, Postępy Nauki i Techniki, 07, 2011, 29-36.

4. Ostrowska K., Szewczyk D., Sładek J.: Wzorcowanie systemów optycznych zgodnie z normami ISO i zaleceniami VDI/VDE, Czasopismo Techniczne, 26, 2012, 167-179

5. Sitnik R. Karaszewski M.: Optimized point cloud triangulation for 3D scanning systems. Graphics & Vision International Journal, 17, 2008.

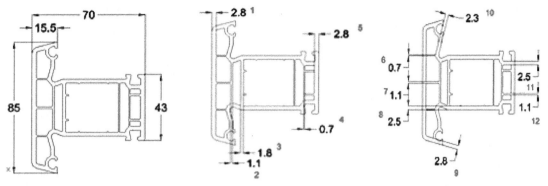

Fig. 15. Nominal dimensions of measured element: external dimensions and thicknesses of selected walls

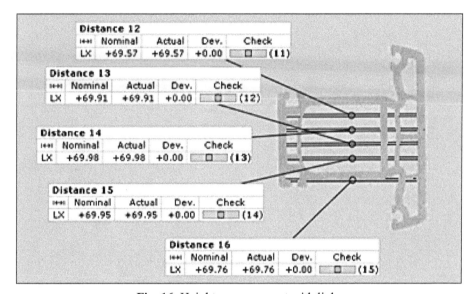

Fig. 16. Height measurement with links

Table 1. Presentation of results of external dimensions measurements

Element name	CAD value [mm]	Value point cloud [mm]					Average
		measurement 1	measurement 2	measurement 3	measurement 4	measurement 5	
Base width	43	42.91	43.03	42.92	43.01	42.71	42.92
Peak width	85	84.71	84.76	84.79	84.66	84.72	84.73
Peak height	15.5	15.12	15.47	15.73	15.66	15.39	15.48
Profile height	70	69.89	69.91	69.98	69.95	69.76	69.90

Table 2. Presentation of results of wall thicknesses measurements

Element number	CAD value [mm]	Value point cloud [mm]					Average
		measurement 1	measurement 2	measurement 3	measurement 4	measurement 5	
1	2.8	3.07	2.81	2.93	3.07	2.94	2.96
2	1.1	1.47	1.59	1.54	1.42	1.43	1.49
3	1.8	2.17	2.14	2.24	2.28	2.27	2.22
4	0.7	0.97	1.01	1.04	0.98	0.94	0.99
5	2.8	3.09	3.06	3.18	3.27	3.15	3.15
6	0.7	1	0.98	1.09	1	0.99	1.01
7	1.1	1.44	1.51	1.56	1.49	1.46	1.49
8	2.5	2.82	2.75	2.73	2.7	2.73	2.75
9	2.8	3.03	3.08	3.06	2.92	3.11	3.04
10	2.3	2.63	2.65	2.63	2.66	2.62	2.64
11	2.5	2.91	3.04	3.2	3.01	3.12	3.06
12	1.1	1.51	1.61	1.59	1.49	1.49	1.54

6. Sładek J., Gawlik J., Ryniewicz A., Krawczyk M., Kupiec R.: Metrologia współrzędnościowa w inżynierii produkcji a dokładność pomiaru i dokładność wytwarzania, Inżynieria Maszyn, 3, 2010, 20-34.

7. Sładek J., Gąska A., Olszewska M., Ostrowska K., Ryniewicz A.: Metoda oceny dokładności pomiarów realizowanych za pomocą ramion pomiarowych wyposażonych w optyczne głowice skanujące. Mechanik, 2, 2012, 133-139.

8. Sładek J., Ostrowska K., Gąska A., Gacek K., Kmita A.: Model matematyczny opisu dokładności Współrzędnościowych Ramion Pomiarowych.

Inżynieria Maszyn, 14(2), 2009. 7-18.

9. Sładek J., Ostrowska K., Gąska A.: Modeling and identification of errors of coordinate measuring arms with use of metrological model. Measurement, 46, 2013, 667-679.

10. Sładek J., Sokal G., Kmita A., Ostrowska K.: Wzorcowanie Współrzędnościowych Ramion Pomiarowych (WRP). Acta Mechanica et Automatica, 1(2), 2007.

11. Sładek J.: Dokładność pomiarów współrzędnościowych. Wydawnictwo Politechniki Krakowskiej, pp. 495, Kraków 2011.

13

THE CONCEPT OF USING EVOLUTIONARY ALGORITHMS AS TOOLS FOR OPTIMAL PLANNING OF MULTIMODAL COMPOSITION IN THE DIDACTIC TEXTS

Marek A. Jakubowski[1], **Michał Charlak**[2], **Michalina Gryniewicz-Jaworska**[3]

[1] Management Faculty, Lublin University of Technology, Nadbystrzycka 38, 20-618 Lublin, Poland.

[2] Fundamentals of Technology Faculty, Lublin University of Technology, Nadbystrzycka 38, 20-618 Lublin, Poland, e-mail: m.charlak@pollub.pl

[3] Faculty of Electrical Engineering and Computer Science, Lublin University of Technology, Nadbystrzycka 38A, 20-618 Lublin, Poland

ABSTRACT

At the beginning we would like to provide a short description of the new theory of learning in the digital age called connectivism. It is the integration of principles explored by the following theories: chaos, network, complexity and self-organization. Next, we describe in short new visual solutions for the teaching of writing so called multimodal literacy 5–11. We define and describe the following notions: multimodal text and original theory so called NOS (non-optimum systems methodology) as a basis for new methods of visual solutions at the classes and audiovisual texts applications. Especially, we would like to emphasize the tremendous usefulness of evolutionary algorithms VEGA and NSGA as tools for optimal planning of multimodal composition in teaching texts. Finally, we give some examples of didactic texts for classrooms, which provide a deep insight into learning skills and tasks needed in the Internet age.

Keywords: algorithm, didactic text, connectivism.

DESCRIPTION OF CONNECTIVISM

Connectivism is a learning theory for the digital age. Learning has changed over the last several decades. The theories of behaviourism, cognitivism, and constructivism provide an effect view of learning in many environments. They fall short, however, when learning moves into informal, networked, technology-enabled arena.

The integration of cognition and emotions in meaning-making is important. Thinking and emotions influence each other. A theory of learning that only considers one dimension excludes a large part of how learning happens.

Learning has an end goal – namely the increased ability to "do something". This increased competence might be in a practical sense (i.e. developing the ability to use a new software tool or learning how to skate) or in the ability to function more effectively in a knowledge era (self-awareness, personal information management, etc.). The "whole of learning" is not only gaining skill and understanding – actuation is a needed element. Principles of motivation and rapid decision making often determine whether or not a learner will actuate known principles.

Learning is a process of connecting specialized nodes or information sources. A learner can exponentially improve their own learning by plugging into the existing network. Learning may reside in non-human appliances. Learning (in the sense that something is known, but not necessarily actuated) can rest in a community, a network, or a database. The capacity to know more is more critical that what is currently known. Knowing where to find information is more important than knowing information. Nurturing and maintaining connections is needed to facilitate learning. Connection making provides far greater returns on effort than simply seeking to understand a single concept.

Learning and knowledge rest in diversity of opinions. Learning happens in many different ways. Courses, email, communities, conversations, web search, email lists, reading blogs, etc. Courses are not a primary conduit for learning. Different approaches and personal skills are needed to learn effectively in today's society. For example, the ability to see connections between fields, ideas, and concepts is a core skill.

Organizational and personal learning are integrated tasks. Personal knowledge is comprised of a network, which feeds into organizations and institutions, which in turn feed back into the network and continue to provide learning for the individual. Connectivism attempts to provide an understanding of how both learners and organizations learn. Currency (accurate, up-to-date knowledge) is the intent of all connectivist learning.

Decision-making is itself a learning process. Choosing what to learn and the meaning of incoming information is seen through the lens of shifting reality. While there is a right answer now, it may be wrong tomorrow due to alterations in the information climate impacting the decision.

Learning is a knowledge creation process... not only knowledge consumption. Learning tools and design methodologies should seek to capitalize on this trait of learning [1].

MULTIMODAL TEXT PARADIGMS FOR CONTEMPORARY EDUCATION

In order to be able to talk about paradigms using multimodal text in the education process much of the term should be explained. The paradigm according to key terms is a philosophy of science, which tries to explain the essence of existence and create the foundations of research programs. The paradigm includes traditional forms of research and the combination of ontology and epistemology, their perspectives and ways of knowing forms of knowledge.

A paradigm is a commitment to cultural practices, reality shows and knowledge. Many of the assumptions, conventions and practices prevailing in a culture are taken for granted, but sometimes they are not understood by other cultures. Furthermore, it is a combination of logic, philosophy of science and research. One of the first who gave meaning to that word today was Thomas Kuhn who defines it as a description of what is to be tested and observed and how to ask questions to get answers.

What are multimodal texts?

In everyday print-based communications like newspapers, mobile phones, TV, words are almost always accompanied by photographs, diagrams or drawings. However, screens are much more familiar not only in the school, but in shops, workplaces and homes. Many everyday texts are now multimodal: combining words as well as sound with mowing images, color and a range of photographic, drawn or digitally created visuals. People of all cultures have always used a range of ways to represent own ideas. In the contemporary 'digital era' the 'newness' is the way that messages are relayed and distributed thorough different media of communication. Even the most familiar and everyday communications are made up of complex combinations of modes. A conversation, whether in face-to-face meetings or viewed on screen is accompanied by movements and gestures; print is often accompanied by pictures; and films and television programs rely on

Table 1. Comparing Systems Theory and Connectivism [1]

Systems Theory	Connectivism
• describes concept formation and mental process in functionalist (goal-driven) ways	• associationist theory; describes how connections are formed
• consequentialist/causal process theory • knowledge is formed through a combination of simple mechanisms	• emergentist theory • knowledge formed by such a system has an impact by virtue of recognition (hence, interaction)
	• distributive theory • concepts have no particular location • no discrete existence (in the mind or elsewhere) • distended across a large number of entities (e.g., neurons) • have fuzzy boundaries • are intermixed with other (distended) concepts and ideas

sound effects and music to add atmosphere and effect. Any multimodal texts might combine elements of:

- gesture, movement, posture, facial expression
- images: moving and still, real or drawn
- sound: spoken words, sound effects and music
- writing, including font and typography.

These elements will be differently weighted in any combination of modes. Children and all people living and grow up in a highly multimodal environment. They are surrounded by texts on screen and on paper which merge pictures, words and sounds. They expect to read images as well as print and, increasingly use computers in seeking information and composing their own texts. This has implications for teaching. The texts that children are familiar with- including computer games and hypertexts- often follow a different structure from sequential narrative, instruction or explanation. Presentational software and websites extend possibilities for hypertextual compositions, and digital technology, with its facility for importing pictures and manipulating text [2].

EVOLUTIONARY ALGORITHMS – SHORT INTRODUCTION

The dynamic development of information technology has caused a great interest in science in the field of artificial intelligence, evolutionary algorithms, genetic or artificial immune systems. Currently the above mentioned scientific disciplines are used in various fields of science and education. For solving technical or engineering tasks the Darwinian theory of evolution is almost universally used Evolutionary algorithms are used in many fields of science, for example in issues typically for engineering, economic, and even investment [3].

Evolutionary algorithms are a group of heuristic methods and optimization, which in its action mimic living organisms. Now we can identify some groups of genetic algorithms, for example:

- Genetic Algorithm *J. Holland in 1975,*
- Evolution Strategy *I. Rechenberg 1973, H. P. Schwefel 1981*
- Evolutionary Programming *L. Fogel 1962*
- Genetic Programming *J. Koza (1992)* [4].

The task of the evolutionary algorithm is to search space of alternatives to select the best or potentially best solution. This search is done by using the mechanisms of evolution and natural selection. The principle of operation of an evolutionary algorithm is based on processing population of individuals, each of which is a proposal to solve a particular task. Each subject is assigned with a value, referred to the adaptation of the subject, moreover, is equipped with a genotype, which is created on the basis of phenotype [5]. The most popular evolutionary algorithms include: algorithm VEGA, NSGA, or swarms of ant colony optimization. The figure below shows a diagram of the evolutionary algorithm according to Eiben and Smith.

An example of using the evolutionary algorithm is an optimization of the schedule for the University. The principle of the algorithm is based on the allocation of rooms and dates of classes in such a way to adjust the time limits for speakers, without unnecessary collisions (rooms or personal) while minimizing discontinuities time in the schedule (free time) [7].

Simulations

At the Technical Universities, students are faced with difficult and complex computational tasks but more efficient and cheaper can be designing an algorithm that simulates arbitrarily

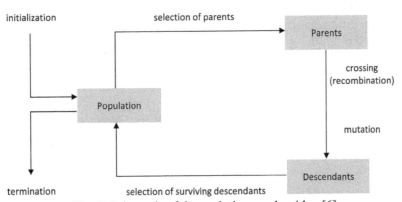

Fig. 1. Schematic of the evolutionary algorithm [6]

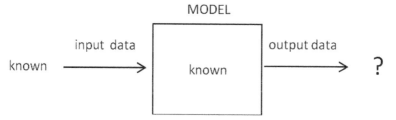

Fig. 2. Diagram of simulation problems [7]

large electrical system to build it in order to investigate and verify its properties.

The simulations rely on generating the output when given input data and model control.

The main advantage of the evolutionary algorithms is not intuitive. The human brain tries to look for solutions in purely schematic, using traditional solutions. In the case of the evolutionary algorithms optimization tasks are not restricted and search solutions in order to select the best or potentially best.

Modeling

In this case sought model describes how the system generates the selected input data to the known output.

Using the above mentioned model we can construct models of certain machines or robots which would perform their tasks. It should be borne in mind when constructing or modeling the function fitted to the data. The input is then independent and output dependent, model -function. The evolutionary algorithms can be used to create zooming function data, which then will serve us as a model. One of the main advantages of the evolutionary algorithms is the lack of ordinary skill enjoyed by a teacher or an expert, in the case of directed evolution algorithms is the choice of the most appropriate function. The mere fact of modeling is done using specific data, without the knowledge of the outside.

The evolutionary algorithms are widely used and are increasingly used in different areas of science and education. They shorten the maximum time and the calculation of complex engineering tasks while minimizing the computational cost and implementation. Moreover, they are often used in the design of various projects in education, for example, when teaching science education, where teaching materials require great knowledge on performing a series of complex calculations. In the evolutionary algorithms for optimization tasks semantic web, organize collections are also met, in the case of the optimization schedule or optimal planning of multimodal texts teaching composition and personalization of information resources on the Internet. The above presented examples of the use of the evolutionary algorithms in addition to the purely computational issues also include such aspects of life as: transportation, management and marketing, scheduling working hours and production.

The concept of using the evolutionary algorithms as tools for optimal planning of multimodal composition in the texts of teaching.

In the case of the development of multimodal composition of didactic texts, we try to use versatility of the evolutionary algorithms. A similar principle of operation can be found at the penetration of the Internet as a source of knowledge and education. Artificial immune systems are moving in the environment, like Internet users move along its resources. Reach their interest of knowledge or information. Taking into account the technical aspects of the Internet or any other group of materials or composition will have to make a few preliminary steps, such as user identification, segmentation and identification of the session. In the case of a cer-

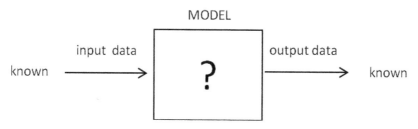

Fig. 3. Schema of modeling problems [7]

tain specificity of which is the graph of resources that have forced us to change in the operation of the algorithm. In the case of the use of the evolutionary algorithms, we can get satisfactory results, which will take into account data from the second part, important for teachers', which in traditional terms may not be taken into account. By creating certain resources or compositions we may try to use the hints that the algorithm suggested bearing in mind that this is an attempt to optimize its assumptions. In the case of solving similar problems of optimization is the most important selection of some of the parameters and rules of the algorithm, not without significance is the way to represent the environment that are to explore artificial immune systems [8].

NEW APPROACH – HIGHER EDUCATION AS FUZZY NON-OPTIMUM SYSTEM

The theory of non-balanced self-organized system, starting from the study of the balanced-open system which the objective world proper possesses, reflects truly the whole internal mechanism and the common principle of the ordered and functional ordered structure in various time-space.

According to the self-organized system principle, an ordered system may go into confusion, and naturally, it is very important to study the reasons, ways and consequence of the ordered system going into confusion. If an ordered system going into confusion is necessary for us, we have to control its speed, so that it may be more fit for our needs; if it is harmful for us, we have to take some measures to prevent it from going into confusion, and manage to make it more ordered. The higher degree of development is the systematic optimization. That is the purpose of studying this system. So the lower degree is the non-optimization. According to the theory of "dissipation structure", as long as the system is open, the non-balanced state may become the source of ordered system. So the non-optimum system is the basis of the optimum. Only when the system goes out of the non-optimum category, can it come into the stage, where we are to seek optimization. The first concept of the optimization was only judged by a comparison with one another and now the concept of the optimization is searching for the very big and very small of the objective function under a certain control. But actually, the optimization

project or system which best represents the objective function bears only relative significance, that is, they are realized under a certain and strict condition. The optimization project or system which best represents the objective function bears only relative significance, that is, they are realized under a certain and strict condition. Because of the complication of mans, social practice (many undetermined and uncertain factors, alternation and the influence by his behaviors) and the feasibility of the pursued goal in present circumstances.

So the traditional optimum methods have their problems which must be analyzed and solved with all dimensions considered. Our purpose is to develop a concept of relative optimum (RO) and thres-optimum hold (OT), with the RO including the "non-optimum" (NO), "sub-optimum" (SO) and the "optimum" (O), following the theory of unity of the opposites. Thus the human practice processes and results are divided, according to their nature, into O, SO and NO sections. From these three directions we can best study the features and rules of system optimization [9].

The types and models in the NOS (Non-optimum System)

In the previous considerations we discussed the relationship between the system no-optimum and the optimum. However, since all systems are sub-optimum in their nature, our aim is set on the problem of system's optimization and non-optimum. Analyzing the general laws behind the systems' movement, we can sum up three different non-optimum (NO) types:

1) Systems formed from the changed states of the systems' old self in the process of system movement.

2) Systems formed because of changes in constraint factors and new constraints can no longer satisfy the operation of the systems.

3) Systems formed from changes in both the system's own states and their constraints, operating in new conditions and thus making it impossible to determine their laws. Then the systems move in the NO category.

Judging these NO system phenomena, we can see that (1) some have obvious NO conditions and can be identified from observation and analysis of the past operations of the system; (2) others are fuzzy NO; people can identify them according to the intrinsic fuzziness of human experiences and reasonings in a system with fuzzy information. They are sets or "grey NO (non-optimum)" and valuable for system operation decision-making and management; (3) potential NO: hidden in the forming stage in a system, has defects in its design but not effecting to functions within certain conditions and its information has not been sensitized.

One rule of scientific research is to develop from the analysis to the quantitative qualitative. To the NOS (non-optimum system), if we discuss at certain level of the understanding of its intension. we can analyze quantitatively.

Suppose the degree of the NO of the system to be n (NO parameter) which is the degree of satisfaction that the system's constraints are given by each factor of the system. This is a typical systematic optimization problem. According to the conventional methods for optimization, it is a process of minimizing the target function while satisfying.

To a NOS can set a value of optimum level which is the optimum threshold determined by the system and statisticalized and processed. If this value equals 1 then the SON (system optimization) accords with the reality, if value is 0 the SO doesn't accord with reality, that is, the system is not optimized. If value of this parameter is between 0 and 1 then the SON is called satisfactory optimum. For example 0.5 means the system is in a sub-optimum (SO) state; if 0.7, then the system is at the 0.7 optimum level.

Because the process of SON is cyclic, the system will, after a cycle, get a group of NO degree values which make up the O threshold, and NO threshold that is A and A no.

If we can evaluate all the NO parameters of the system, that is, get the O threshold and NO threshold, then we can control the operation of the system and keep it off the NO threshold, thus gaining satisfactory O target.

If the system is clearly NO with clear information, then it can definitely be called as "generally NO".

1) Common probability model. It is a basic NO system model structured from the values of NO parameters with a certain logic relationships The system calculated and discussed by them all belong to the narrow-sensed NO. The methods used for predicting the NOS parameters include those of mathematic calculation, Monte Carlo methods, limit line methods and Boolean logic methods.

2) Regressive model of NOS. Suppose there are P number of constraints whose variables are x_1, x_2, ..., x_p, that shape a NOS from which each constraint and linear interrelating divisors of state variables and constant divisors can be analyzed. Then based on the appearing probability of as few as possible typical constraints x_1, x_2, ..., x_n, we can predict the level and probability of the NO phenomenon.

So the degree of satisfaction of the constraint conditions determines the reciprocal conversions of the NO and O (optimum) of the system and differentiate the various level system optimization [9].

The practical implications of the NOS methods

According to the self-organizing principle of the systematology. The development of human society is forever in the dynamic process of moving from the less ordered toward the more ordered larger system, or toward it destination point cycle.

However we must be aware of the hidden danger under the vigorous reform stream which may bring about mistakes and failures. Meanwhile we have already suffered a few mistakes and setbacks in some areas to some extent. What is more serious is that some mistakes and setbacks suffered have been repeated and what could be avoided was not.

Even if some model is considered optimum under the present circumstances, it is hard to be a stable one because it is in the midst of a dynamic process with quite a few hidden threats lurching and many horizontal or vertical relations between factors and their specific laws unknown. The so-called optimum model is only at a SO state. So, if we try to set goals for the reform, make plans and take measures and advocate some optimum models simply following the optimum thinking methods out of blind subjective wish, we'll be actually putting the reform on an unreliable and unrealistic basis.

Applying the principle of multiple perspectives of the university can be viewed from different points of view. From the government's point of view the university can be seen as an optimal system (curriculum), while from the student's point of view is important to their experience (hidden curriculum). Based on this experience, we can develop a non-optimal system [10]. This can be seen to be extremely useful NOS systems.

We can also see the education in terms of historical development as a developing system. As we have said, a system that is optimum in one time and space environment may be non-optimum in another. The behavior of a system is almost circling around the cycle from the unbalanced state to the balanced from the disordered to the ordered, overcoming "ups and downs" and "disruptions" to reach its "destination point" or "destination ring" in its reciprocal space. So the non-optimum cases under different conditions are different.

CONCLUSIONS

1. Connectivism is a learning theory for the digital age. Learning has changed over the last several decades. The theories of behaviourism, cognitivism, and constructivism provide an effect view of learning in many environments but not for 'new digital age'.

2. In everyday print-based communications like newspapers, mobile phones, TV, words are almost always accompanied by photographs, diagrams or drawings. However screens are much more familiar not only in the school, but in shops, workplaces and homes.

3. Evolutionary algorithms VEGA and NSGA as a tools for optimal planning of multimodal composition in teaching texts.

4. Applying the principle of multiple perspectives of the university can be viewed from different points of view. From the government point of view of the university can be seen as the optimal system (curriculum), while from the student's point of view is important to their experience (hidden curriculum). Based on this experience, we can develop a non-optimal system [10]. This can be seen to be extremely useful NOS systems.

REFERENCES

1. http://www.connectivism.ca/about.html
2. Bearne E., Wolstencroft H.: Visual approaches to teaching writing. Paul Chapman Publishing, London 2007.
3. http://mpra.ub.uni-muenchen.de/31620/1/MPRA_paper_31620.pdf
4. http://www.zam.iiar.pwr.wroc.pl/index.php?option=com_content&view=article&id=11&Itemid=19
5. Michalewicz Z.: Algorytmy genetyczne + struktury danych = programy ewolucyjne. WNT 1999.
6. http://aragorn.pb.bialystok.pl/~wkwedlo/EA1.pdf
7. http://www.michal.ejdys.pl/nauka/emh-pg.pdf
8. Technologie wiedzy w zarządzaniu publicznym. Zeszyty Naukowe Wydziałowe Uniwersytetu Ekonomicznego w Katowicach, Katowice 2012.
9. Ping He: Fuzzy non-optimum system theory and methods. Fuzzy sets, IFSA-EC, Warsaw 1986.
10. Charlak M., Jakubowski M.A.: The concept of integrated engineering and business (EB) education system. Advances in Science and Technology Research Journal, Vol. 7 (20), 2013, 99–103.

14

SYNCHRONIZATION OF DATA RECORDED USING ACQUISITION STATIONS WITH DATA FROM CAMERA DURING THE BUBBLE DEPARTURE

Paweł Dzienis[1], Romuald Mosdorf[1]

[1] Department of Mechanics and Applied Informatics, Faculty of Mechanical Engineering, Bialystok University of Technology, Wiejska 45c, 15-351 Bialystok, Poland, e-mail: dzienis.pawel@gmail.com; r.mosdorf@pb.edu.pl

ABSTRACT

In this study the first part of the experimental data was recorded in a data acquisition station, and another one was recorded with a high speed camera. The data recorded using the acquisition station was recorded with higher frequency than the time between two subsequent frames of the film. During the analysis of the experimental data the problem was related to the synchronization of measurement from acquisition station and data recorded with a camera. In this paper the method of synchronization of experimental data has been shown. A laser- phototransistor system has been used. The data synchronization was required in scaling of sampling frequency in the investigated time series.

Keywords: experimental data synchronization, time series, video analysis, bubble departure.

INTRODUCTION

During the study of dynamics of bubble chain formation in liquid the data were recorded using the acquisition station and with a high-speed camera at the same time [1–4]. During the analysis of the experimental results the data synchronization was required. There are few methods of data synchronization [4, 5]. In the first method the specialized cameras which can be connected to the data acquisition station are used. Another method is based on a connection between the camera and acquisition station using PC computer. These methods allow us for the simultaneous data acquisition and the recorded video, but these methods require additional and expensive hardware. These methods need also the same sampling frequency.

In the paper the method of data synchronization, which is based on laser- phototransistor system, has been shown. This method is cheaper than the previously described methods of data synchronization. The method consisted of two stages. The first stage of data synchronization was based on the phenomenon of voltage change during the time when the laser beam was interrupted. The second stage of synchronization was based on characteristic points inside the analysed time series. The data which were recorded using acquisition systems were sampled at frequency equal to 1 kHz. The videos were recorded with the speed of 600 fps. The time series of pressure changes in air supply system, which were recorded using acquisition systems synchronized with changes of liquid penetration into the nozzle, which were recorded with a high speed camera.

EXPERIMENTAL SETUP AND MEASUREMENT TECHNIQUE

In the experiment, bubbles were generated in the tank whose dimensions were 300×150×700 mm. The experimental setup, for which the dynamics of bubble departing was investigated, has been shown in Figure 1.

The bubbles were generated from glass nozzle with inner diameter 1 mm. The glass nozzle was placed at the bottom of the tank. The tank

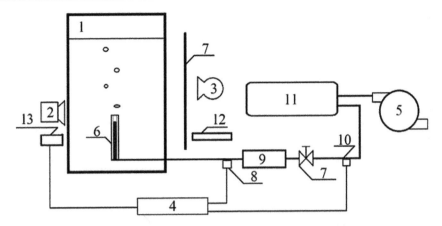

Fig. 1. Experimental setup: 1 – glass tank, 2 – camera, 3 – light source, 4 – computer acquisition system, 5 – air pumps, 6 – glass nozzle, 7 – air valve, 8 – overpressure sensor, 9 – air flow meter, 10 – pressure sensor, 11 – air tank, 12 – laser, 13 – phototransistor

was filled with distilled water. During the experiment the temperature of water was constant at about 20°C. The air volume flow rate was changed from 0.0045 l/min to 0.125 l/min. The changes of air pressure in air supply system were measured using pressure sensor MPX12DP. The time series of pressure changes in the supply system were recorded using data acquisition station DT9800 Series USB Function Modules for Data Acquisition Systems. Sampling frequency was 1 kHz. Videos were recorded using a high speed camera (Casio EX FX 1). The films were recorded in grey scale with the speed of 600 fps. The duration of each video was 20 s. The lighting was based on LED, which gave cold white light. This kind of lighting made it possible to obtain high contrast between liquid and gas. On the videos the gas phase was a dark grey and the liquid phase was light grey. This kind of lighting allows obtaining a clear boundary between liquid and gas. The light source was powered by a DC power supply. Therefore, the light intensity could be adjusted. Between the lights and tank,

the glass plate was placed. The plate was made of translucent glass.

The recorded videos were divided into frames. Using the frames, the time series of liquid penetration were obtained. The technique of the obtained time series has been presented in the paper [1].

THE SYNCHRONIZATION OF THE EXPERIMENTAL RESULTS

In Figure 2 examples of the time series of pressure changes in the gas supply system has been shown. The exemplary time series of changes of depth of liquid penetration inside the nozzle has been shown in Figure 3.

The experimental results (liquid penetration inside the nozzle and pressure changes) were recorded with different sampling frequencies (600 Hz and 1 kHz). Adjustment of sampling frequency for the analysed time series was required. The sampling frequency of pressure changes has been

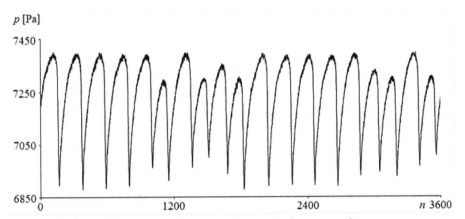

Fig. 2. Time series of pressure changes in the gas supply system

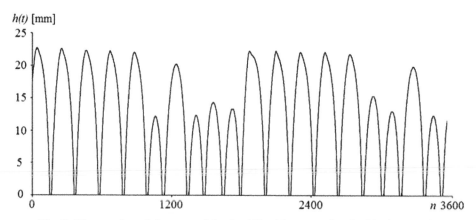

Fig. 3. Time series of changes of depth of liquid penetration inside the nozzle

modified using a computer program. The time series, which were recorded using data acquisition system, had a higher sampling frequency. In this method two samples, recorded with the data acquisition station, determined the straight line equation. The value of pressure in time between these two points was calculated using this equation. The example of the output of the algorithm is shown in Figure 4. The original points has been shown which were marked with rhombuses. The new points were plotted on a graph – marked with squares.

In the first stage of the synchronization a laser-phototransistor system has been used. The schema of electronic circuit of the laser-phototransistor system has been shown in Figure 5. The integrated circuit LM317 was used to power the laser which allowed us to achieve the stable op-

eration of the laser. Laser module was equipped with aperture. The laser beam diameter was approximately 0.1 mm. The phototransistor that was used (BPYP22) allowed the registration of the signal with a frequency above 75 kHz. The phototransistor was equipped with a cover whose length was equal to 30 mm and was made of a tube with inner diameter of 4 mm.

The laser beam was directed to the translucent plate of glass. On the other side of the glass plate the phototransistor was set. The part of the laser beam was passed through the translucent plate of glass and the next part was reflected, which gave the effect of a spots on the videos (Figure 6a). A signal from phototransistor as a time series of changing of voltage, which was generated in phototransistor, was recorded by the data acquisition station.

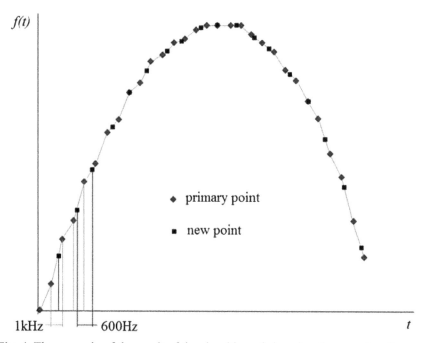

Fig. 4. The example of the result of the algorithm of changing the sampling frequency

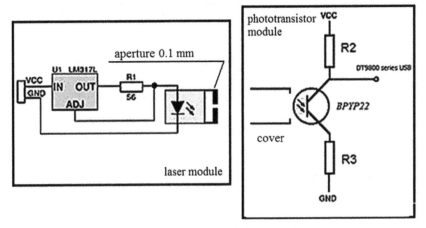

Fig. 5. The schema of electronic circuit of the laser-phototransistor system

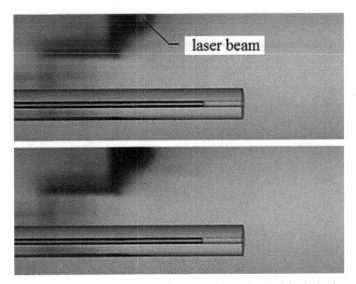

Fig. 6. The frames of the video a) visible laser beam, b) the block the laser light

Before the start of the measurement the laser was on and the voltage generated by phototransistor was equal to 2.5V. During the measurement the laser beam was temporarily blocked by a shutter. The shutter was made from a rod with an outside diameter of 5 mm. The time when the laser beam was invisible was about 0.3 s – about 180 frames. The frame in which there was no light of laser is shown in Figure 6.b. The moment when the laser beam was blocked was also observed in the signal recorded by the data acquisition station as a voltage change (Figure 7). The moment in which the voltage was re-stabilized on phototransistor (2.5 V) and the re-emergence of light on the video frame was treated as the starting of the synchronized time series.

The data obtained from the high-speed camera was analysed from the frame where the re-emergence of laser beam was noticed. In this way, the changes of liquid penetration into the nozzle and the time of bubble growth connected with the pressure changes in the supply system.

The time of voltage rise of the signal from the laser was about 0.05 s, therefore, the accuracy of the first phase of synchronization was about 30 frames. As a result, the time series of pressure changes have been shifted to the time series of liquid penetration into the nozzle. In the second phase of synchronization the beginning of those time series have been corrected using characteristic points in those time series.

Second phase of synchronization of changes of pressure in the supply system and the time series of changes of liquid penetration into the nozzle is shown in Figure 8. Point A and point B in Figure 8 were the characteristic points of the two time series - changes in pressure in the supply system and change of the depth of liquid penetration in to the nozzle, so those points were used in second part of synchronization. In the time se-

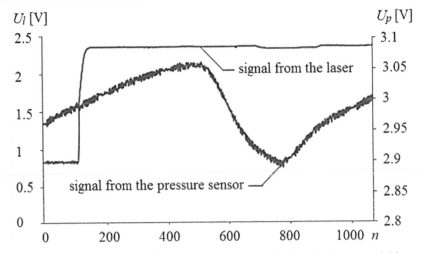

Fig. 7. Voltage change observed in the time series recorded by the data acquisition station

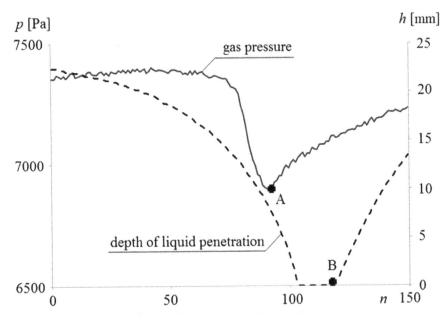

Fig. 8. Second phase of synchronization of changes of pressure in the supply system and the time series of changes of liquid penetration into the nozzle

ries of gas pressure changes in the supply system the lowest pressure value determines the time of bubble departure (A). During the bubble growth, the value of liquid penetration into the nozzle was zero. The moment when the liquid penetration increased, the time of gas bubble departing (B) is Determined. The number of samples with the lowest pressure value and the number of frames where the process of liquid penetration was starting become new onset points of time series. Using these points in the time series the experimental data was synchronized. Points A and B in those time series were set on the same values of the samples (x-axis). The samples corresponding to the presented values, at points A and B, was beginning of the analysed time series.

CONCLUSIONS

The presented method of data synchronization allowed us to fit the pressure time series recorded using the data acquisition station and the time series of changes of liquid penetration into the nozzle, recorded by the high-speed camera.

The method described in this paper can be applied only to the time series, which contain characteristic points. In this case, these points were the characteristic pressure conditions in which the bubble departured and characteristic depth of liquid penetration into the nozzle before bubble departure. Synchronization accuracy was about 0.0017 s, which is the duration of one frame.

A great advantage of the presented method of data synchronization is that additional specialized equipment is unnecessary. This reduces the costs required to perform the studies. This method enables the analysis of the time series recorded at different intervals.

REFERENCES

1. Dzienis P., Mosdorf R., Wyszkowski T. The dynamics of liquid movement inside the nozzle during the bubble departures for low air volume flow rate. Acta Mechanica et Automatica, 2012, 6(3): 31-36.

2. Zang L., Shoji M. Aperiodic bubble formation from a submerged orifice. Chemical Engineering Science, 2001, 56: 5371-5381.

3. Mosdorf R., Wyszkowski T., Dąbrowski K.K. Multifractal properties of large bubble paths in a single bubble column. Archives of Thermodynamics, 2011, 32(1): 3-20.

4. Ruzicka M.C., Bunganic R., Drahos, J. Meniscus dynamics in bubble formation. Part I: Experiment. Chem. Eng. Res. Des. 2009, 87: 1349–1356.

5. http://www.visionresearch.com/Products/High-Speed-Cameras/v1610/ 03.04.2013.

15

THE USE OF COMPUTER ALGEBRA SYSTEMS IN THE TEACHING PROCESS

Mychaylo Paszeczko[1], Marcin Barszcz[1], Ireneusz Zagórski[2]

[1] Department of Fundamentals of Technology, Fundamentals of Technology Faculty, Lublin University of Technology, 38 Nadbystrzycka Str., 20-618 Lublin, Poland, e-mail: m.paszeczko@pollub.pl

[2] Department of Production Engineering, Mechanical Engineering Faculty, Lublin University of Technology, 36 Nadbystrzycka Str., 20-618 Lublin, Poland, e-mail: i.zagorski@pollub.pl

ABSTRACT

This work discusses computational capabilities of the programs belonging to the CAS (Computer Algebra Systems). A review of commercial and non-commercial software has been done here as well. In addition, there has been one of the programs belonging to the this group (program Mathcad) selected and its application to the chosen example has been presented. Computational capabilities and ease of handling were decisive factors for the selection.

Keywords: computer algebra systems, Mathcad, engineering calculations.

INTRODUCTION

It is difficult to imagine the work of designers and technologists without computers and specialist software nowadays. They are used at all levels of design and manufacturing. On the one hand, they facilitate and accelerate these processes and on the other they have a positive influence on the final result of the product. There is a whole range of computer programs supporting the work of engineers at present. Among them the special place is occupied by calculation programs referred to as computer algebra systems CAS. These are mathematical packages designed to perform symbolic calculations in various technical disciplines. They allow for numerical calculations as well. Programs of this type have a built-in own programming language that allows to use own algorithms and create application programs [1, 2]. Therefore, they can be used as an integrated development environment for creating, modifying and testing usable software. They are also used to solve various problems in different fields [1–8].

Therefore, teaching CAS programs is important. It is fundamental to use them as tools in the teaching process. It will help to prepare young people to use them actively in everyday life and to solve a number of engineering problems. It will

increase their chances on the labour market. The introduction of these programs in teaching additionally enables education through an active use such tools and to lead author's lessons by lecturers using not only the blackboard and the chalk. CAS programs can be taught in high school, vocational school and in college. They can be used for courses in subjects such as Mathematics, Physics, Electronics, Electrical Engineering, Mechanical Engineering, Strength of Materials, Statistics, Computer Aided Engineering Calculations, etc.

CHARACTERISTICS OF CAS PROGRAMS

CAS program is the result of work on artificial intelligence. The operations on the mathematical expressions were carried out (elementary functions, matrices, derivatives, calculations related to the number theory, mathematical statistics, calculations for modelling, graphical presentations of graphs, etc.). Basic operations performed by CAS programs include [9]:
- simplifying expressions,
- substitution of symbolic expressions for variables and reduction of similar words,
- developing products,
- distribution of expressions into factors,

- symbolic differentiation,
- symbolic and numerical integration – definite and indefinite integrals,
- symbolic and numerical solving of equations and their systems,
- solving differential equations,
- calculating the limits of functions and sequences,
- calculating the sums of series,
- developing functions into series,
- operations on matrices,
- calculations related to the theory of groups,
- calculations related to mathematical statistics,
- operations on lists and sets of elements,
- export of the results of calculations to TeXa and EPS formats.

Currently there are about 30 different CAS packages available on the market. Some of them are distributed under free software licences, while the rest are commercial programs. The examples of such programs are: Maple, Mathematica, MuPAD, Mathcad, Derive, Fermat, Macsyma and Magma work under a paid licence. In contrast, the free equivalents of these programs include: Sage, Maxima, CoCoA, Axiom, Cadabra, GAP, Macaulay, OpenAxiom, PARI/GP, Reduce. These programs are implemented with the latest algorithms from various fields of mathematics. They provide programming languages which allow the users to write their own programs as well. They plan an important role in the formation of the new field of science, which is called experimental mathematics.

CHARACTERISTICS OF MATHCAD PROGRAM

Mathcad is a commercial computer algebra system (CAS) created by Mathsoft company. Its capabilities are similar to Mathematica or Maple programs. It is an environment of huge computational capabilities, which are characterised by incredible ease and intuitiveness of use, compared to e.g. those two aforementioned. This environment is like a white sheet of paper. Although there is a difference between Mathcad and a sheet of paper. On paper, we have to perform all the calculations by ourselves, while Mathcad will do most of them for us. Documents prepared in Mathcad program can contain not only text and equations, but also various types of graphs (Figure 1). Each arithmetic expression, text paragraph or graph is an independent region. Worksheet allows you to combine created regions in one document. All of these areas create one document, in which the modification of any region changes the entire calculation procedure. Thanks to it, this program allows you to create one, a few or several pages of a document [7, 8, 10].

The program allows you to perform both simple and very complex calculations. It offers the opportunity to create technical documentation in the form of a text document. Program environment enables engineers of all fields to use its options effectively at all the stages of designing. Unique computational tools and built-in programming language make advanced mathematical calculations in view of the most important aspects of creating documentation, which are: security, efficiency and productivity, possible. Mathcad enables you to shorten the design process, to increase efficiency, to improve the quality of the product considerably and allows better adaptation to the existing regulations. It is an environment that certainly stands from others in terms of work ergonomics. Using it does not require the knowledge of syntax of any programming language, since almost everything may be "cursed" and the record of the problems

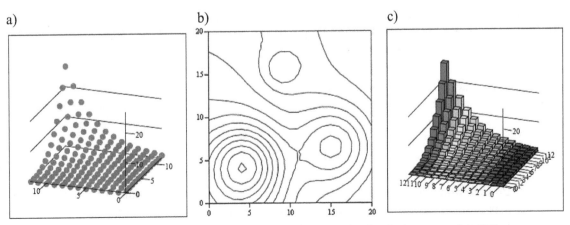

a) b) c)

Fig. 1. Examples of three-dimensional graphs: a – point, b – isohypse; c – bar [11]

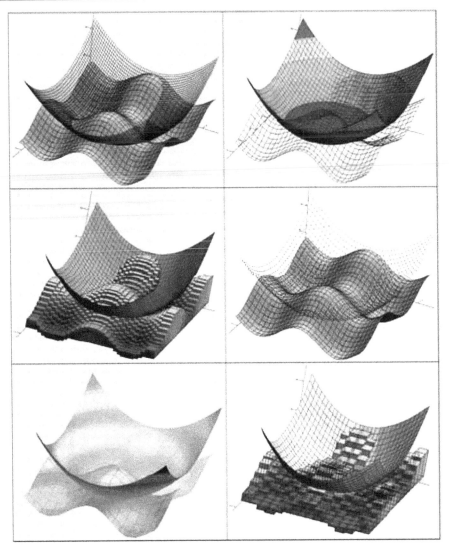

Fig. 1d. Examples of three-dimensional graphs – surface [11]

to be solved is identical with the commonly used mathematical notation. This environment makes it possible to perform complex calculations and to document them in a form, which is readable even for those who are unfamiliar with Mathcad, simultaneously. It is very convenient, because you may share the results of analysis and calculations with others almost immediately. In addition, it is much easier to carry out the verification of the correctness. An important distinguishing feature of Mathcad against the others mathematical computational environments is the ability to perform mathematical operations in a symbolic way, which, in combination with an impressive collection of built-in primary and special functions options for carrying out tasks from various fields of mathematics, makes this environment versatile. Furthermore, the opportunity to work with units of measure and create their own programming procedures make Mathcad a program, which is used for engineering

calculations exceptionally often. It fully supports the Unicode character set, which includes all the scripts used in the whole world. It makes national characters are displayed in worksheets correctly, regardless of operating system version, local settings and language selection.

Thus, its advantages undoubtedly include: ease of use, transparent representation of the data and graphs as well as natural mathematical notation in the record of all formulas. Mathcad allows to transfer data and texts to other programs as well as to import files of different formats. Program environment is equipped with many additional moduli that extend computational capabilities in specific directions:

• Data Analysis – contains functions in the field of data analysis, which include, among others: data imports processes, data scheduling, nonlinear curve fitting algorithms, principal component analysis PCA;

- Signal Processing – includes over 70 functions supporting the analysis and processing of signals, among others: correlation, FFT, filtration, signal windows, spectral analysis;
- Image Processing – includes over 140 functions for analysing and processing images, among others: morphology operations, edge detection, image segmentation, quantitative descriptions of objects;
- Wavelets – contains a set of examples of the use of 1D and 2D wavelet transformations in a form of interactive electronic book and more than 60 functions, which are crucial to wavelet signal analysis.

AN EXAMPLE OF THE PRACTICAL APPLICATION OF MATHCAD PROGRAM

Practical possibilities of using Mathcad on the example of solving the issues of durability of materials. You need to calculate the elongation at break for a steel rod of a rapidly varying diameter and loaded as shown in Figure 2. You should construct graphs of normal forces, a normal stress range and cross-sectional area changes as well. Adopt the following data: $d_1 = 40$ mm, $d_2 = 1/2d_1$, $d_3 = 2/3d_1$, $l_1 = 1,2$ m, $l_2 = 1,2$ m, $l_3 = 0,8$ m, $F_1 = 42$ kN, $F_2 = 40$ kN, $F_3 = 8$ kN, $q_1 = 10$ kN/m, $E_1 = 2,1 \cdot 10^5$ MPa, $E_2 = 2,1 \cdot 10^5$ MPa, $E_3 = 3/4E_1$ and $l_{F1} = 0,6$ m, $l_{F2} = 2,8$ m.

Before starting to solve the above issue in Mathcad program, you need to define each load acting on the given rod, the points of application of these loads, rod diameter, cross-sectional changes, Young's moduli and the length of the individual sections of the rod (additionally, you need to define the scope of function and step of calculation on the length of rod L):

- individual sections of the rod and its total length:
$$l_1 = 1.2 \text{ m}, l_2 = 1.2 \text{ m}, l_3 = 0.8 \text{ m},$$

$$L := \sum_{i=1}^{3} l_i \quad L = 3.2 \text{ m}$$

- scope of function x and step of calculation on the length of rod L:
$$x := 0 \cdot L, 0.001 \cdot L .. L$$

- forces acting on the rod and the distances of their application from restraint point A (forces acting according to the direction of the x-axis are identified by "+" and the opposite ones by "–"):
– concentrated forces:
$$F_1 = 42000 \text{ N}, F_2 = 40000 \text{ N}, F_3 = -8000 \text{ N}$$
$$l_{F_1} := \frac{1}{2} l_1 \quad l_{F_2} := \sum_{i=1}^{2} l_i + \frac{1}{2} l_3 \quad l_{F_3} := L$$

– spread forces:
$$q1 := 10000 \frac{\text{N}}{\text{m}} \quad l_{q_1} := l_2 \quad a_{q_1} := l_1$$

- Young's moduli for each section of the rod:
$$E_1 := 2.1 \cdot 10^5 \text{MPa} \quad E_2 := 2.1 \cdot 10^5 \text{MPa} \quad E_3 := \frac{3}{4} E_1$$

- diameters of individual rod sections and their cross-sectional area:
$$d_1 := 0.040\text{m} \quad d_2 := \frac{1}{2} d_1 \quad d_3 := \frac{2}{3} d_1$$
$$S_1 := \frac{\pi (d_1)^2}{4} \quad S_2 := \frac{\pi (d_2)^2}{4} \quad S_3 := \frac{\pi (d_3)^2}{4}$$

- distance in changes cross-sectional from the point A
$$l_{S_1} := l_1 \quad l_{S_2} := \sum_{i=1}^{2} l_i \quad l_{S_3} := L$$

Once each size is defined, you can calculate:
- reaction of restraint point of the rod in point A:
$$R_A := \sum_{i=1}^{3} F_i + \sum_{i=1}^{1} \left(q_i \cdot l_{q_i} \right)$$
$$R_A = 8.6 \times 10^4 \text{N}$$

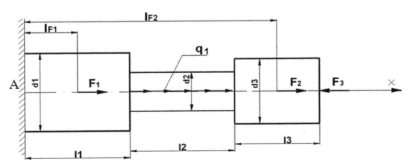

Fig. 2. Scheme of tie rod

- forces coming from both external concentrated and spread forces acting on the rod:

$$N_F(x) := \sum_{i=1}^{3} \left[F_i \left(x \geq l_{F_i} \right) \right]$$

$$N_q(x) := \sum_{i=1}^{1} \left[\left[q_i \left(x \geq {}^a q_i \right) \right] \mathrm{if} \left[x \geq \left({}^a q_i + l_{q_i} \right), l_{q_i}, x - {}^a q_i \right] \right]$$

- normal forces N for each section of the rod:

$$N(x) := R_A - N_F(x) - N_q(x)$$

- cross-sectional areas changing in the range of function X:

$$S(x) := \sum_{i=1}^{1} \left[S_i \left(x \leq l_{S_i} \right) \right] + \sum_{i=2}^{2} \left[S_i \left(l_{S_1} < x \leq l_{S_i} \right) \right] + \sum_{i=3}^{3} \left[S_i \left(l_{S_2} < x \leq l_{S_i} \right) \right]$$

- distribution of stresses in the area of function X:

$$\sigma(x) := \frac{N(x)}{S(x)}$$

- Young's modulus changing in the range of function X:

$$E(x) := \sum_{i=1}^{1} \left[E_i \left(x \leq l_{S_i} \right) \right] + \sum_{i=2}^{2} \left[E_i \left(l_{S_1} < x \leq l_{S_i} \right) \right] + \sum_{i=3}^{3} \left[E_i \left(l_{S_2} < x \leq l_{S_i} \right) \right]$$

- total elongation:

$$\Delta l_c := \int_0^L \frac{\sigma(x)}{E(x)} \, dx$$

$$\Delta l_c = 1.092 \times 10^{-3} \, m$$

For checking, construct a graph for normal forces, cross-sectional changes, normal stresses occurring in the rod (Figure 3).

As it was presented above, Mathcad allows to write computational procedures, or independent programs. They may contain many assigning functions, all kinds of conditional instructions and various options for local and global variables. These programs (procedures) perform calculations automatically.

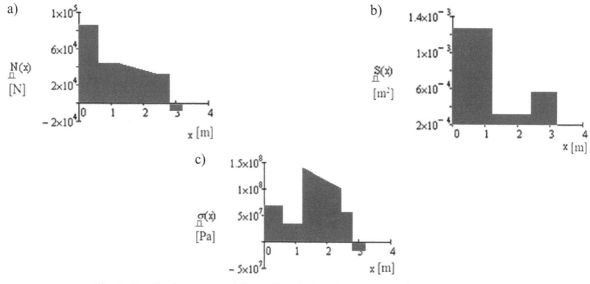

Fig. 3. Graph of: a – normal force distribution; b – cross-sectional area changes;
c – changes of normal stresses of the rod

Change in any record makes the whole procedure change. The user can interfere with its record. They can analyse the changes in solving the given issue with different parameters (e.g. variables, values, etc.) on prepared programs. Changes may be presented and analysed in the graphical form. Students, pupils or engineers can use it to solve all kinds of problems in various fields. You can use it to solve more or less advanced issues, because of its fairly extensive computational capabilities, which include [11]:

- calculating expressions and functions including derivatives, integrals and limits,
- solving equations and inequalities,
- solving systems of linear and non-linear equations,
- solving ordinary and partial differential equations,
- performing numerical and symbolic calculations,
- calculations on vectors and matrices,
- finding vectors and eigenvalues of the matrix,
- curve fitting to a given system of points on a surface,
- creating graphs of 2D and 3D functions,
- creating three-dimensional animations,
- performing operations on complex numbers,
- built-in probability distribution and statistical functions,
- use of SI, MKS, CGS and US units of measure,
- built-in set of functions (DoE) that reduces time and cost of conducting and analysing experiments,
- creating your own subprograms,
- use of upper and lower case letters of the Greek alphabet in expressions,
- comparison of two worksheets,
- data exchange with other programs,
- analysis and synthesis of audio files,
- work on bitmaps,
- cooperation with data files,
- supporting Unicode,
- additional modules of data analysis, signals, images and wavelet transformations,
- access to the online libraries providing technical information and tools from the fields of engineering,
- transfer of physical quantities and parameter values between the applications in an unified way.

CONCLUSIONS

We can use the computational capabilities of CAS programs in everyday work that requires frequent and repeatable use of more or less advanced mathematical calculations. The opportunities of using Mathcad, which were discussed in this work, can greatly facilitate, improve and accelerate solving different kinds of problems in various fields.

Automation of complex calculations, faced by engineers, helps avoid errors while reducing computation time, which, in turn, translates into the quality and profitability of the project. Therefore, it is very important and advisable to teach CAS programs in vocational and high schools, technical schools and in colleges. They can be used for courses in subjects such as Mathematics, Physics, Electronics, Electrical Engineering, Mechanical Engineering, Strength of Materials, Statistics, Computer Aided Engineering Calculations, etc.

REFERENCES

1. Kruczek W.: The electrical characteristics of a catenary system in electric rail vehicles, the calculation of traction load and short – circuit currents. IAPGOŚ 4, 2013, 22–25.

2. Radzieński M., Noga K.: Digital image processing in Mathcad. Scientific Papers of the Faculty of Electrical and Control Engineering Gdansk University of Technology, 25, 2008, 135–139.

3. Hałat W.: Use of computer algebra system for beams' bending problems. Mining and Geoengineering, 3, 2007, 171–182.

4. Gosowski B., Redecki M.: Solution of torsion problems of continious I-sections using Mathematica package. Scientific Papers Rzeszów University of Technology. Construction and Environmental Engineering, 9(3/II), 2012, 357–364.

5. Galon Z.: Mathcad 13 – application for managing engineering design documents. Electrical Review, 82(6), 2006, 87–88.

6. Noga K.M.: Analog and digital modulations in MATHCAD and VISSIM environment. Scientific Papers of the Faculty of Electrical and Control Engineering Gdansk University of Technology, 36, 2013, 137–140.

7. Pashechko M., Bartnicki J., Barszcz M., Kiernicki Z.: Computer-aided in the engineering calculations – Mathcad. Publisher PWSZ, Zamość 2013.

8. Pashechko M., Barszcz M., Dziedzic K.: The use Mathcad program to solve of selected engineering issues. Publisher Lublin University of Technology, Lublin 2011.

9. Website: http://www.helionica.pl (Access: Apr. 2014).

10. Motyka R., Rasał D.: MathCAD from the calculations for programming. Publisher Helion, 2012.

11. Website: http://www.mathcad.pl (Access: Dec. 2013).

16

A COMPUTATIONAL SOFTWARE PROGRAM FOR DETERMINING THE COMBUSTION TEMPERATURES OF SOLID FUELS

Marta Kowalik[1], Jarosław Boryca[1]

[1] The Department of Industrial Furnaces and Environmental Protection, The Faculty of Process & Material Engineering and Applied Physics, Technical University of Czestochowa, Al. Armii Krajowej 19, 42-200 Czestochowa, Poland, e-mail: kowalikm@wip.pcz.pl

ABSTRACT

The combustion temperature is one of parameters influencing the efficiency of combustion process. The analytical, model and design calculations of processes related to fuel combustion and heat exchange intensity require the combustion temperature to be correctly determined. These are, however, complex, and, as a consequence, burdensome and time-consuming requirements. Developing an appropriate software program will considerably streamline the calculation procedure. Based on analytical relationships for the combustion process, a computational software program has been developed within this study, which enables the determination of the calorimetric, theoretical and actual combustion temperatures of solid fuels.

Key words: combustion of solid fuels, combustion temperature, computational software program.

INTRODUCTION

A basic combustion process control parameter, aside from the excess air factor, is temperature. The temperature of combustion is a factor determining the efficiency of heat transfer. Normally, efforts are made to increase the combustion temperature with the aim of increasing the heat transfer efficiency. There are several methods that allow the increase of this parameter, namely [1, 2]:

- heating up the fuel and incoming air,
- enriching the air with oxygen,
- thermal insulation of the combustion chamber,
- assuring the complete and total combustion with the lowest possible value of the excess air factor, α.

The proper selection of the combustion temperature allows the correctness of analytical, and in a particular model and design combustion process-related calculations, to be maintained. Determining the combustion temperatures conditions, inter alia, model studies of the combustion of solid fuels in the context of reducing atmospheric pollutant emissions. Hence, it seems to be of paramount importance to determine this parameter in an efficient and, at the same time, expeditious manner.

COMBUSTION TEMPERATURE

The temperature that combustion gas attains at the end of the combustion process is called combustion temperature. Three combustion temperature types are distinguished [3–6].

The calorimetric combustion temperature is the highest temperature achievable by undissociated combustion gas as a result of the adiabatic and isobaric combustion of fuel with theoretical amount of air [3, 5]:

$$t_{kal} = \frac{i_0 + i_r}{c_{sp}} \qquad (1)$$

where: c_{sp} – mean specific heat of combustion gas, J/(μm^3·K),

i_0 – enthalpy of 1 μm^3 of wet theoretical combustion gas ($\alpha = 1,0$), J/μm^3,

i_r – combustion substrates enthalpy per 1 μm^3 wet theoretical combustion gas, $J/\mu m^3$.

The enthalpy of wet theoretical combustion gas is expressed by the relationship [3, 5]:

$$i_0 = \frac{Q_d}{V_s''} \tag{2}$$

where: V_s'' – unit of wet combustion gas volume, $\mu m^3_{\text{sp. wilg}}/kg_{\text{fuel}}$,
    Q_d – calorific value, J/kg:

$$Q_d = \left[33900 \cdot c + 144030 \cdot \left(h - \frac{o}{8} \right) + 10400 \cdot s - 2500(w_c - 9h) \right] \cdot 10^3 \tag{3}$$

where: c, s, h, o, w_c – mass fractions of liquid and solid fuel components.

The enthalpy of combustion substrates per 1 μm^3 of theoretical wet combustion gas is determined from the relationship [3]:

$$i_r = \frac{V_{a\min} \cdot c_{pow} \cdot t_p + c_{fuel} \cdot t_{fuel}}{V_s''} \tag{4}$$

where: c_{pow} – mean specific heat capacity of combustion air, $J/(\mu m^3 \cdot K)$,
    c_{fuel} – mean specific heat capacity of combustion gas, $J/(kg \cdot K)$,
    t_p – combustion air temperature, °C,
    t_{fuel} – fuel temperature, °C,
    $V_{a\min}$ – minimum combustion air demand, $\mu m^3_{pow.}/kg_{fuel}$,

The theoretical (initial) combustion temperature is the highest temperature achievable by dissociated combustion gas [3, 5]:

$$t_{teor} = \frac{i_\alpha + i_r - i_d}{c_p} \tag{5}$$

where: i_α – enthalpy of 1 μm^3 of wet real combustion gas allowing for the value of the excess air factor, $J/\mu m^3$,
    i_d – enthalpy of dissociation of 1 μm^3 of real combustion gas, $J/\mu m^3$.

The enthalpy of wet real combustion gas, while allowing for the value of the excess air factor, is expressed by the relationship [3, 5]:

$$i_\alpha = \frac{Q_d}{V_s''} \tag{6}$$

The enthalpy of real combustion gas dissociation is determined from the relationship:

$$i_d = 12470 \cdot \alpha_{CO_2} \cdot r_{CO_2} + 10620 \cdot \alpha_{H_2O} \cdot r_{H_2O} \tag{7}$$

where: r_{CO_2}, r_{H_2O} – volumetric fractions of combustion gas components,
    $\alpha_{CO_2}, \alpha_{H_2O}$ – dissociation coefficients.

For combustion temperatures below 1700 °C the enthalpy of dissociation is negligible and its influence on the combustion temperature can be omitted.

The actual combustion temperature is also called flame temperature. This is a temperature at a given moment and in a given location in the flame (furnace). It allows for the effect of heat radiation into the furnace space. It is determined from the relationship [3, 5]:

$$t_{rzecz} = \mu \cdot t_{teor} \tag{8}$$

where: μ – pyrometric combustion factor.

The values of the pyrometric combustion factor is provided in literature [3] for different types of furnace.

COMPUTATION METHODOLOGY

For developing the program, analytical relationships for the combustion temperature were used. The implementation of these relationships in the program required mathematical functions describing the following quantities to be formulated:
- the mean specific heat capacity of the gas, air and combustion gas;
- the coefficients of dissociation of CO_2 and H_2O.

The value of mean specific heat capacity of the solid fuel, expressed in kJ/(kg .K), was determined from the relationship:

$$c_{paliwa} = 0.708 \cdot c + 14.195 \cdot h + 0.915 \cdot o + 1.039 \cdot n + 0.699 \cdot s + 0.795 \cdot p + 4.186 \cdot w_c \qquad (9)$$

where: p – ash mass fraction of fuel.

The value of the mean specific heat capacity of air and combustion gas, expressed in kJ/($\mu m^3 \cdot K$), was determined from the relationship:

$$c = \sum \overline{c_i} \cdot r_i \qquad (10)$$

where: $\overline{c_i}$ – mean specific heat capacity of air or combustion gas component, kJ/($\mu m^3 \cdot K$),

r_i – volumetric fraction of an air or combustion gas component.

Based on the value of mean specific heat capacity for individual air and combustion gas components, mathematical functions describing the effect of temperature on their heat capacities were formulated. The general relationship assumes the form as below:

$$\overline{c_i} = A + B \cdot t + C \cdot t^2 \qquad (11)$$

where: A, B, C – constant values,

t – temperature, °C.

The solid values to calculations of average proper warmth for individual components of gas and air and the fumes summarized in Table 1.

The dissociation coefficients represent a function of temperature and partial pressure being dependent on the CO_2 and H_2O contents of combustion gas. The energy balance equation enabling computations to be performed with the method presented herein and the problems related to the dissociation of CO_2 and H_2O are described in a greater detail in references [7–9]. For particular partial pressure ranges, relationships for the dissociation coefficients as a function of temperature were developed. The general relationship adopts the following form:

$$\alpha = A_1 + B_1 \cdot t + C_1 \cdot t^2 + D_1 \cdot t^3 \qquad (12)$$

where: A_1, B_1, C_1, D_1 – constant values.

The solid values to calculations of dissociation H_2O coefficients for individual ranges of partial pressure summarized in Table 2.

Table 1. The solid empirical values to calculations of average proper warmth for individual components of gas and air and the fumes

Components	The solid values		
	A	B · 10³	C · 10⁷
CO_2	1.61957	0.844664	-2.5154100
H_2O	1.48957	0.201901	0.3196780
O_2	1.29731	0.225157	-4.6761200
N_2	1.28986	0.084818	1.7209400
SO_2	1.71520	0.773119	-2.7719800
Air	1.28957	0.113784	0.0353641
CO	1.28882	0.113424	0.0546218

Table 2. The solid empirical values to calculations of dissociation CO_2 coefficients for individual ranges of partial pressure

Partial pressure CO_2 in fumes, kPa	The solid values			
	A_1	$B_1 \cdot 10^3$	$C_1 \cdot 10^7$	$D_1 \cdot 10^{10}$
3	1.0769795	-1.5647	5.62075	0
4	1.2074031	-1.6814	5.83561	0
5	1.2856280	-1.7473	5.93966	0
6	1.3233584	-1.7727	5.94880	0
7	1.3760369	-1.8167	6.01631	0
8	1.3985608	-1.8310	6.01588	0
9	1.4233874	-1.8483	6.02667	0
10	1.4440101	-1.8628	6.03492	0
12	1.4567568	-1.8623	5.98104	0
14	1.4782624	-1.8732	5.96471	0
16	1.4724573	-1.8583	5.89191	0
18	1.4510133	-1.8272	5.78002	0
20	1.4630247	-1.8325	5.76571	0
60	-0.0158115	0.4452	-5.45004	1.72170
100	-0.1273187	0.5825	-5.83210	1.69451

Table 3. The solid values to calculations of dissociation H_2O coefficients for individual ranges of partial pressure

Partial pressure H_2O in fumes, kPa	The solid values			
	A_1	$B_1 \cdot 10^3$	$C_1 \cdot 10^7$	$D_1 \cdot 10^{10}$
3	-0.7364956	1.4376	-9.62587	2.21989
4	-1.0296681	1.8584	-11.54020	2.48524
5	-0.8522410	1.5838	-10.10520	2.22688
6	-0.6930881	1.3379	-8.82552	1.99883
7	-0.7293497	1.3821	-8.95886	1.99728
8	-0.7181641	1.3609	-8.80892	1.95824
9	-0.7496520	1.4005	-8.94406	1.96426
10	-0.7169212	1.3437	-8.60804	1.89549
12	-0.7338214	1.3595	-8.60589	1.87277
14	-0.7216266	1.3362	-8.44132	1.83081
16	-0.6944776	1.2922	-8.18712	1.77720
18	-0.7296117	1.3336	-8.31393	1.77953
20	-0.7199730	1.3262	-8.29773	1.77486
60	-0.7236804	1.2654	-7.51713	1.52914
100	-0.6085711	1.0674	-6.35763	1.29584

The solid values to calculations of dissociation H_2O coefficients for individual ranges of partial pressure summarized in Table 3.

Using the described mathematical functions allowing for the effect of temperature, the dissociation coefficients were determined from the relationships:

$$\alpha_{CO_2} = \alpha_{(i+1)\,CO_2} + \left\{ \left(\alpha_{i\,CO_2} - \alpha_{(i+1)\,CO_2} \right) \cdot \left[p_{(i+1)CO_2} - p_{CO_2} \right] \right\} \tag{13}$$

$$\alpha_{H_2O} = \alpha_{(i+1)\,H_2O} + \left\{ \left(\alpha_{i\,H_2O} - \alpha_{(i+1)\,H_2O} \right) \cdot \left[p_{(i+1)H_2O} - p_{H_2O} \right] \right\} \tag{14}$$

where: $\alpha_{i\,CO_2}$, $\alpha_{i\,H_2O}$ — the coefficients of dissociation of CO_2 and H_2O for the lower partial pressure value from the range under consideration,

$\alpha_{(i+1)CO_2}$, $\alpha_{(i+1)H_2O}$ — the coefficients of dissociation of CO_2 and H_2O for the higher partial pressure value from the range under consideration,

p_{CO_2}, p_{H_2O} — the actual partial pressure of CO_2 i H_2O, kPa,

$p_{(i+1)CO_2}$, $p_{(i+1)H_2O}$ — the higher CO_2 and H_2O partial pressure value from the range under consideration, kPa.

COMPUTATIONAL SOFTWARE PROGRAM

For developing the software program, computational procedures were employed, as illustrated in Figure 1. Considering the analytical relationships and the determined mathematical functions, a computational software program has been developed, whose screenshot is shown in Figure 2.

According to the procedures shown in Figure 1, the input data in a form of the oxygen content of combustion air, the excess air factor value, the temperatures of combustion air and fuel as well as fuel composition needs to be entered in the program (Figure 3). The procedure for the calorimetric temperature provides combustion process computation results for $\alpha = 1.0$ and specific heats and enthalpies necessary for determining the temperature sought for (Figure 3). The assumed calorimetric temperature should be selected so that its value be approximate to the obtained result.

The procedure for the theoretical temperature provides combustion process computation results for the actual value of the excess air factor α and specific heats and enthalpies necessary for determining

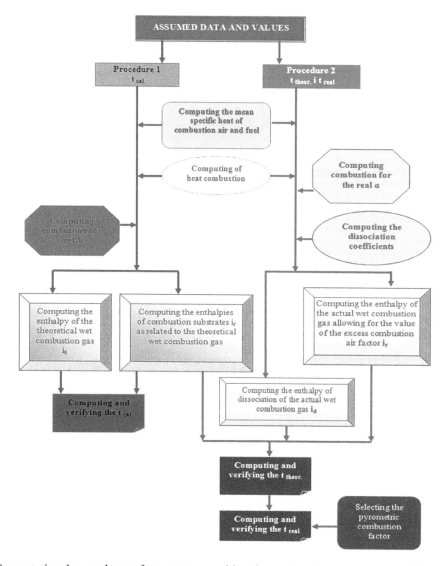

Fig. 1. Computational procedures of program to marking the combustion temperatures of the solid fuels

the temperature sought for (Figure 4). The assumed theoretical temperature must be approximate to the obtained result, whereas the actual temperature results from the theoretical temperature. The design of the program enables fast determination of solid fuel combustion temperatures; however, it requires basic theoretical knowledge of combustion processes.

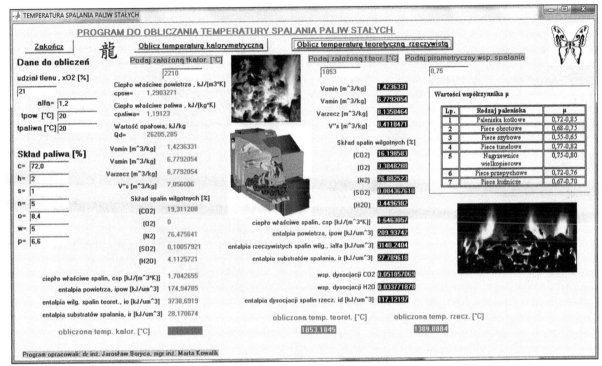

Fig. 2. A screenshot of program for calculations of combustion temperature of the solid fuels

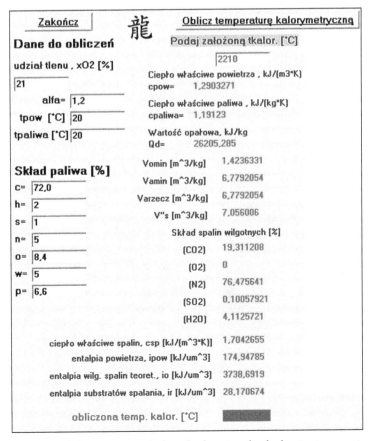

Fig. 3. Part of the program window for input and calorimeter temperature

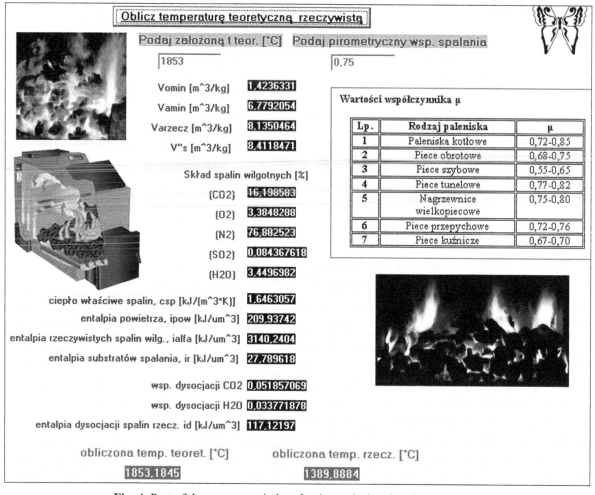

Fig. 4. Part of the program window for theoretical and real temperature

EXAMPLE COMPUTATION RESULTS

For the fuel composition shown in the program window (Figure 3), the theoretical temperature was computed for the variable value of the excess combustion air factor and the calorimetric, theoretical and actual temperatures for the variable combustion air temperature, with an excess combustion air factor of $\alpha = 1.2$.

The computation results are summarized in Figures 5 and 6. By examining Figure 5 it can be stated that with the increase in the excess air factor value, the theoretical combustion temperature decreases, whereas increasing the air temperature (Figure 6) causes an increase in the calorimetric, theoretical and actual combustion temperatures.

SUMMARY

The paper has presented basic assumptions used for the development of a software program that will enable the user to determine the solid fuel combustion temperature in an easy and expeditious manner. An asset of the program is the fact that, in addition to the ease of operation, provides the capability to readily change the input data in the form of the excess air factor value, combustion substrate temperature, fuel composition and the oxygen fraction of the feed air. The possibility of entering a variable oxygen fraction is extremely important in case of computation concerning combustion in an oxygen-enriched atmosphere. For the actual temperature, it is also possible to select an appropriate pyrometric coefficient.

The presented computation results enable the authors to state that the theoretical and the actual combustion temperatures depend on the value of the excess air factor. With the increase in α, the above-mentioned temperatures decrease. In turn, the increase in substrate temperature causes an increase in combustion temperatures, including also the calorimetric temperature. The results obtained for different fuels are approximate to those provided in the literature, which evidences the correctness of operation of the developed program.

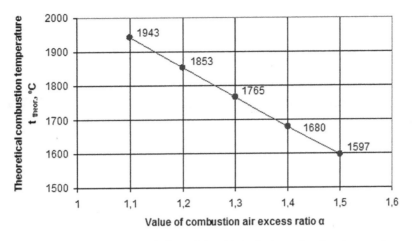

Fig. 5. The results of calculation of the theoretical combustion temperature

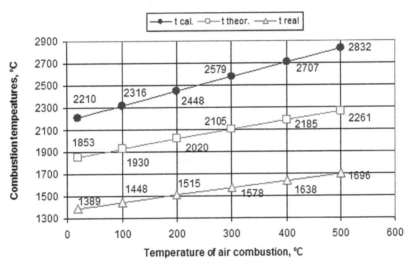

Fig. 6. The results of calculation of the calorimetric, theoretical and real combustion temperatures for variable of air temperature

The presented computational program can provide a useful tool for both teaching and research purposes. Indeed, combustion temperature computation results are an essential input data element in the modelling of combustion processes, as well as in designing combustion chambers.

REFERENCES

1. Szargut J.: Termodynamika techniczna. Wydawnictwo Politechniki Śląskiej, Gliwice 2010.

2. Pastucha L., Mielczarek E.: Podstawy termodynamiki technicznej. Wydawnictwo Politechniki Częstochowskiej, Częstochowa 1998.

3. Kieloch M., Kruszyński S., Boryca J., Piechowicz Ł.: Termodynamika i technika cieplna – ćwiczenia rachunkowe, Skrypt. Wydawnictwo Politechniki Częstochowskiej, Częstochowa 2006.

4. Senkara T.: Obliczenia cieplne pieców grzewczych w hutnictwie. Wydawnictwo „Śląsk", Katowice 1991.

5. Słupek S., Nocoń J., Buczek A.: Technika cieplna – ćwiczenia obliczeniowe. Wydawnictwo AGH, Kraków 2002.

6. Nocuń J., Poznański J., Słupek S., Rywotycki M.: Technika cieplna, przykłady z techniki procesów spalania, Uczelniane Wydawnictwo Naukowo-Dydaktyczne, Kraków 2007.

7. Szkarowski A.: Spalanie gazów, Wydawnictwo Uczelniane Politechniki Koszalińskiej, Koszalin 2009.

8. Pudlik W.: Termodynamika. Wydawnictwo Politechniki Gdańskiej, Gdańsk 2011.

9. Wiśniewski S.: Termodynamika techniczna, WNT, Warszawa 2005.

17

APPLICATIONS OF CLOUD COMPUTING SERVICES IN EDUCATION – CASE STUDY

Tomasz Cieplak[1], Mirosław Malec[2]

[1] Department of Company Organisation, Lublin University of Technology, Nadbystrzycka 38, 20-618 Lublin, Poland, e-mail: t.cieplak@pollub.pl

[2] Department of Fundamentals of Technology, Lublin University of Technology, Nadbystrzycka 38, 20-618 Lublin, Poland, e-mail: m.malec@pollub.pl

ABSTRACT

Applications of Cloud Computing in enterprises are very wide-ranging. In opposition, educational applications of Cloud Computing in Poland are someway limited. On the other hand, young people use services of Cloud Computing frequently. Utilization of Facebook, Google or other services in Poland by young people is almost the same as in Western Europe or in the USA. Taking into account those considerations, few years ago authors have started process of popularization and usage of Cloud Computing educational services in their professional work. This article briefly summarizes authors' experience with selected and most popular Cloud Computing services.

Keywords: cloud computing, education.

INTRODUCTION

In Poland, wide usage of application of computational software in education has started in 1980's. The software was used in vary ways, depending of its purpose. But, the software always needed expanded IT infrastructure to be used effectively. Also, activity with traditional software systems were limited to the area of school building or one classroom. Students could not have access to their educational materials, homeworks or statistics related to their activity in school. The solution for those limitation were Web-based educational systems. Yet, in this case the IT infrastructure became even more complicated and more difficult in administration.

To gain effective educational systems, educational institution had to spend a lot of financial resources for server infrastructure, administrative staff, Internet connection and of course professional software. In this case, teachers were able to prepare educational materials and share them with students but this process had few important limitations. The first limitation was the way how educational material must be prepared. There were many standards and even more complex tools for preparation of those materials. This situation required from teachers to get familiar with standards of materials preparation and most often caused teachers to be attached to one selected system.

Another limitation standing on the way of popularization of educational systems was complicated administration of IT resources, as well as educational materials. And last but not the least, curtailment were problems with access to educational systems in case of server infrastructure hardware problem. Mostly, educational systems were located on one physical server and its failure resulted in a stoppage of the learning process, or caused a lot of problems in the smooth conduct of classes. The final solution for elimination of the previously mentioned limitations as well as simplifying the process of preparation of materials and availability of resources are educational system based on Cloud Computing services.[1]

BRIEF OVERVIEW OF CLOUD COMPUTING

The term of Cloud Computing was recorded for the first time as early as in 1997, when during INFORMS conference Rama Chellappa – a professor at the University of Maryland defined cloud computing as "the emerging computer paradigm, whose computation limits are established not by technical boundaries, but by justified requirements" [2].

The first research articles concerning the issue were published in 2008. Cloud Computing is a new, yet dynamically developing branch of computer science. Moreover, it may strike as surprising that Cloud Computing has quickly come to enjoy great popularity in many other fields, influencing such areas as social networking, which can be exemplified by Facebook and Twitter services.

The basic classification Cloud Computing was divided into three layers. The first layer – IaaS (Infrastructure as a Service), lies closest to hardware. The next layer – PaaS (Platform as a Service), does not allow the user access to Operating System, but offers an elastic and scalable framework for creating and running their applications. SaaS (Software as a Service) constitutes the third layer of application, which are made available as services.

Although both solutions belong to the same class, their implementation and capabilities are strikingly different. The first difference is the number of operating systems available that the user can utilize. EC2 (Elastic Compute Cloud), true to its name, is a very flexible solution. It enables the user to install one of Linux platforms or Microsoft Windows Server. Apart from that the user has a selection of a few hundred of OS images, configured and prepared for specific tasks. In case of Windows Azure the OS choice is limited to implementations of Microsoft Windows Server images. The billing scheme is another significant difference. It is characterized by different set of parameters, which influence the final price. On account of the character of this publication authors will refrain from comparing both solutions. This will be the subject of another work. In case of IaaS, its essential advantage is enabling the user to full access to the purchased system which he can then managed as he pleases and run any software on it. Nonetheless, with IaaS cloud it is vital to remember that many of Cloud features such as

scalability and failover mechanisms are not available there by default. They can be utilized only if the programmer knows how to implement them in a given solution.

For that reason, if the user does not require full control over the system, but puts scalability and reliability above it he should consider using PaaS solution. PaaS services are offered on a number of platforms: Google App Engine. Microsoft Windows Azure, Ruby on Rails IN Cloud and Force.com – Salesforce.com. One of the key advantages of PaaS is its separation from hardware infrastructure and operating system, thanks to which the issues of hardware malfunction, licensing and installing updates are non-existent. Although the user has to abide certain rules and limitations in the created software, he does not need to utilize specialized techniques enabling him to tap onto scalability of available resources.[3]

Cloud Computing does not restrict its capabilities to programmers. The users may count on ready, pre-made solutions adapted to their needs. This service model is called SaaS. It does not allow for creating applications. Instead it permits using ready software which runs and is made available within the cloud. Google Apps, Microsoft Office 365 and Windows Live are the best examples of this model. Perhaps the most renowned SaaS applications are community based social portals and apps such as Facebook, Flickr, Picasa and many more.

CLOUD COMPUTING SERVICES IN DAILY TEACHERS WORK

Examples shown in this part of article are based on authors' experience and, in most cases, are consistent with the results of other researchers but detailed implementation of services may vary depending on the teacher [4].

Author's first experience with implementation of Cloud Computing services into educational process began in 2010. As in case of many other teachers, the first step was to convince students to use email as communication to exchange their homework as well as questions and other matters connected with learning process. Seemingly, this very simple process required some time and discipline needed to develop the certain habits among students. At the same time Google Apps for Education were implemented. Study was conducted to determine the suitability of specific cloud computing services – in this case Google Apps – in the teaching process. The activities carried out with the use of Google Apps were compared with the previous experience of the authors of online learning systems, such as eg. Moodle. However, due to the nature of the article, these systems will not be compared.

As mentioned earlier, the email communication should have some rules to fully utilize Gmail function. To keep track of students work received on the email box, it was needed to implement filters and labels in Gmail. Without certain students habits this process would fail. Next, maybe less important, was fact that most of student were using their private email addresses, without properly described first and last names. Almost simultaneously, after the implementation of Google Apps, an educational website built on Google Sites service was launched. What was very important for authors, the implementation time was very short comparing to time needed to run educational service based for example on on Moodle. To start the service and fill it with educational materials, Google user needed just about one hour. But simplicity sometimes means less opportunity in case of educational means. In the case of site based on Google, teacher has no possibility to track who and when uses materials. The solution could be Google Analytics, but also in this case information is very limited. Teacher has no possibility to prepare in easy way tests, flashcards and other interactive materials that are implemented into Moodle. So at the first sight, Google was good but not sufficient. When a simple communication via email, file sharing and ads were needed, Google services were sufficient. But in the case where a teacher needs more sophisticated tools, further research was needed to be carried out. A natural step was to search for applications, which are available as an extension proposed for Google Apps for Education.

In year 2011 such extension was available as Web application called Docebo E-Learning. Unfortunately, the cost of the application was too high. After extended research, the authors found very flexible and very cost effective e-learning solution called Engrade on the market. This system has been used for three years until now. The total number of registered classes equals sixty four and registered students equals about eight hundred. During this time the system was very stable and, what is very important – especially

in the case of Cloud Computing services – the rules of use of this system were unchanged. Because Engrade is not widely known, at least in Poland, it will be described in more detail later in the article.

Engrade, as a very useful tool to teach yet, it does not meet all the requirements. The authors sought additional applications that, for example, may allow for conducting classes remotely – Remote seminars or consultations. The solution was an AnyMeeting system. AnyMeeting is a Cloud Computing service, too. It allows one to conduct meetings and conference – share the view of the screen, text chat and voice conversations. For the authors, this system was used by a group seminar. Such a method of conducting classes, familiarizes students with teleconferences and presentations.

The last tool used in the teaching process is Facebook. It may be a surprising statement, but Facebook appears to be an excellent tool to stay in touch with current or former students. For current students, allows for quick contact with a person or a group of students – which happens extremely rarely. However, in the case of former students v especially graduates v Facebook gives you the ability to track their careers after graduation, as well as a tool to obtain an opinion on the activities undertaken.

During the research on Cloud Computing application in education, authors have tested many other services such as Mojo Helpdesk, SlideRocket, Do, Youtube, but their usefulness in the education process was limited. Of course in the case of Youtube one can find this tool very useful as a tool to assist the teaching process, but in case of authors, application of that service was very rare.

Using SlideRocket service as an example, you should pay attention to a very important aspect of Cloud Computing services usage, namely the stability of the operations of the service, and the immutability of license usage rights. As we all know the teaching process takes a fairly long period of time, once prepared classes should be modernized, not totally rebuilt or reconstructed. The most serious threat in the case of free access to the service is change of the terms of service. The user has the choice to cease the use of the service or pay a certain fee for the use. In the case of the aforementioned system Engrade or Google Apps for Education this situation has not occurred. However, one should always reckon with the possibility that the terms of service may change.

BENEFITS AND RISKS OF USING CLOUD COMPUTING

As mentioned at the end of previous part of the article, Cloud Computing gives the educational institution many benefits but also brings some risks. With previously mentioned example of SlideRocket service is directly connected the risk called Lock-in. This risk is that an institution will become "locked-in" to the products of a particular provider. There are significant costs in migrating from any used system to another. While some providers make claims about the interoperability of their products it is rarely easy to transfer content from one system to another. Institutions which start to integrate business or educational processes with the cloud systems will find it even more difficult to migrate. If a better rival product emerges or the cloud provider decides to impose or increase charges on institutions it may be too late to change the service.

In many cases of services – especially those provided for free – with software there are also associated advertising. That fact causes the next risk appears called "unsolicited advertising". This is especially important in EU countries where unsolicited advertising is illegal and institutions must take steps to ensure this does not happen. In addition, the accumulation of usage data by the providers may be of value for onward selling to third parties, though it may be anonymized. The inclusion of appropriate clauses in the contract may minimize the risk of abuse.

A major concern is around the security of data. Institutions may consider that their data is more secure if it is hosted within the institution. Transferring data to a third party in a remote data center, not under the control of the institution and the location of which may not be known, presents a risk. Strict data protection laws in Poland, as a part of the EU, restrict the storage of personal data to countries with which agreements have been signed (those countries are Argentina, Bailiwick of Guernsey, Faroe Islands, Isle of Man, Jersey, Switzerland and – if the provider is accept certain conditions – Canada, USA).[5] Some cloud providers now provide guarantees in their contracts that personal data will only be stored in particular countries.[6]

Benefits of use of Cloud Computing services are as follow:

- Economies – services such as email are offered for free by external providers; hardware can be redeployed or removed, potentially freeing up valuable real estate; personnel costs can be cut.
- Elasticity – allows for rapid escalations in demand at peak times, such as at the start of the academic year or during exam periods.
- Enhanced availability – less downtime due to the superior resources and skills available to cloud providers.
- End user satisfaction – range of new applications being provided; students can use such applications as Office for free without having to purchase, install and keep these applications up to date on their computers; collaboration; data is accessible from any location or from a range of devices; technologies such as HTML5 will increasingly allow users to work offline when Internet access is intermittent.

ENGRADE AS A TOOL FOR TEACHERS

Engrade is a secure, web-based online gradebook and class management tool, free of charge. This software allows teachers to post and track students information in one place, as well as allows students and their parents to check grades and attendance. Engrade also offers mobile site access to provide access from mobile devices. For those who need more advanced features, like collecting and viewing data from third-party providers, there is paid version, for a per-student annual fee.

As it was said, Engrade is a free of charge for teacher as well as for students and their parents. In the research, in case of use of Engrade by authors, parents accounts were not taken into account. Yet, this utility was used to carry on all documentation of students from all classes. Engrade was tested for three years and during this time occurred no problem with system stability. Also, the design and usability was not changed.

After very easy registration – were few possible account types to choose (to prepare Engrade for an institution it was better to choose and establish a school account of administrator than teacher account) – administrator could register teachers belonging to one school. Figure 1 shows the dashboard of Engrade prepared for testing purpose.

In case of presented test school, seventeen teachers were registered. Not everyone was conducting classes during summer semester of academic year 20013/14. Some of teachers were using whole teaching process where some of them were using Engrade just in some cases eg. for stu-

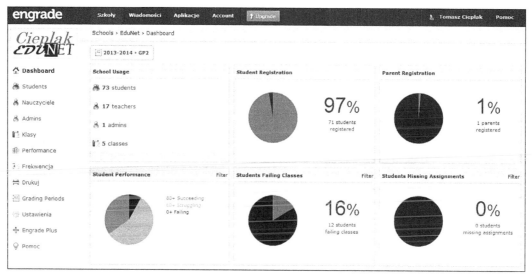

Fig. 1. Administrator dashboard of school

dents testing purpose. Teachers faced few problems with adaptation their classes style for online method of teaching. Some of them no needed computers on their classes and used Engrade as a supporting tool to share materials with students. In case of authors, Engrade was used to: share materials, communicate with students, keep track of students assignments and finally to collect suggestions about student progress and support decision on final grade of student .

All features of Engrade are divided into Apps. Figure 2 shows Class Apps with following sections: gradebook, assignments, calendar, attendance, list of students, tests turn-ins, discussion, standards, comments to lessons, seating chart. Teacher can also set settings for chosen class –

settings (class name, school year, grading scale, main apps) were configured during class addition of a class, but they could always be adjusted by teacher during a school year.

To proper set a class inside Engrade, after adding class name and students to the class, teacher needed to put subjects of lessons and dates of deadline for each lesson (see Figure 3). This was very useful to keep self-discipline of teacher as well as discipline of class. After setting all lessons, students can see all assignments and they know the date when turn-in must be send to get score of an accomplished lesson. Figure 3 shows dates of turn-ins sent by students as well as scores for each student. After completion all turn-ins at the end of semester, teacher was having informa-

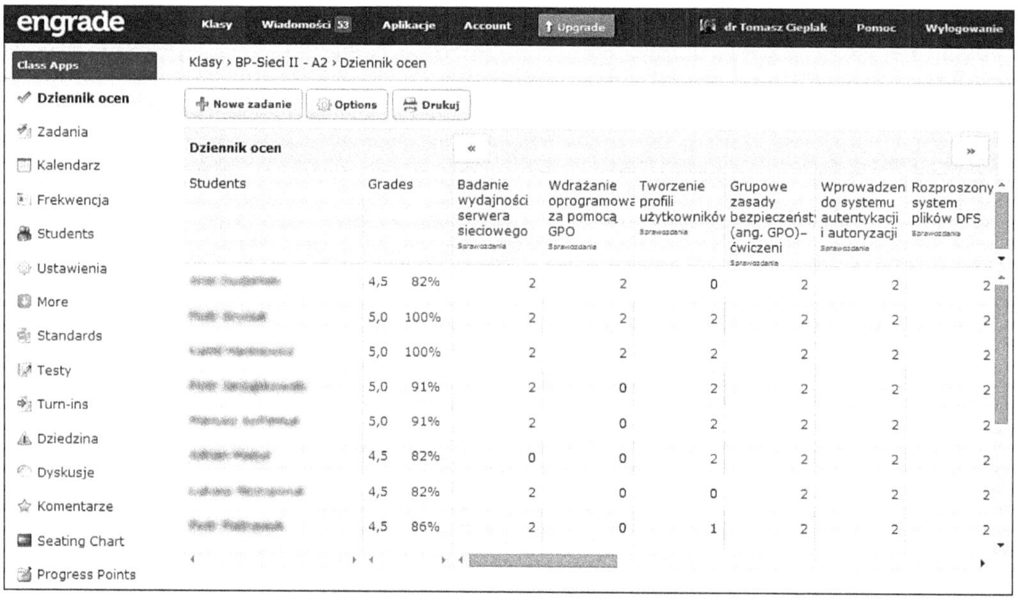

Fig. 2. View of teachers dashboard

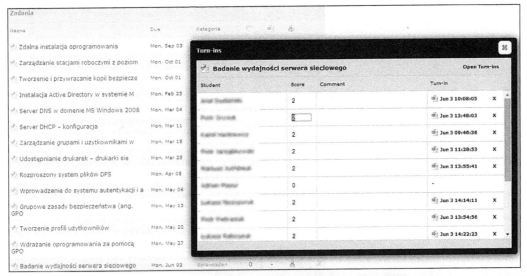

Fig. 3. Assignments screen with subjects and turn-ins

tion about each student progress and in the same time a proposition of the final grade.

Frequently, authors were using flash cards as a tool to prepare student for tests or other methods of knowledge verification. For each class was also checked attendance, which at the end of the semester was a factor in the final evaluation (see Figure 2).

CONCLUSIONS

Application of Cloud Computing services was researched and different solutions were tested during three years. Systems like Engrade, AnyMeeting, Google Apps for Education were found as a very useful tools in everyday practice of teachers. According to students opinion on classes, carried out with use of these services, students always knew what would be the course of the lesson, their scores and other information of class progress. That fact made them clear about the rules of gaining credit in a given subject. From point of view of teachers and administration, analyzed systems were easy to set and maintain.

However, it should also be noted that systems operating in a cloud computing have a number of drawbacks. First, the user must have access to the Internet to be able to use these systems. Must be paid attention to the license agreement and the changes in conditions and prices of service. User may be locked in a specific, single solution and move to another provider may be a process quite difficult and time consuming. When choosing a system, should be paid attention to

the language versions of the system. English is available in almost all services, but eg. Polish language is available in only a few. The most important note, user must always pay attention to where his data will be collected and how it will be secured in the system.

Already in the course of writing the article, Google has launched a new service called Classroom. Thus, further studies in the academic year 2004/15 will focus on the use of new solutions running in the cloud computing. These services will be Google Classroom and EDU 2.0.

REFERENCES

1. Sultan N.: Cloud computing for education: A new dawn? International Journal of Information Management, Vol. 30 (2), 2010.

2. Chellappa R.: Cloud computing – emerging paradigm for computing. Institute for Operations Management and Research (INFORMS), Dallas, 1997.

3. Cieplak T., Malec M.: Practical usage of cloud computing in computer integrated manufacturing. In: New methods in industrial engineering and production management, Lublin University of Technology 2012.

4. Sclater N.: Cloud computing in education. UNESCO Institute for Information Technologies in Education, Moscow 2010.

5. European Commission, http://ec.europa.eu/justice/data-protection/document/international-transfers/adequacy/index_en.htm (on day 08.20.2014).

6. Zissis D., Lekkas D.: Addressing cloud computing security issues. Future Generation Computer Systems, Vol. 28 (3), 2012.

18

CFD MODEL OF THE CNG DIRECT INJECTION ENGINE

Zbigniew Czyż[1], Konrad Pietrykowski[1]

[1] Department of Thermodynamics, Fluid Mechanics and Aviation Propulsion Systems, Faculty of Mechanical Engineering, Lublin University of Technology, 36 Nadbystrzycka Str., 20-618 Lublin, Poland, e-mail: z.czyz@pollub.pl

ABSTRACT

The paper presents CFD analysis of fuel flow in the CNG injector. The issues such a pressure drop along an injector channel, mass flow through the key sections of the injector geometry, flow rates, the impact of the needle shape on the deflection of the sprayed gas cone and the impact of the wall head are analyzed in the article. The simulation was made in the transient states conditions for full injection process, including the opening and closing of the injector. An injection time of 6 ms, velocity of 0.33 mm/ms and a lift of 0.5 mm were selected for opening and closing of injector based on experimental test. The simulation shows that the volume inside the injector is a kind of fuel accumulator, and the opening process of the needle influence the flow parameters in an inlet cross-section after a certain time, depending on a channel cross section. The calculations allowed to select the ratio of an injector duct cross sectional area to the aperture area of the injection capable of the reducing pressure loss. The unusual location of the injector in the socket of a glow plug in the Andoria ADCR engine makes a stream be impaired by a part of the head. This research result would be useful in developing an injector construction which will be used for an investigation of CNG addition into diesel engine.

Keywords: simulation and modeling, gas injection, methane injection, direct injection.

INTRODUCTION

Performance of internal combustion engines is largely dependent on the characteristics of the fuel injection system. Transient nature of the flow through these systems and their small sizes makes it very difficult to analyze them experimentally. Simulation tests are often used to analyze the flow inside the injectors and provide the physical flow processes visibility that occurs in them and the entire fuel system [1, 2, 3, 4, 5]. Because of that, computational flow dynamics analysis (CFD) of flow through the injector was performed. In the past, most of the fuel injector CFD analysis was limited to the steady state time conditions. This approach is simplistic and does not fully reflect the phenomena occurring in the undetermined flow. In order to improve computing technologies, the moving mesh is used nowadays. Depending on the computing solver, there are many

ways to simulate the movement of the elements. In work of Margot et al. and Payri et al. [6, 7], the moving mesh was done using STAR CD software in which the movement does not affect the change in the number of elements. Lee and Reitz [8] used a special algorithm of needle movement, which contained the structural grid consisting of hexahedral elements. However, such an approach increases the difficulty of mesh generation for complex shapes of injectors. It is possible to carry out the whole analysis including the geometry preparation and model discretization, not only in STAR CD software, but also in Ansys Fluent software. In the case of transient time analysis (taking into account the time-varying phenomena), there are two possibilities of moving mesh behavior. The first one does not make any changes to the finite element of mesh and is called Sliding Meshes. The second one modifies the elements (remeshing, layering, smoothing). In the simulation, the layering moving mesh was used. This method allows for dynamic layering of hexahedral or wedge mesh elements. This makes it possible to add or remove cells layer placed near the movement surface, based on the thickness of the layer adjacent to the moving surface [9]. Certainly, the development of model discretization methods and movement simulation increases design options.

Injector designing is still challenged by constant striving to improve economic and ecological aspects in combustion engines, alternative-fuel supply and varied injection pressure. This paper focuses on the development of the model of compressed natural gas injector, using Ansys Fluent. CFD tools are often applied to simulate parameters, difficult and sometimes impossible to measure experimentally, of the flow inside the injector and injection. The injector investigated in this paper was developed for dual-fuel supply in a compression ignition engine. Methane seems to have fairy high heating value, so as an additional fuel, it requires special injection conditions to power an engine, mainly for its relatively low density and large-volume flows. Therefore, developing a model that can help to identify and exclude any structural mistakes in flow channel geometry.

RESEARCH OBJECT

The assumptions of a geometric numerical model were based on real geometry and experimental studies. It will be used to supply the CNG fuel to Andoria ADCR diesel engine. The injector will be placed in the cylinder head in glow plug socket. Other cases of construction solutions for dual-fuel engine were presented in [10]. Figure 1 presents an injector used for experimental research along with its longitudinal cross section.

The actual geometry of the injector was used to prepare the geometric model shown in Figure 2.

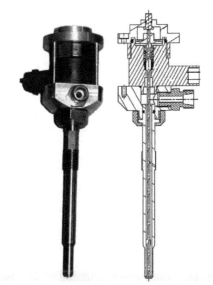

Fig. 1. The actual design of the injector (left) and its longitudinal cross section (right)

In addition, different geometries of injectors were used for numerical calculations (Figures 2 and 3). The second version is completely changed by the injector nozzle, but the third version has an expanded needle nozzle, in comparison to the first version. This is a consequence of previously performed tests on the first version of the injector and is intended to inject the gas correctly to the cylinder. In all of the cases, there is the same cross-section area (5.1 mm²) of the outlet channel at the outlet of the injector. Simulation studies carried out on other versions of injector were made to provide an injector characterized by small pressure drop over the length of the flow channel with a relatively large mass flow rate and the correct shape of the gas spray injected into the cylinder.

The experiments on real injector determined the characteristics of the injector opening and closing which leads to a simplified model of the needle movement that had been assumed in CFD analysis. Similarly to Czarnigowski [11], table 1 and in Figure 4 present the time of injector open-

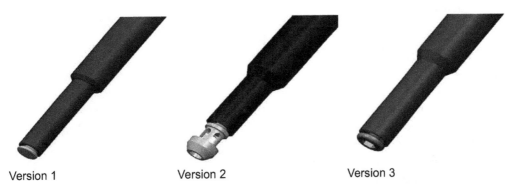

Version 1   Version 2   Version 3

Fig. 2. Digital models of studied injectors – first from the left compatible with the real geometry

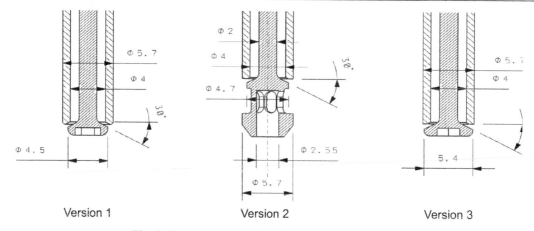

Version 1   Version 2   Version 3

Fig. 3. Cross–sections of studied version of injectors

ing and closing, which was calculated on the basis of the opening and closing velocity that was chosen on the basis of the experiment equal to 0.33 mm/ms for the needle lift of 0.5 mm. Injection time 6 ms was assumed for the calculation.

Table 1. Time of opening and closing of injector form the experiment

Time [ms]	Stroke [mm]
0	0
0.18	0
1.68	0.5
5.18	0.5
6.68	0
7.18	0

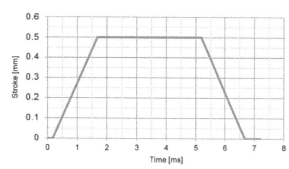

Fig. 4. Opening and closing characteristics of the injector

NUMERICAL METHOD AND BOUNDARY CONDITIONS

In order to reduce the number of elements and the calculation time it was decided to perform the calculation of the symmetric half geometrical (Fig. 5). In order to make transient type analysis with moving parts it was necessary to divide of the geometry that will be useful for the develop-

ment of a moving mesh (Fig. 6). The usage of layering method requires to have a structural mesh in the moving surfaces. Structural mesh enables the separation of rows and columns of elements belonging to a given volume. This kind of the geometry results in the distribution of regular and uniform formation of new layers. As it is illustrated in figure 7 in the area of injector needle seat, moving elements consist of a hexahedral type, and at different locations they are tetrahedral with the inflation boundary layer on the walls of the flow channel (Fig. 8).

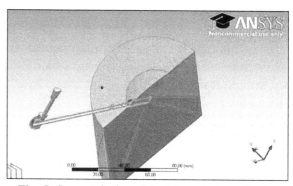

Fig. 5. Geometrical model of the injector with the cylinder

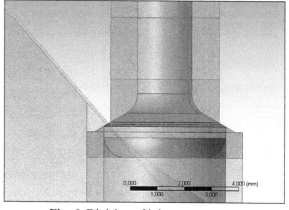

Fig. 6. Division of injector geometry

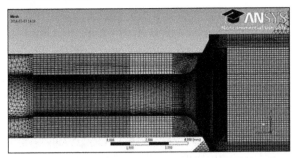

Fig. 7. Computational mesh in the area of injector needle seat

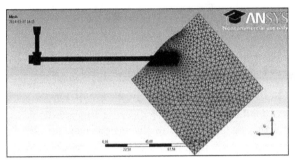

Fig. 8. Computational mesh

Using computational solver Fluent, flow phenomena simulation with transient time conditions was prepared. Due to the nature of flow, to solve the phenomena of turbulence, equation of energy and turbulence were assumed. In all analyzes turbulence model Realizable k-ε (RKE) was used. The flowing gas was, in the first step, the ambient air while in the second step it was methane, for which the ideal gas model was adopted. As a reference pressure, a normal pressure with a value of 101325 Pa was assumed.

In the simulations, the following boundary conditions were assumed:
- for inlets: pressure-inlet, air pressure at the inlet 10 bar,
- the air outlets: pressure-outlet, the air pressure at the outlet was equal to ambient pressure 101325 Pa.

As a solver pressure-based solver was selected. In the solution settings as momentum equation algorithm and default SIMPLE algorithm was selected. For the equations of momentum, energy, dissipation energy of turbulence, kinetic energy of turbulence, the interpolation schemes of the second row were chosen. The convergence calculation solution for the above mentioned equations, as well as the pressure and the velocity on the plane of the injector symmetry were monitored during the simulation. To prepare the movement, it was necessary to develop the profile file

as a text file describing the position of the moving components of the geometry depending on the time. Below a sample file is presented while table 2 contains its description:

((movement_of_valve 6 point)
(time 0 0.00018 0.00168 0.00518 0.00668 0.00718)
(y 0.0 0.0 -0.0005 -0.0005 0.0 0.0))

Table 2. Description of the motion profile

Designation		Description
Movement of valve		Name of this profile
6 point		Number of points of the curve shown in figure 5
Time [s]	0	Moments of time the individual moves in seconds
	0.00018	
	0.00168	
	0.00518	
	0.00668	
	0.00718	
y [m]	0.0	Changing the position of the Y axis in meters for given points in time
	0.0	
	-0.0005	
	-0.0005	
	0.0	
	0.0	

Sliding mesh layers on each other and the exchange of information between them without having to connect the nodes of each cell is guaranteed by the use of interfaces. This situation required to choose the interfaces cooperating with each other, so it was necessary to create a pair of interfaces on the contact place, one for each of the adjoining. The next step was to set move components and dynamically changing mesh by layering options. The appropriate properties of rigid body or stationary were given to the surfaces or volumes. The first properties correspond to moving elements and for them, previously developed profile: movement_of_valve was assigned. In the case of moving mesh it was necessary to determine the side from which layers will be built or deleted, dealing with the size of newly formed layers.

RESULTS AND DISCUSSIONS

The following figures illustrate exemplary results of the simulation in a form of contours of velocity, pressure and volume rendering for the

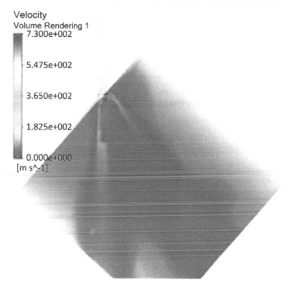

Fig. 9. The shape and the gas velocity profile exiting the first injector version

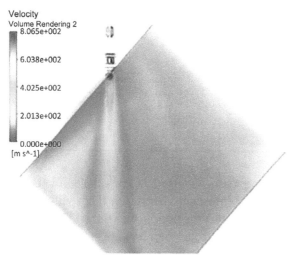

Fig. 10. The shape and the gas velocity profile exiting the second injector version

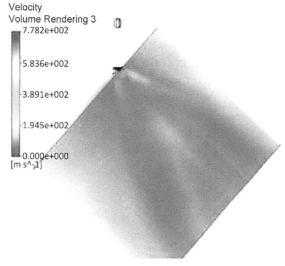

Fig. 11. The shape and the gas velocity profile exiting the third injector version

full opening of the injector. Exemplary velocity contours in the same cross section where methane was injected are presented in Figures 9, 10, 11. The figures show that the maximum flow velocity for methane reaches the value of 730 m/s to 805.1 m/s. The first version is characterized by the smallest value of the flow velocity. The velocities also translate into mass flow rate. This is due to the occurrence of flow accumulations. However, these are only local increases in speed and they are not indicative of the size of the mass flow rate. They depend on the average flow speed. As it can be seen from Figure 15, version 1 is characterized by the largest mass flow rate of both air and methane. By comparing different versions of injector supply by the air and methane, it was found that for the first version the mass flow rate difference between air and methane supply is the smallest 4% in air is preferrable. In the latter case, this is much higher, up to 27%, while in the third it is 19% (relative to air). Thus, the mass flow rate of the injector version 1 is about 40.5% higher than version 2 and 24.9% from version 3.

Differences air mass flow and methane are mainly due to the physical and chemical properties of these gases. Density of methane amounting to 0.717 kg/m^3 and air equals 1.205 at 20 °C significantly affect the mass flow rate. During the incompressible flow through the duct the injector the required volume of methane is 68% greater while the mass flow rate remained unchanged. As the critical velocity of these gases are varied but it is not a proportional correlation so the same value of mass flow rate cannot be obtained. As is apparent from Figure 12 and 13 the maximum speed of the flow of methane from the injector is from 30% to 40% higher with respect to the air. This implies that the speed ratio does not compensate for the difference in density. In addition, the volume of elasticity ratio which amount to 1.42 × 105 Pa, and 1.013 × 105 must be considered respectively for air and methane. As shown, methane is more compressible and translates this unfavorably to the mass flow, especially in terms of gas injection at high positive pressure and flow at high speeds.

The first stage of the research allowed to choose the best shape of the injector nozzle of the three tested versions. On this basis, an analysis of the complete cycle of the injection for the first version was made. This version mass flow characteristics result from calculations and are shown in Figure 15. Red line "Inlet" corre-

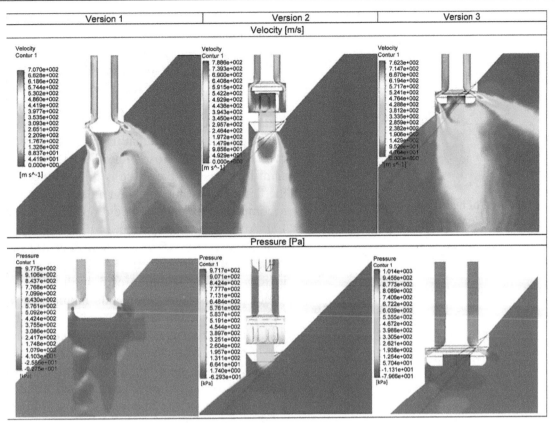

Fig. 12. The contours of velocity and pressure of methane around the needle seat of the injectors for the three versions of design solutions

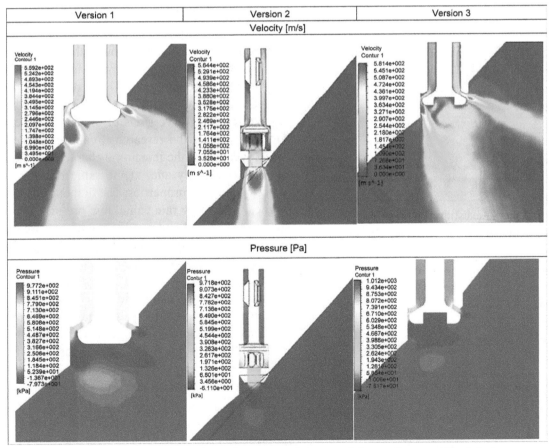

Fig. 13. The contours of velocity and pressure of air around the needle seat of the injectors for the three versions of design solutions

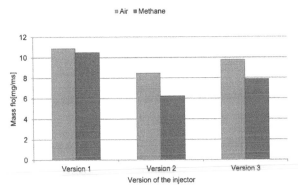

Fig. 14. Comparison of mass flow [mg/ms] examined three injector needle valves for air and methane

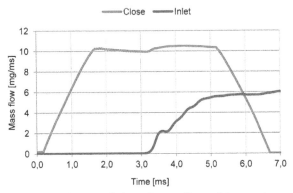

Fig. 15. Characteristics of mass flow of the version 1 injector for methane

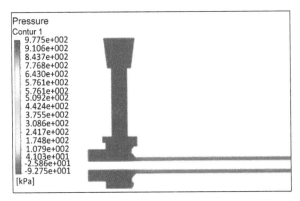

Fig. 16. The pressure distribution in the longitudinal cross-section of the injector close to the inlet

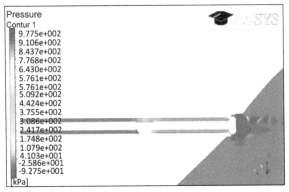

Fig. 17. The pressure distribution in the longitudinal cross-section of the injector close to injector nozzle

sponds to the mass flow in the inlet cross section of the injector, while the blue line "Close" corresponds to the mass flow in the cross-section in the valve seat, i.e. cross section of the flow channel at the outlet of the injector. The Close line values correspond to the injector outflow. Analyzing the mass flow at the time of injection it can be observed that in the cross-section corresponding to "close" line there is no constant flow, even if the valve is fully opened. In the first phase of the injection a decline occurs, accompanied by the pressure drop (Fig. 16 and 17). After some time period, in this case equal to approximately 1.5 ms, a slight increase occurs. The moment when the increase occurs coincides with the initiation of flow through the "Inlet" cross-section. From this moment, flow in this cross-section begins. Injection duration without affecting the "Inlet" cross-section depends on the flow channel volume. The value of mass flow through "Inlet" cross-section, for the tested injection time, has reached a value of about 58% of the maximum "close" cross-section mass flow.

CONCLUSIONS

The main purpose of this simulation was to determine the mass flow through the needle of the injector at a define overpressure, depending on the injection time. The scope of work included the analysis of the flow through the injector with three versions of injector nozzles. On the basis of the research it can be decided which version of the injector is characterized by simplest geometry and, at the same time, preserves good flow properties. The first one has the highest mass flow rate value, low pressure drop along the channel and good shape of gas stream coming for the injector nozzle. The changes in the injector nozzles geometry, while maintaining the same cross-sectional area of injector outlet, cause the big changes in the characteristics of the gas flow. It turned out, that the change in shape, and thereby change of the local loss flow coefficients for the same pressure supply, leads to the changes in the mass flow rate even by 40%. With regard to the study of gases with different physical and chemical properties, such as air and methane, it is possible to obtain approximately the same values of the mass flow by adjusting the shape of the flow channel. In each of the tested versions, the methane mass flow value is smaller, but for the first version, this difference is very small, just over 4%. In relation to the second and third testes version, where the difference between the mass flow of air and methane is in the range 19–27%, the value for the first version is optimistic, so the next step is to verify the results obtained by simulation with experimental studies.

The study also shows the impact of the injection time on the value of the mass flow in the outlet section of the injector. The gas accumulated in the injector channel, in the moment of valve opening flows into the combustion chamber, thereby generating a pressure drop in the area of the outlet nozzle. The pressure drop is noticeable during the injection process and goes farther and farther from the nozzle inside into the injector. Consequently, the mass flow in the outlet cross-section reduces its value in the initial phase of the injection (when the injector valve is fully open). This effect is caused by a feedback pressure wave. Only after a certain time, which for the tested geometry was at about 1.5 ms, changes of the pressure wave direction occurs and the pressure increases moving in the direction of the outlet. The consequence of this is phenomenon is a small mass flow increase at the injector outlet what is presented in figure 15. The pressure drop depends on the volume of the injector channel, and its cross-section area. As shown in figure 17 and 18, the pressure decrease does not reach the inlet cross-section. To reduce its range, the cross-section of the channel must be increased. However, in this case it is limited due to the mounting of the injector onto a glow plug socket.

Acknowledgments

This work has been financed by the Polish National Centre for Research and Development, under Grant Agreement No. PBS1/A6/4/2012.

REFERENCES

1. Mitcham II C.E., at al., Simulations and Analysis of Fuel Flow in an Injector Including Transient Needle Effects. ILASS-Americas 24th Annual Conference on Liquid Atomization and Spray Systems, San Antonio, TX, May 2012.

2. Salvador F.J., Hoyas S., Novella R., Martinnez-Lopez J., Proceedings of the Institution of Mechanical Engineers. Part D: Journal of Automobile Engineering, 225, 2011, 545–556.

3. Tonini, S., Gavaises, M., Theodorakakos, A., Cossali, G.E., Numerical investigation of a multiple injection strategy on the development to high-pressure diesel sprays. Proc. IMechE, Part D: J. Automobile Engineering, 224 (1), 2010, 125–141.

4. Som S., Aggarwal S.K., El-Hannouny E.M., Longman, D.E., Investigation of Nozzle Flow and Cavitation Characteristics in a Diesel Injector. J. Eng. Gas Turbines Power, 132(4), 2010, (12 pages).

5. Schmidt D.P., Corradini M.L., The internal flow of diesel fuel injector nozzles: a review. Int. J. Engine Res., 2(1), 2001, 1–22.

6. Margot X., Hoyas S., Fajardo P., Patouna S., Mathematical and Computer Modelling. 52, 2010, 1143–1150.

7. Payri F., Margot X., Patouna S., Ravet F. et al., A CFD Study of the Effect of the Needle Movement on the Cavitation Pattern of Diesel Injectors. SAE Technical Paper 2009-24-0025, 2009.

8. Lee W.G., Reitz R.D., A Numerical Investigation of Transient Flow and Cavitation Within Minisac and Valve-Covered Orifice Diesel Injector Nozzles. Transactions – ASM Journal of Engineering for Gas Turbines and Power; 132, 5, 052802.

9. HELP program AVL Boost.

10. Pietrykowski K., Grabowski Ł., Sochaczewski R., Wendeker M., The CFD model of the mixture formation in the Diesel dual-fuel engine. Combustion Engines, 154(3), 2013, 476–482.

11. Czarnigowski J., Effect of calibration method on gas flow through pulse gas injector: Simulation tests. Combustion Engines, 154(3), 2013, 383–392.

DIDACTIC AUTOMATED STATION OF COMPLEX KINEMATICS

Mariusz Sosnowski[1], Jędrzej Jaskowski[1]

[1] West Pomeranian University of Technology in Szczecin, Department of Automated Manufacturing Systems Engineering and Quality, Al. Piastów 19, 70-310 Szczecin, Poland, e-mail: mariusz.sosnowski@zut.edu.pl; jjaskowski@zut.edu.pl

ABSTRACT

The paper presents the design, control system and software that controls the automated station of complex kinematics. Control interface and software has been developed and manufactured in the West Pomeranian University of Technology in Szczecin in the Department of Automated Manufacturing Systems Engineering and Quality. Conducting classes designed to teach programming and design of structures and systems for monitoring the robot kinematic components with non-standard structures was the reason for installation of the control system and software.

Keywords: the automated station, industrial computer, Ethernet PowerLink, servo drive

INTRODUCTION

Certain experiments are too dangerous, difficult, or expensive to conduct in a classroom. However, the emergence of innovative technological tools yields some possibilities [4]. Educational theorists believe that robotics has tremendous potential to improve classroom teaching. Educators have started to generate ideas and develop activities to incorporate robotics into teaching various subjects, including math, science, and engineering. However, without research evidence to support their direct impact on students' academic performance, robotics activities may be just a "fad" [5].

The control system of the didactic automated station of complex kinematics has been designed and constructed in the Department of Automated Manufacturing Systems Engineering and Quality of West Pomeranian University of Technology in Szczecin, with student participation.

Developing construction of automated station has been ordered in Norwegian company IMS by Szczecin company SONION manufacturing medical instruments for people with hearing impairment [1]. Due to many faults in the control system, the company has donated the robot to university, where the construction was supposed to serve didactic or scientific purposes, thus the concept of adapting the construction to new control system on Bernecker&Rainer components.

Currently, automated station may serve as independent unit for didactic and/or scientific purpose, especially learning to program non-standard automated structures.

STATION CONSTRUCTION

The automated station is characterised by non-standard mechanical solution, presented in Figure 1. A station with two degrees of freedom allows manipulative operations in the space of 379×67 mm.

Station's construction is based on two arms: horizontal and vertical. There is a slider mounted on the horizontal arm, along which the body (actuator) moves; the vertical arm is fixed inside the body. Both arms are controlled with M1and M2 motors, which, by means of axis gears, drive one cogbelt transmitting the drive and moving end "arm" of the machine, as presented in Figure 2.

The layout of cogbelts and pulleys provides proper „winding" ensuring proper movement of

Fig. 1. The automated station with complex kinematics; A) external appearance B) actuator

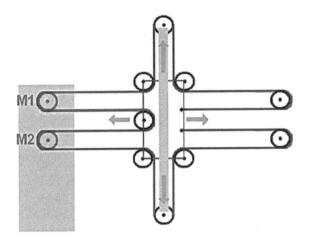

Fig. 2. Layout of the machine work

the arm. Both ends of belt driver are fastened in two points, as presented in Figure 2. Arm movement depends on movement and rotational speed of the motors. For the basic vertical and horizontal movements the engines must operate in the following manner:

- M1 right, M2 right – upward movement,
- M1 left, M2 left – downward movement,
- M1 right, M2 left – leftward movement,
- M1 left, M2 right – rightward movement.

The movement of actuator is thus a combination of the movements of M1 and/or M2 motors.

On the basis of abovementioned analyses, formulas have been developed for all directions, describing change of actuator's in the lower part of vertical "arm", based on changes in motor shaft position:

$$\Delta X = \frac{1}{2} N_{M1} - \frac{1}{2} N_{M2} \qquad (1)$$

where: N_{M1} and N_{M2} defines shaft position.

These equations proved significant for the whole project, as they allowed to develop translocation and movement at random angle.

The whole structure is encased in glass box and rests on a stable bench with control system installed beneath the bench.

CONTROL SYSTEM

For the developed structure of automated station, a new control system has been designed, controlling and supervising robot's work. The concept of control has been presented in Figure 3.

The control system contains: visualisation panel (industrial computer), servodrives, digital input/output modules and two synchronous motors of alternating current. The control system is connected to an industrial computer, where control software is installed. The program sends and reads control signals to and from servodrives and other modules with Ethernet PowerLink.

The system controls the work of synchronous motors of alternating current and cooperation with other devices, e.g. peripheral, robot.

The whole control system is based on a proper number of drivers (control modules) coupled parallelly. Basic version requires two servodrives and two digital input/output modules. All elements except visualisation panel are placed in control cabinet, as shown in Figure 4.

Control Panel

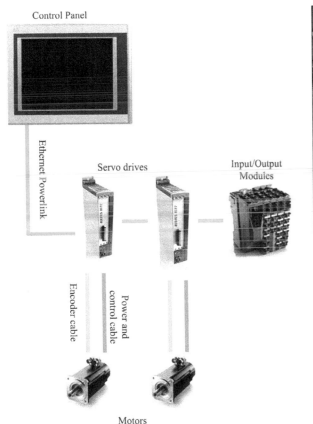

Fig. 3. Block diagram of control system

Fig. 4. The control cabinet

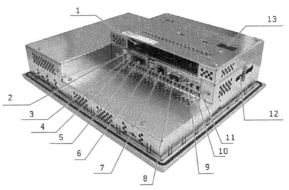

The main foundation of control system is open module structure and free extension and modification of the control system. Control of automated station is unrestrained, depending on scientific or research aim and task, thus customized to the user's needs.

Industrial computer

Industrial computer is a driver integrated with PP420 panel manufactured by Bernecker&Rainer, presented in Figure 5. The driver has 15" colour touchscreen, with 32-bit Geode LX processor. TFT Green with 1024×768 resolution enables graphic display and the processor allows fast arithmetic-logic calculations with 400 μs time interval. To ensure fast transmission between servodrives and modules, additional interface Ethernet PowerLink has been used [2].

Servodrives ACOPOS

Servodrives ACOPOS 1016 series have been selected to control automated station due to their unusual flexibility in terms of programming. The outer appearance of servodrive is presented in

Fig. 5. Computer appearance; 1) slot for communication terminal, 2,3,4) sequentially – buttons for connecting, reset and diagnostics of computer 5) power jack, 6) USB, 7), Ethernet jack, 8) serial link RS232, 9) diode signaling the work of computer, 10-11) configuration switches, 12) card slot for a saved program, 13) battery socket backup memory.

Figure 6.

Servodrive is powered by alternating current 230V and proper lead cap plate enables control, signal exchange with other servodrives and fast communication with industrial computer. Servodrives cooperate with all kinds of synchronous motors as well as the asynchronous ones with built-in encoders. The most significant advantages are:

Fig. 6. ACOPOS 1016 servodrive

- functional blocks, enabling realization of system of limit switches resulting in faster and more reliable work, independent of control program,
- movement system on *CAMAutomat* cams,
- possibility to implement virtual axes and drives synchronization,
- possibility to change key drive parameters directly from control program, using service channel,
- tools for testing and analyzing the work of the drive.

Digital input/output modules

All modules have similar external construction, which facilitates installation and simplifies replacement. The appearance of individual control modules has been show in Figure 7.

The whole module comprises of Ethernet PowerLink gate (Figure 7a) and digital input and output (Figure 7b).

The modules are connected to Ethernet PowerLink gate and communicate by its means, sending/receiving control signals to/from the industrial computer. The reaction speed of these modules is below 100 µs.

Each module has 12 clamps, where additional control signals can be connected.

Synchronous motors of alternating current

The actuator is a synchronous motor of alternating current, type 8LSA25, as shown in Figure 8. The motor has good dynamic parameters and built-in encoder.

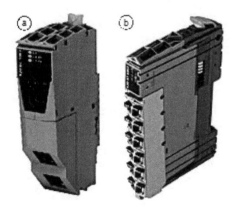

Fig. 7. Modules; a) the PowerLink gate, b) digital input module

Fig. 8. AC drive

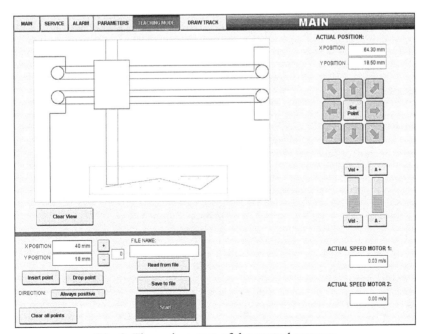

Fig. 9. The main screen of the control program

SOFTWARE

Program controlling automated station designed in Automation Studio 3.0 has been implemented into the developed control system. The operator communicates with the program using main touch panel. Complete control program contains six tabs, presented in Figutre 9.

The tabs are as follows: service screen, page displaying alarms on the station displayed automatically when error appears, screen showing changes in movement parameters and teaching and visualization of the robot.

Every tab is divided into three sections in order to establish communication with the automated station, placing it in base position, operating robot's positions database and writing program for the robot to execute.

The most advanced is the tab used for teaching movement path of robot arm. There are two methods of movement realisation. The first is based on sequential saving arm positions with cursors in the screen. The second option is teaching by drawing it on the screen. This method allows fast generating of complex trajectories.

Implemented program in visualization panel ensures easy and intuitive use. When using visualization panel, not only may the operator generate certain movements, but also change their parameters, e.g. speed, acceleration, etc. Before activation of the robot, it is possible to verify previously loaded movement using virtual window. Additionally, the program uses interpreter of record/readout of the trajectory to/from the file, by means of so-called G-codes taken from CNC systems [3]. Exemplary G-code generated by control system has been published in Listing 1.

Listing 1. The sample trajectory in a form of the G-code generated by the control system

```
G01 X 0   , Y 0
G01 X 116 , Y 45
G01 X 46.9, Y 23.4
G01 X 155 , Y 23.4
G01 X 119 , Y 41.4
G01 X 91.0, Y 41.4
M30
```

Each program containing G code and X and Y position ends with M30 command, finishing movement of the robot. Additionally, in every line after X and Y positions it is possible to introduce parameter M0÷9 informing the system about interactions of control system with peripherals.

The concept of control system is based on main control algorithm, presented in Figure 10.

After activating industrial computer, main control algorithm runs reference positioning procedure and awaits operator's command. There

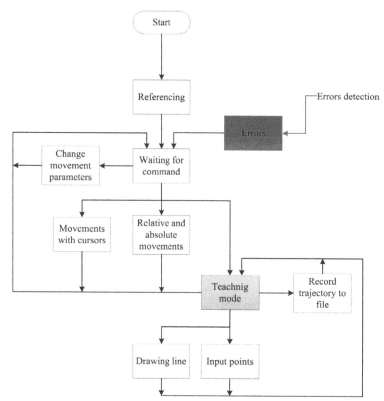

Fig. 10. The main algorithm of the station

are two modes of work available. Basic mode means sequential input of steps using control buttons on computer screen. The extended mode includes drawing paths with option of creating own trajectories.

Regardless of generating mode, each path can be saved/read on memory stick connected to USB1, as text file or G-codes. It is also possible to change parameters of movement, speed and acceleration. The program has a built-in alarm system informing about possible mistakes in the servodrive.

SUMMARY

Automated station designed and constructed in cooperation with student may serve as a learning tool for controlling and programming robots, but also enable realization of simple production processes for research application, including co-operation with real machines. It is possible due to the following features:

- Precision in robot's positioning allows precise manipulative functions.
- Control system with drivers based on PLC technology allows programming automated station using operator's panel or PC computer.
- Presented concept of robot construction and control system create opportunities for engaging students in development and, more importantly, experience-based verification of software, customized to user's needs.
- Control of automated station is unrestrained, depending on didactic aim and task, that is customized to the user's needs

The station enables conducting classes, mainly for Engineer and Master's Papers, related to programming, control and design of robots.

REFERENCES

1. Online resources: http://www.sonion.com/
2. Online resources: www.br-automation.com/
3. Grzesik W., Niesłony P., Bartoszuk M., Programowanie obrabiarek NC/CNC. Wydawnictwo Naukowo-Techniczne, 2006.
4. Jonassen D., Peck K., Wilson B. Learning with technology: A constructivist perspective. Englewood Cliffs, NJ: Prentice-Hall, 1999.
5. Barreto F., Benitti V. Exploring the educational potential of robotics in schools: A systematic review. Computers & Education, 58, 2012, 978–988.

20

AUTHENTICATION ARCHITECTURE USING THRESHOLD CRYPTOGRAPHY IN KERBEROS FOR MOBILE AD HOC NETWORKS

Hadj Gharib[1], Kamel Belloulata[2]

[1] Mathematics laboratory, Djillali LIABES University, Sidi Bel Abbes, Algeria, e-mail: gharib2@gmail.com
[2] RCAM laboratory, Djillali LIABES University, Sidi Bel Abbes, Algeria, e-mail: k_belloulata@yahoo.fr

ABSTRACT

The use of wireless technologies is gradually increasing and risks related to the use of these technologies are considerable. Due to their dynamically changing topology and open environment without a centralized policy control of a traditional network, a mobile ad hoc network (MANET) is vulnerable to the presence of malicious nodes and attacks. The ideal solution to overcome a myriad of security concerns in MANET's is the use of reliable authentication architecture. In this paper we propose a new key management scheme based on threshold cryptography in kerberos for MANET's, the proposed scheme uses the elliptic curve cryptography method that consumes fewer resources well adapted to the wireless environment. Our approach shows a strength and effectiveness against attacks.

Keywords: authentication, attacks, Kerberos, MANET, threshold cryptography.

INTRODUCTION

Background

A mobile ad hoc network is formed by a population of wireless nodes without preexistent network infrastructure or central administration. This nature makes it easy to deploy especially in environments where it's difficult to implement a regular network. MANET networks can be used in both civilian and military applications where security of exchanges must be ensured.

Motivation

User authentication is an important security measure to protect confidential data. Without a way to check a user, data access can be granted to users or groups which are not normally allowed. If the number of nodes is small, an authentication node to node is relatively easy to implement, but if the number of nodes becomes large, a total security strategy must be carefully implemented. The introduction of a Trusted Third Party (TTP) is highly recommended. Pirzada and McDonald in [1] used a TTP based on Kerberos, which inspired our idea. Although this model is widely used, it has inherited all the weaknesses of the Kerberos authentication system [2], such as guessing and replay attacks; but the most important is the presence of a single point of failure, it requires continuous availability of a central server. When the Kerberos server is down, no one can log in. This can be mitigated by using an improved distribution of authentication servers using threshold cryptography on elliptic curves that produces less computation which is well suited to MANETs.

Related work

Secret sharing scheme was first introduced by Shamir in [3] and now widely used in many cryptographic protocols as a tool for securing information [4, 5, 6, 7, 8, 9, 10]. Zhou et al. in [4] proposed the use of threshold cryptography for providing security to Ad-Hoc networks and enumerate challenges in the design of such a scheme. In [5] Azer et al. describes a survey on the authentication technique based on the same principle and also described some challenges to take into account. In [6] Govindan and Mohapatra present a detailed survey on various trust computing approaches that are geared towards MANETs. A distributed key management and authentication approach by deploying the concepts of identity-based cryptography and threshold secret sharing was proposed in [7]. In [8] RSA-threshold cryptography-based scheme for MANETs using verifiable secret sharing (VSS) scheme is presented. Another scheme presented in [9] proposes a fully distributed public key certificate management system based on trust graphs and threshold cryptography. In [10] the authors use a threshold Signature in Anonymous Cluster-Based MANETs. However none of the above works use kerberos [11] as TTP in threshold cryptography in MANETs. To the best of our knowledge, our proposed security architecture is the first in which the authentication is based on the distribution of Kerberos TGS combined with threshold cryptography in mobile ad hoc networks (MANETs).

Challenging issues

The main vulnerability of MANETs comes from their open architecture. Unlike wired networks that have dedicated routers, each mobile node in an ad hoc network can function as a router and forwards packets for other nodes [12]. The wireless channel is accessible to both legitimate network users and malicious attackers. The security of wireless networks is sensitive to a series of non-existent problems in wired networks, in wireless networks, data flows in the air, which makes it easy to sniff by eavesdroppers who can inject malicious messages. Wireless networks also have fuzzy boundaries difficult to control. Wireless devices in the network can be the target of physical attacks. Consequently, the secrets and sensitive data could be extracted. The computational capacity of a mobile node is also a constraint as the node can hardly perform computationally intensive tasks as asymmetric cryptographic calculation due to the limited energy resources of the batteries.

The network topology is very dynamic as nodes frequently join and leave the network. The wireless channel is also subject to interference and errors which affect the bandwidth and delay. Despite such dynamics, mobile users may request for anytime, anywhere security services as they move from one place to another.

Security solution must take into account all these aspects for the performance and quality of service desired.

The ideal solution must take into account:
- The collaboration of all mobile nodes is involved in thwart attacks.
- The solution must extend across all layers of networks each layer contributing to a line of defense.
- Security solution must thwart internal and external threats.
- Finally and most importantly, the security solution must be feasibly adapted to the network to be secured.

Organization

The rest of the paper is organized as follows: First we present a brief overview of the Kerberos authentication system and ElGamal threshold cryptosystem. Then, we present our proposed model with security analysis. Finally, we compare our proposal with threshold-RSA based schemes.

PRELIMINARIES

The Kerberos authentication protocol

Kerberos is a network authentication protocol created by MIT utilizing a symmetric key cryptography to authenticate users to network services. Kerberos uses tickets instead of passwords, thus avoiding the risk of fraudulent interception of users' passwords.

Kerberos credentials. Kerberos has two types of credentials: tickets and authenticators. A ticket is used by a user to authenticate itself to a server from which it requests a service, it contains the server ID (Identifier), the user ID, a timestamp, a lifetime, and a session key encrypted by the authentication server key. An authenticator is used to prevent replay attacks. Generally, an authenticator contains the user's ID and a timestamp encrypted with a session key shared between the user and the authentication server.

Kerberos exchanges. The Kerberos protocol consists of three exchanges: the authentication server (AS), the Ticket Granting Service (TGS) and the application server (AP). The AS exchange allows the client to obtain credentials to prove his identity at TGS. The TGS exchange allows the client to authenticate itself to the TGS and obtain

KDC

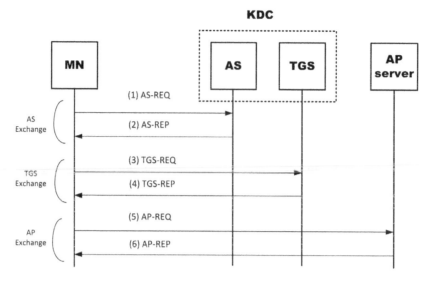

Fig. 1. The Kerberos protocol exchanges

a service ticket for the desired service. AP exchange is performed between the client and the service to authenticate the client before granting access to resources (Figure 1).

Shamir's Secret Sharing

Secret sharing refers to methods for distributing a secret among a group of participants (also called shareholders), each of which is assigned a share of the secret. The secret can be reconstructed if a sufficient number of shares are combined. In the *(k, n)* threshold secret sharing, the secret is distributed to *n* shareholders, and any *k* out of these *n* shareholders can reconstruct the secret, but any collection of less than *k* partial shares can't get any information about the secret [13].

Description. Dealing phase:
- Let *s* be a secret from some Zp, *p* prime
- Select a random polynomial
  $$f(x) = f_0 + f_1 x + f_2 x^2 + \cdots f_{k-1} x^{k-1}$$

under the condition that $f(0) = s$:
- Select $f_1, \dots, f_{k-1} \leftarrow R \, Zp$ randomly
- Set $f_0 \leftarrow s$
- For $i \in [1, n]$, distribute the share $s_i = (i, f(i))$ to the ith party

The secret *s* can be reconstructed from every subset of *k* shares by the Lagrange formula,
  Given *k* points (x_j, y_j), $i = 1, \dots, k$,

$$f(x) = \sum_{i=1}^{k} y_i \prod_{j=1, j \neq i}^{k} \frac{x - x_j}{x_i - x_j} \, (mod \, p)$$

and

$$s = f(0) = \sum_{i=1}^{k} y_i \prod_{j=1, j \neq i}^{k} \frac{-x_j}{x_i - x_j} \, (mod \, p)$$

Any subset of up to *k*–1 shares does not leak any information on the secret.

Elliptic Curve ElGamal threshold cryptosystem

ElGamal cryptosystem is based on the difficulty of solving the discrete logarithm problem [14]. We'll assume that we have a Trusted Third Party *(TTP)* – Kerberos in our case – that sets up the system.

Phase 1: Key generation for (t, n)
- Choose a large prime: *a* prime *p* such that $p = 2q + 1$, *q* also prime.
- Find a generator *g* of order *q*.
- Choose a random $a \in \mathbb{Z}q$ and compute $y = \beta^x$.
- Compute a random degree $t - 1$ polynomial
  $$f(x) = a + \sum_{j=1}^{t-1} a_i x^i \, mod \, p$$

The a_i are chosen randomly.
- Compute *n* shares of *a*: $s_i = f(x_i)$ for each user *i*.

The public key is $pk = (p, g, \beta)$ and the master private key is $sk = (x)$. The master private key is not given to anyone.

Phase 2: Encryption
- Choose a random $k \in \mathbb{Z}q$ and compute $c_1 = g^k \, mod \, p$.
- Compute $c_2 = m\beta^k \, mod \, p$.
- The ciphertext is:
  $$c = (c_1, c_2) = (g^k, m\beta^k).$$

Phase 3: Decryption

To decrypt a ciphertext $c = (c_1, c_2)$, t participants must ask the *TTP* for their decryption shares for this ciphertext.

TTP compute $d_i = c_1^{s_i} = \left(g^k\right)^{s_i} mod\ p$, for each user i that asks for decryption share.

Suppose that I is the set of t participants that requested a decryption share. Once each user has their decryption share $d_i = g^{ks_i} = g^{kf(x_i)}$, the users cooperate to compute:

$$d = \prod_{i \in I} d_i^{\Lambda_i} \equiv \prod_{i \in I} \left(g^{kf(x_i)}\right)^{\Lambda_i} \equiv \prod_{i \in I} g^{kf(x_i)\Lambda_i} \equiv g^k \sum_{i \in I} f(x_i)\Lambda_i \equiv g^{kf(0)} \equiv g^{ka} (mod\ p).$$

The participants must cooperate so that can
- Compute the Λ_i values, and
- Compute g^{ka}.

The plaintext is computed as [15]:

$$m = c_2 d^{-1} = \left(m\beta^k\right)\left(g^{ka}\right)^{-1} = mg^{ka} g^{-ka} = m\ mod$$

Phase 4: Elliptic Curve ElGamal Threshold

This operation can be done by converting message to a point on an elliptic curve and vice-versa using the Koblitz's method [16, 17].

Phase 5: Finally, we use the Lagrange interpolation formula to recover the message.

Table 1. Notations used in this paper

Notations	Descriptions
MN	Mobile Node
AS	Authentication Server
TGS	Ticket-Granting Server
ID_x	Identity of *x*
TKT_x	Ticket *x*
T^i	Timestamp i = ',',''',''','''''
E_k	Encryption by using key
$K_{x,y}$	The shared key between *x* and *y*
$AUTH_{x,y}$	Authenticator between *x* and *y*

OUR PROPOSAL

Mobile node sends resource ticket and authenticator to the service encrypted with the MN/AS key (pre-distributed via a secure channel in the registration phase). The AS confirms the identity of MN, if valid, it responds back to MN with a modified version of timestamp in the authenticator encrypted with MN/AS key. In this phase instead of using only one TGS, we use the ECC-ElGamal Threshold Cryptosystem to divide TGS into multiple parts to allow threshold authentication, it means one TGS cannot ensure the completion of the authentication process without the participation of a number predefined of TGS.

Algorithm: Distributed TGS

1- MN sends *TGT* request to *AS*
$$MN \rightarrow AS: ID_{MN} \parallel ID_{TGS} \parallel T'$$

2- *AS grants* a *TGT* to *MN* and if ID_{MN} *valid continue else reject request*
$$AS \rightarrow MN: ID_{MN} \parallel TKT_{TGS} \parallel E_{kMN}[K_{MN,TGS} \parallel T'' \parallel ID_{TGS}]$$
$$TKT_{TGS} = E_{KTGS}[K_{MN,TGS} \parallel ID_{MN} \parallel T'' \parallel ID_{TGS}]$$

Repeat
{ k: (*Number of TGS*)
3- $MN \rightarrow TGS: ID_{AP} \parallel TKT_{TGS} \parallel AUTH_{MN,TGS}$
$$AUTH_{MN,TGS} = E_{K(MN,TGS)}[ID_{MN} \parallel T''']$$

4- $TGS \rightarrow MN: ID_{MN} \parallel TKT_{AP} \parallel E_{K(MN,TGS)}[K_{MN,AP} \parallel T'''' \parallel ID_{TGS}]$
$$TKT_{AP} = E_{KAP}[K_{MN,AP} \parallel ID_{MN} \parallel ID_{AP} \parallel T'''']$$

5- $MN \rightarrow AP: TKT_{AP} \parallel AUTH_{MN,AP}$
$$AUTH_{MN,AP} = E_{K(MN,AP)}[ID_{MN} \parallel T''''']$$

6- $AP \rightarrow MN: E_{K(MN,AP)}[T'''''']$

$k = k + 1$
until $k = r$ (*r: the min of shareholders*)
$k < n$ (*n: number total of TGSs*)

Details of the proposal description

1. The *MN* (Mobile Node) asks for a *TGT* (Ticket Granting Ticket), the *MN* send a message to the *AS* requesting services, which includes the *MN ID* and *TGT ID*.

2. The *AS* grants a *TGT* to *MN*. The *AS* will check the *MN's ID*. If the *MN* is valid, the *AS* create a *TGT Ticket tgs* and generate a Session key $K_{MN,TGS}$ encrypted by the *MN* key K_{MN} to protect communication between *MN* and *TGS*, and send all this to *MN*. The *Ticket TGS* includes *MN ID*, the *TGS ID* – of *shareholders TGS* – timestamp, ticket validity period, and the $K_{MN,TGS}$ session key. The K_{MN} is only known by the *MN* and the *AS*.

3. After receiving the message from *shareholders TGS*, the *MN* decrypts the message to obtain the *Ticket TGS* and $K_{MN,TGS}$. When asking for a *Ticket AP*, the *MN* must send a request message to *TGS*, which includes *AP's ID*, the *Ticket TGS* and the encrypted authenticator $AUTH_{MN,TGS}$ by using $K_{MN,TGS}$.

4. *Shareholders TGS* grant *Ticket AP* to *MN*. Upon receiving the *MN's* request message, the *TGSs* decrypts *Ticket TGS* using its own secret key to get $K_{MN,TGS}$, then uses it to decrypt $AUTH_{MN,TGS}$, thus it can confirm the *MN* through the decrypted message and if the operation is right they generate a session key $K_{MN,AP}$ for the communication service between *MN* and the *AP*, then create a *Ticket AP*, which includes *MN's ID*, *AP's ID*, new timestamp, *Ticket AP* validity period and $K_{MN,AP}$. Then *TGS* encrypts *Ticket AP* using K_{AP} and session key $K_{MN,AP}$ using $K_{MN,TGS}$ and sends them to *MN* which can decrypt the replay message by using $K_{MN,TGS}$ to obtain *Ticket AP* and $K_{MN,AP}$.

5. The *MN* forwards the *Ticket AP* to the application server with a new authenticator $AUTH_{MN,AP}$.

6. *AP* decrypts *Ticket AP* and $AUTH_{MN,AP}$ separately, and judges whether the requests is effective by comparing the all containing information and more precisely the timestamps to prevent a replay attack.

Advantage of our proposed architecture

Our scheme ensures the availability of the service; in traditional kerberos the KDC is single point of failure, by dividing the TGS into n parts

and at least k parts are need to achieving the authentication operation, doing this we provide a deterministic security guarantees. Besides these, our ECC-TC architecture can provide equivalent security with shorter processing time and smaller key size [18] (Table 2).

Table 2. Key sizes in bits for equivalent levels

RSA	Elliptic Curve
1024	160
2048	224
3072	256

ANALYSIS

Measuring the security level for distributed TGSs

Assuming the distributed TGS nodes are anonymous and an adversary cannot discover their identity, the best approach for the adversary is to compromise as many nodes as possible in a given amount of time, hoping that enough TGS nodes are included among the compromised nodes. The following equation captures this situation [19], which was simulated with the R language [20] (Figure 2):

$$Security\ Level = 1 - \frac{\sum_{c}^{i=k}\binom{n}{i}\binom{M-n}{c-i}}{\binom{M}{c}}$$

Emphasize that if the difference between *n* and *k* is too large, the system security is deteriorating.

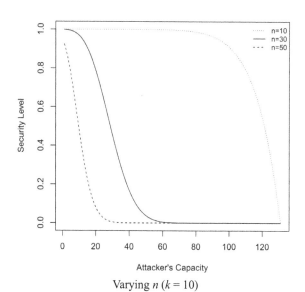

Varying *n* (*k* = 10)

Fig. 2. Security level

Computational complexity

The computations in our proposal depend on key generation and operations such as encryption, decryption, distribution and verification. The master key generation uses threshold secret sharing, and the computational complexity comes from the number of shareholders.

Processing time

According to the results presented in [21, 22, 23]. It is very clear that the use of elliptic curves cryptography is very suitable for wireless environments, as shown in Figure 3. At the 192-bit ECCEG-TC is roughly 2 to 3 times as fast as an 1024-bit RSA private key operation which is higher than the required security level security level (Table 2).

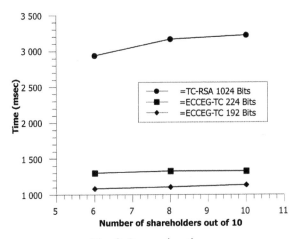

Fig. 3. Processing time

Guessing attacks prevention

Our system is resistant to guessing attacks, the introduction of encrypted timestamps in exchanged messages, make the task difficult for an attacker trying to enter guessed passwords. [24, 25, 26, 27].

Replay attack prevention

We use a synchronized timestamp embedded in the message within acceptance time window to prevent replay attack; this countermeasure ensures the freshness of messages in a session.

CONCLUSION

It has been demonstrated that the use of RSA based authentication scheme in wireless environ-

ments is not preferable. The proposed authentication scheme based on Elliptic curve ElGamal threshold cryptosystem offers both availability and strong security level required in mobile Ad hoc networks and has proven to be a best method for resistance at offline guessing attack and reply attack. By using elliptic curve cryptography, our scheme is efficient to be implemented in mobile devices. Future work focuses on validation of our study by simulations.

REFERENCES

1. Asad A., Pirzada McDonald C., Kerberos Assisted Authentication in Mobile Ad-hoc Networks. In: CRPIT '04 Proceedings of the 27th conference on Australasian computer science, Vol. 56, 41–46, Australian Computer Society, Inc., 2004.

2. Bellovin S.M., Merritt M. Limitations of the Kerberos authentication system. ACM SIGCOMM Computer Communication Review, vol. 20(5), 1990, 119-132.

3. Shamir A. How to share a secret. Communications of the ACM, Vol. 22(11), 1979, 612-613.

4. Zhou L. and Haas Z.J., Securing Ad Hoc Networks. IEEE Network., vol. 13, 1999, 24-30.

5. Azer M.A., El-Kassas S.M. and El-Soudani M.S. Threshold cryptography and authentication in ad hoc networks survey and challenges. In: Systems and Networks Communications, ICSNC 2007. IEEE Second International Conference on, p. 5.

6. Govindan K. and Mohapatra P. Trust computations and trust dynamics in mobile adhoc networks: a survey. Communications Surveys & Tutorials, IEEE, 14(2), 2012, 279-298.

7. Deng H., Mukherjee A., and Agrawal D.P. Threshold and identity-based key management and authentication for wireless ad hoc networks. In: Information Technology: Coding and Computing, Proceedings. ITCC 2004. IEEE International Conference on, p. 107-111.

8. Sarkar S., Kisku B., Misra S., Obaidat M.S. Chinese Remainder Theorem-Based RSA-Threshold Cryptography in MANET Using Verifiable Secret Sharing Scheme. Wireless and Mobile Computing, Networking and Communications. WIMOB 2009. IEEE International Conference on, p. 258-262.

9. Omar M., Challal Y., and Bouabdallah A. Reliable and fully distributed trust model for mobile ad hoc networks. Computers & Security, 28(3), 2009, 199-214.

10. Park Y. and Moon S. Anonymous cluster-based MANETs with threshold signature. International Journal of Distributed Sensor Networks, Article ID 374713, 9 pages, 2013.

11. Neuman T.Y., Hartman S., and Raeburn K. The Kerberos Network Authentication Service (V5). RFC 4120, July 2005.

12. Yang Hao, Luo Haiyun, Ye Fan, et al. Security in mobile ad hoc networks: challenges and solutions. Wireless Communications, IEEE, vol. 11(1), 2004, 38-47.

13. Dey H. and Datta R. A threshold cryptography based authentication scheme for mobile ad-hoc network. In: Advances in Networks and Communications. Springer Berlin Heidelberg, 2011. p. 400-409.

14. ElGamal T. A public key cryptosystem and a signature scheme based on discrete logarithms. Information Theory, IEEE Transactions on, vol. 31, 1985, p. 469-472.

15. https://www.scs.carleton.ca/sites/default/files/course_page/secretsharing.pdf, Last accessed: 14-02-2014.

16. Koblitz N. A Course in Number Theory and Cryptography (Graduate Texts in Mathematics, No 114), Springer-Verlag, 1994.

17. Padma B.H., Chandravathi D. and Roja P. Prapoorna. Encoding and decoding of a message in the implementation of Elliptic Curve cryptography using Koblitz's method. International Journal on Computer Science and Engineering, vol. 2(5), 2010.

18. http://www.nsa.gov/business/programs/elliptic_curve.shtml, Last accessed: 27-01-2014.

19. Yi Seung and Kravets R. MOCA: Mobile certificate authority for wireless ad hoc networks. In: 2nd Annual PKI Research Workshop Program (PKI 03), Gaithersburg, Maryland 2003, p. 3-8.

20. http://www.r-project.org/ Last accessed: 02-03-2014.

21. Ertaul L., and Chavan N.J. RSA and Elliptic Curve-ElGamal Threshold Cryptography (ECCEG-TC) Implementations for Secure Data Forwarding in MANETs. Threshold, vol. 7(8), 2007, p. 9.

22. Ertaul L. and Lu Weimin. ECC based threshold cryptography for secure data forwarding and secure key exchange in MANET (I). In: NETWORKING 2005. Networking Technologies, Services, and Protocols; Performance of Computer and Communication Networks; Mobile and Wireless Communications Systems. Springer Berlin Heidelberg, 2005, 102-113.

23. Lauter K. The advantages of elliptic curve cryptography for wireless security. Wireless Communications, IEEE, vol. 11(1), 2004, 62-67.

24. Li Chun-Ta and Chu Yen-Ping. Cryptanalysis of Threshold Password Authentication Against Guessing Attacks in Ad Hoc Networks. IJ Network Security, vol. 8(2), 2009, 166-168.

25. Corin R., Malladi S., Alves-Foss J., et al. Guess what? Here is a new tool that finds some new guessing attacks. Twente Univ. Enschede (Netherlands), Dept of Computer Science, 2003.

26. Chai Zhenchuan, Cao Zhenfu and Lu Rongxing. Threshold password authentication against guessing attacks in ad hoc networks. Ad Hoc Networks, vol. 5(7), 2007, 1046-1054.

27. Ruan Na, Nishide Takashi and Hori Yoshiaki. Elliptic curve ElGamal Threshold-based Key Management Scheme against Compromise of Distributed RSUs for VANETs. Journal of Information Processing, vol. 20(4), 2012, 846-853.

21

REDUCING TRANSFER COSTS OF FRAGMENTS ALLOCATION IN REPLICATED DISTRIBUTED DATABASE USING GENETIC ALGORITHMS

Navid Khlilzadeh Sourati[1], Farhad Ramezni[2]

[1] Department of Computer Engineering, Sari Branch, Islamic Azad University, Sari, Iran, e-mail: mr.khlilzadeh@gmail.com

[2] Department of Computer Engineering, Sari Branch, Islamic Azad University, Sari, Iran, e-mail: f.ramezani@gmail.com

ABSTRACT

Distributed databases were developed in order to respond to the needs of distributed computing. Unlike traditional database systems, distributed database systems are a set of nodes that are connected with each other by network and each of nodes has its own database, but they are available by other systems. Thus, each node can have access to all data on entire network. The main objective of allocated algorithms is to attribute fragments to various nodes in order to reduce the shipping cost. Thus, firstly fragments of nodes must be accessible by all nodes in each period, secondly, the transmission cost of fragments to nodes must be reduced and thirdly, the cost of updating all components of nodes must be optimized, that results in increased reliability and availability of network. In this study, more efficient hybrid algorithm can be produced combining genetic algorithms and previous algorithms.

Keywords: distributed database, genetic algorithms, communication costs, GA, data segmentation, Fitness, Crossover, node, fragment data.

INTRODUCTION

Advances in networking and database technology in recent decades has led to development of distributed database systems. Data assignment is used in distributed database in order to achieve the objectives. The first objective is to minimize the total cost of transmission for processing and the second objective is to unify implementation strategy. The primary concerns of distributed database systems are fragmentation and allocation of fragments in main database. Data fragment unit can be a file; in this case, allocation subject is file allocation problem that is NP degree which requires fast heuristics in order to produce effective solutions. In addition, the optimal allocation of database fragments are strongly dependent on query execution strategy that have been implemented by distributed database. Fragments allocation problem has been done in many ways, including repetitive and non-repetitive distributed database, in this article, we have discussed this approach combined with genetic algorithm.

RELATED WORKS

Fragments allocation solution can be divided into two categories including static and dynamic and articles related to static method are briefly examined and its advantages and disadvantages are discussed.

STATIC ALLOCATION ALGORITHM

In 2002, Quang Cook & Goode Berg et al., presented a genetic algorithm; fragments can be distributed by this method among sites so that it results in transmission cost reduction. These papers evaluate update costs in order to reduce transmission costs when allocating fragments of

two basic parameters named fragments transmission cost reduction.

Transmission cost reduction

Node that requests a fragment must send its request to a node holding the fragments that do not lead to increased shipping costs.

Update cost

Since the fragments are provided for several sites in each period, then updating the fragment after writing operation on each fragment will be necessary that must be done automatically by the system. Meybodi et al. [2010] presented the genetic algorithm and two considered like previous method factors of reducing the transmission costs as well as updating factor as a parameter for fitness function; another parameter called machine- based learning separated system from other systems.

We will discuss on combining the genetic algorithm with algorithm in distributed database discuss, all sites are formed in a set called $F = \{S1, S2, ..., Sn\}$. Each distributed database is made of an array ArrSizeNode [], each Si is determined by its capacity which is the sum of all fragments size $S_i = \{$Fragment 1 + Fragment 2 + ... + Fragment n$\}$.

REQUIREMENT MATRIX

Each fragment may be required for at least one of sites in the near future. Each site need for each fragment will be determined by a matrix called requirement matrix, where Rij represents the site i need for fragment j which does not have this fragment in its local database, then it must put this demand in requirement matrix so that distributed system becomes aware of this practice. For example, the node number 5 has the demand for fragment number 25. In general, this requirement will be displayed by means of an actual amount that is weight, but another way is to use a binary value. Then, row 5 and column 25 will change requirement matrix amount from 0 to 1 (Figure 1).

Transmission Cost Matrix

This matrix contains the cost of fragments transmission from one node to other nodes. Gen-

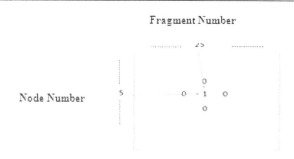

Fig. 1. Requirement Matrix

eration function of random numbers is used in order to determine the weight and random value of this function will be greater than 50 and less than 100, what is determined as below.

Rand.Next (50, 100);

It must be noted that according to vast communications of World Wide Web each node can communicate with other nodes that follow from the protocols of distributed system. The cost of transmission from one node to target node does not differ, so in this case we can reduce transmission cost of matrix, and this means that a matrix instead of having rows and columns of the size equal to number of nodes, the matrix can be outlined up triangular or lower triangular.

It must be noted that according to vast communications of World Wide Web each node can communicate with other nodes that follow from the protocols of distributed system. The cost of transmission from one node to target node does not differ, so in this case we can reduce transmission cost of matrix, and this means that a matrix instead of having rows and columns of the size equals to the number of nodes, the matrix can be outlined up triangular or lower triangular.

As shown in the Figure 2, the transmission cost will be 67 in order to transfer fragment from node 1 to node 2. According to the definitions given in previous sections, evaluation formula in order to allocate fragments will be formed of three relationships:

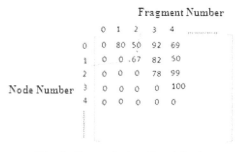

Fig. 2. Transmission Cost Matrix

1) The size of fragment does not exceed the capacity of site.

$$\sum_{j=1}^{n} r_{i,j} s_j \leq c_i \qquad \forall i | 1 \leq i \leq m$$

2) The transmission cost will be optimal.

$$\sum_{i=1}^{m} \sum_{j=1}^{n} r_{i,j} t_{i,p_j}$$

3) The node that will do transmission with the lowest cost of transmission and update.

$$\sum_{i=1}^{i=s} \sum_{j=1}^{j=f} \left[(\min(Transmission(i,k)))required(i,j) + \sum_{l} update(i,l)required(i,j) \right]$$

Chromosomes view in genetic algorithms

1) The function of initial population

In this function, the number of rows is equal to the number of chromosomes and number of columns is equal to number of fragments and the number of genes within chromosomes will be equal to the number of nodes that have used these fragments as well as we have considered the initial population for each generation as 50 (Figure 4).

2) Combinational function

In the combinational function, according to conventional methods of function in this paper, two parents one point method is used for this algorithm, and combinational rate is considered equal to 0.7 (Figure 5).

3) The mutation function

The mutation is a one parent one point method, however, in mutation method random numbers between 0 and 1, are produced using generation function; if this number is equal to 1 it indicates that add a node to nodes having this fragment, but we must not forget one thing and that is whether the node that is going to be owner of this fragment has had it previously or not, and if it is true replace new node, otherwise select

Number of sites including fragment 1	Number of sites including fragment 2	Number of sites including fragment 2	. . .	Number of sites including fragment n-1	Number of sites including fragment n-2	Number of sites including fragment n

Fig. 3. The structure of a chromosome

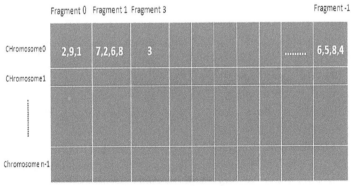

Fig. 4. Generation population

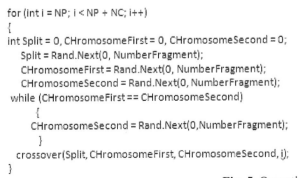

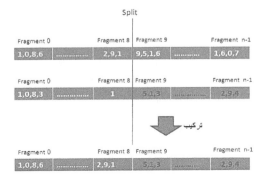

Fig. 5. Operation CrossOver

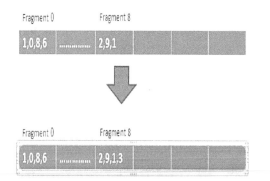

Fig. 6. Operation Mutation

the same node; in below figure, adding node 3 to list of nodes having fragment 8.

But if the generated random value is equal to 0, this indicates that mutation operation will remove a node among the current nodes, then a problem will occur; for solving this problem, it will firstly be checked whether the number of nodes that have this fragment is more than one or not, if this is true, remove the node, otherwise if elimination is done, certainly the availability of distributed system will be disappeared and the system will fail in the near future. It is better to choose another gene from the chromosome and this will be repeated until the problem is resolved and desired result is reached. The mutation rate is considered equal to 0.3. In figure below, removing node 5 from list of nodes having fragment 9 (Figure 7).

Fitness function

In fitness function according to the parameters established in the previous method and were tested, that is transmission cost and update cost, two other parameters have been added it in order to increase efficiency in selection of optimal chromosome. If the node that has the desired fragment fails for any reason, we

can restore the node fragments that are provided for other sites. As you know, hardware fragments are not put together in distributed systems, so that they can be repaired, so the fragment and the site will be out of control and availability of the distributed system will be in crisis, and the whole systems may fail; for solving this problem we will use an counter for counting the number of genes in chromosomes that face the problem.

Another idea that was discussed in this paper is when the information is fragmented by a system, it is better to number fragments by the same number which have inter dependency to each other. At this time, nodes that demand these fragments when assigning the fragments, they are asked whether dependent fragments are sent to this fragment or not. If the node accepts the demand, the fragment will be sent to node with related parts. Now, this practice helps all the fragments to be sent in a package to the destination and reduces the cost of transmission. Since the transaction of fragment may need fragments related to the main fragment which reduces the cost of resending fragment. This means, the node that demands fragment will obtain fragments in a package instead of searching twice nodes and paying costs.

Selection function

Choosing the best chromosome is done by tournament from population of chromosomes. Tournament calculates each generation chromosomes according to the main parameters, such as minimum transmission cost, the cost of update, the number of available fragments of a node, and chromosome that can do allocation operation with the lowest cost will be selected as optimal chromosome.

```
for (int i = NP + NC; i < NP + NC + NM; i++)
{
   int Split = 0, Chromosome = 0;
   Split = Rand.Next(0, Number Fragment);
   CHromosome = Rand.Next(0, NP);
   Mutation(CHromosome, Split, i);
   ArrayRequiredUpdate[50, NumberUpdate++]
=  CHromosome.ToString();
}
```

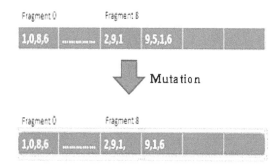

Fig. 7. Operation Mutation

SIMULATION RESULTS

Tests are shown for two proposed measurement factors separately on simulation software and finally, applying these two parameters the transmission cost will be evaluated in the previous and proposed method.

Applying the first measurement parameter of fragments that belong to a node. As the results show, in the proposed GA-F algorithms, a number of fragments that are available for a node are declining and directly effects on availability and reliability (Figure 8).

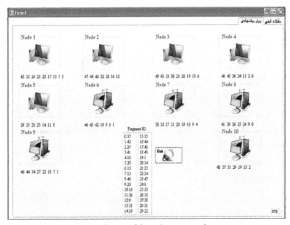

Fig. 11. A view of implemented program

Applying the second parameter of measurement

Number of fragments that are provided for node with determined ID number (Fig. 9, 10, 11).

Recommendations and future works

This paper provides complete descriptions on different methods of reducing transmission cost when assigning fragments of duplicate distributed database using genetic algorithm. In addition, our proposed method could affect the optimality of GA. For future work, we intend to offer our partners to research on the following:

- combining cellular automata with genetic algorithm in order to increase the efficiency,
- examining non-randomized and intelligent methods for initial population of GA,
- using clustering method for this system and combining it with GA.

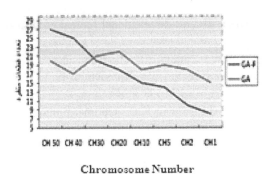

Fig. 8. First measurement parameter

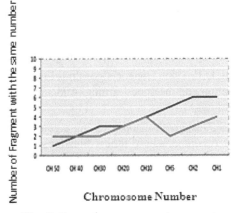

Fig. 9. Second measurement parameter

CONCLUSION

In this paper, we examine the transmission cost reduction when allocating fragments of duplicate distributed database using a genetic algorithm, in addition to previous methods that have implemented this algorithm; we have decided to try advantages of each method and add more effective measurement parameters so that generated output become more effective. Also, we changed some states of genetic algorithm which were specified as hypotheses. As a result, the output of proposed method will show that if the allocation of fragments is done reasonably at the basic steps, they can be very effective in reducing the cost of transmission. We must note that the needed cost for doing this must not be so high.

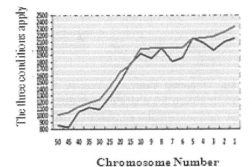

Fig. 10. Evaluating cost of transmission in proposed and previous method

REFERENCES

1. Hu Y., Chen J., Fragment allocation in distributed database design. Journal of Information Science and Engineering 17, 2001, 491–506.

2. Dokeroglu T., Cosar A., Dynamic programming with ant colony optimization meta heuristic for the optimization of distributed database queries. [In:] Proceedings of the 26th International Symposium on Computer and Information Sciences (ISCIS), London 2011.

3. Lee Z., Su S., Lee C., A heuristic genetic algorithm for solving resource allocation problems.Knowl. Inf. Syst. 5 (4), 2003, 503–511.

4. Schwartz R.A., Kraus S., Negotiation on data allocation in multi-agent environments. Autonomous Agents and Multi-Agent Systems, 5 (2), 2002, 123–172.

5. Chin A.G., Incremental data allocation and reallocation in distributed database systems. Journal of Database Management, 12 (1), 2001, 35–45.

6. Huang Y.F., Chen J.H., Fragment allocation in distributed database design. Journal of Information Science and Engineering, 17 (3), 2001, 491–506.

7. Morgan H.L., Levin K.D., Optimal program and data locations in computer networks. Communications of the ACM, 20 (5), 1977, 315–322.

8. Jin Hyun Son, Myoung Ho Kim, An adaptable vertical partitioning method in distributed systems. The Journal of Systems and Software. Elsevier 2003.

9. Shemshaki M., Shahhoseini H.S., Energy efficient clustering algorithm with multi-hop transmission. IEEE, Scalable Computing and Communications; Eighth International Conference on Embedded Computing, 2009, 459–462.

10. Wai Gen Yee, Donahoo M.J., Shamkant B., Navathe, A framework for server data fragment grouping to improve server scalability in intermittently synchronized databases. CIKM 2000.

11. Chun-Hung Cheng, Wing-Kin Lee, Kam-Fai Wong, A genetic algorithm-based clustering approach for database partitioning. IEEE Transactions on Systems, Man and Cybernetics, Part C: Applications and Reviews, 32 (3), 2002.

12. Srinivas M., Patnaik L.M., Genetic Algorithms: A Survey. IEEE Computer, 2002, 17–26.

13. An introduction to genetic algorithms. Kanpur Genetic Algorithms Laboratory (KanGAL). Sadhana, 24 (4-5), 1999, 293–315.

14. Basseda R., Fragment allocation in distributed database systems. Database Research Group 2006.

15. Basseda R., Data allocation in distributed database systems. Technical Report No. DBRG. RB-ST. A50715, 2005.

16. Ulus T., Uysal M., Heuristic approach to dynamic data allocation in distributed database systems. Pakistan Journal of Information and Technology 2 (3), 2003, 231–239.

17. Baseda S., Tasharofi M.R., Near neighborhood allocation: A novel dynamic data allocation algorithm in DDB, CSICC, 2006.

18. Safari A.M., Meybodi M.R., Clustering of software systems using new hybrid algorithms. Proc. Int. Conf. on Computer and Information Technology (CIT 2009), Xiamen, China, 2009, 20–25.

19. Oommen B.J., Ma D.C.Y., Deterministic learning automata solutions to the equi partitioning problem. IEEE Trans. on Computers, Vol. 37, 1998, 2–13.

20. Ahmed I., Karlapalem K., Kowok Y.K., Evolutionary algorithms for allocating data in distributed database systems. International Journal of Distributed and Parallel Databases, 11 (1), 2002, 5–32.

21. Chu W.W., Optimal file allocation in a multiple computer system. IEEE Transactions on Computers, C-18 (10), 1969, 885–889.

22. Morgan H.L., Levin K.D., Optimal program and data locations in computer networks. Communications of the ACM, 20 (5), 1977, 315–322.

23. Chu W.W. 1969. Optimal file allocation in a multiple computer system. IEEE Transactions on Computers, C-18 (10), 885–889.

24. Ishfaq Ahmad, Yu-Kwong Kwok, Siu-Kai So, Distributed and parallel databases. Kluwer Academic Publishers, 11, 2002, 5–32,

25. Srinivas M., Patnaik L.M., Genetic algorithms: A survey. Computer, 27 (6), 1994, 17–26.

26. Goldberg D.E. 1989. Genetic algorithms in search, optimization and machine learning. Addison-Wesley: Reading, MA.

27. Hurley S., Taskgraph mapping using a genetic algorithm: A comparison of fitness functions. Parallel Computing, 19, 1993, 1313–1317.

28. Mahfoud S.W., Goldberg D.E., Parallel recombinative simulated annealing: Agenetic algorithm. Parallel Computing, 21, 1995, 1–28.

29. Jing L., Michael K.N., Huang J.Z., Knowledge-based vector space model for text clustering. 2009.

30. McClean S., Scotney B., Shapcott M., Using domain knowledge to learn from heterogeneous distributed databases. Springer-Verlag, Berlin Heidelberg 2004.

31. Xiuxia Yu, Yinghong Dong, Li Yue, A study of optimized algorithm for distributed database half-join query and knowledge engineering. Springer-Verlag, Berlin Heidelberg 2012.

32. Moghaddam H., Mamaghani S., Mahi M., Meybodi M., A novel evolutionary algorithm for solving static data allocation problem in distributed database systems. IEEE 2010.

22

NOISY IMAGE SEGMENTATION USING A SELF-ORGANIZING MAP NETWORK

Saleh Gorjizadeh[1], Sadegh Pasban[2], Siavash Alipour[3]

[1] Student in the Department of Computer Engineering, Islamic Azad University, Sari, Iran, e-mail: Gorjizadeh. saleh@gmail.com

[2] Department of Computer Engineering at Birjand University, Birjand, Iran, e-mail: sadegh.info@gmail.com

[3] Department of Electrical and Electronic Engineering at Malek-Ashtar University of Technology, Tehran, Iran, e-mail: siavash.alipur@gmail.com

ABSTRACT

Image segmentation is an essential step in image processing. Many image segmentation methods are available but most of these methods are not suitable for noisy images or they require priori knowledge, such as knowledge on the type of noise. In order to overcome these obstacles, a new image segmentation algorithm is proposed by using a self-organizing map (SOM) with some changes in its structure and training data. In this paper, we choose a pixel with its spatial neighbors and two statistical features, mean and median, computed based on a block of pixels as training data for each pixel. This approach helps SOM network recognize a model of noise, and consequently, segment noisy image as well by using spatial information and two statistical features. Moreover, a two cycle thresholding process is used at the end of learning phase to combine or remove extra segments. This way helps the proposed network to recognize the correct number of clusters/segments automatically. A performance evaluation of the proposed algorithm is carried out on different kinds of image, including medical data imagery and natural scene. The experimental results show that the proposed algorithm has advantages in accuracy and robustness against noise in comparison with the well-known unsupervised algorithms.

Keywords: image segmentation; unsupervised algorithms; noise; statistical features; SOM neural network.

INTRODUCTION

This Image segmentation is the process of image division into regions with similar attributes [1, 2]. It is an important step in image analysis chain with applications to satellite images, such as locating objects (roads, forests, etc.), face recognition systems, and Medical Imaging [3]. The objective of segmentation is to simplify and/or change the representation of an image into something that is more meaningful and easier to analyze [3]. The result of image segmentation is a set of regions that collectively cover the entire image, or a set of contours extracted from the image. Each pixel in a region is similar with respect to some characteristic or computed property, such as color, intensity, or texture.

Image segmentation can be considered to be a kind of clustering, which clusters similar pixels into same group. Clustering by supervised and unsupervised learning [4] is considered as the most popular segmentation technique. Until recently, most of the segmentation methods and approaches are supervised such as Maximum Posteriori (MAP) [5] or Maximum Likelihood (ML) [6] with an average efficiency rate of about 85% [7, 8]. In the supervised methods a priori knowledge is needed to get a successful segmentation process and sometime the required information may not be available.

On the other hand, in unsupervised technique inherent features extracted from the image is used for the segmentation. Unsupervised segmentation based on clustering includes K-means, Fuzzy C-Means (FCM) and ANN. K-means algorithm is a hard segmentation method because it assigns a pixel to a class or it does not [4]. FCM uses a membership function so that a pixel can belongs to several clusters having different degree. One important problem of these two clustering methods is that the clustering numbers must be known beforehand. ANN can change their responses according to the environmental conditions and learn from experience. Self-Organizing Map (SOM) [9, 10] or Kohonen's Map is an unsupervised ANN that uses competitive learning algorithm. The SOM features are very useful in data analysis and data visualization, which makes it an important tool in image segmentation [4]. Although the use of SOM in image segmentation is well reported in the literature [9, 11], its application under noisy condition is not widely known.

This paper proposes a developed self-organizing-map to segment images under noisy cases with high performance. Using two Statistical features, mean and median, calculated according to a block of pixels, and all pixels in this block as part of SOM input learning data for each pixel, leads to a suitable segmentation with respect to noise.

SELF-ORGANIZING MAP

The SOM introduced by Kohonen [12], is an unsupervised learning neural network. SOM projects a high dimensional space to a one or two dimensional discrete lattice of neuron units. Each node of the map is defined by a vector Wij, whose elements are adjusted during the training. An important feature of this neural network is its ability to process noisy data. The map preserves topological relationships between inputs in a way that neighboring inputs in the input space are mapped to neighboring neurons in the map space [13].

In SOM, the neurons are arranged into the nodes of a lattice that is shown in Figure 1 [14]. The basic SOM model consists of two layers. The first layer contains the input nodes and the second one contains the output nodes. The output nodes are arranged in a two dimensional grid [15, 16]. Every input is connected extensively to every output via adjustable weights [17].

Best matching unit and finding the winner neuron determined by the minimum Euclidean distance to the input. Let x be the input and W_{ij} be the weight vector to the nodes. Vector x is compared with all the weight vectors. The smallest Euclidian distance (d_{ij}) is defined as the best-matching unit (BMU) or winner node.

$$d_{ij} = \min \|x(t) - w_{ij}\| \qquad (1)$$

Adjustment of the weight vector for the winning output neuron and its neighbors are calculated as followed:

$$w_{ij}(t+1) = w_{ij}(t) + \alpha(t)[x(t) - w_{ij}(t)], \quad i \in N_c$$
$$w_{ij}(t+1) = w_{ij}(t), i \notin N_c \qquad (2)$$

Where for time t, and a network with n neurons: α is the gain sequence ($0 < \alpha < 1$) and N_c is the neighborhood of the winner ($1 < N_c < n$).
The basic training algorithm is quite simple:
1) Each node's weights are initialized.
2) Vector is chosen at random from the set of training data.
3) Every node is examined to calculate which node's weight is most alike the input vector. The winning node is commonly known as the Best Matching Unit
4) Then the neighborhood of the BMU is calculated. The amount of neighbors decreases over time.
5) Update weights to node and neighbors according to equation (2).
6) If $N_c \neq 0$ then repeat step 2.

PROPOSED SOM METHOD

Although normal SOM has sufficient result through its features such as learning capability from examples, generalization ability, and non-parametric estimation, it suffers from two main problems. First, it is highly dependent on the training data representatives [18], especially in noisy situations. So, choosing a suitable training data is one of the most important parts in SOM. Second, Normal SOM cannot recognize segment or cluster's numbers automatically. This section proposes a new SOM algorithm to segment input images in both noisy and non-noisy cases. This algorithm consists of two steps:

First, training data for each pixel are chosen via a pixel with its block values and two statistical features as well. A block of each pixel is made by its spatial neighbors. Moreover, two statistical features, median and mean values, which are computed according to intensity values of the block, are employed to recognize a model of noises. Median value helps the proposed SOM model to identify salt & pepper noise and means value help it to identify Gaussian noise too. In fact, the proposed SOM does take spatial information and two statistical features into account in order to recognize model of noise and consequently segment noisy image as well.

Second, we use a maximum cluster number instead of a predefined number of SOM output cluster. In addition, a two cycle thresholding process is used at the end of SOM learning phase to remove the unnecessary cluster. In fact, by using these two thresholds, we would not need to a prior knowledge about the number of clusters in SOM method. These two cycles process are describe as below.

In the first cycle, we remove clusters which their data numbers are less than a specific threshold, $T1$, (clusters with few pixels). $T1$ is computed via the number of image pixels. Then, the data whose clusters are removed will put into a cluster according to the nearest Euclidean distance between the data and center of clusters. To reduce over segmentation problem, in the second cycle, two clusters are combined if the distance between their cluster centers is less than a predefined threshold T. Figure 2 shows a scheme of proposed method.

EXPERIMENTAL RESULT

This section presents several results of the simulation on the segmentation of medical and famous public Berkeley segmentation dataset (Fig. 3). These results illustrate the ideas presented in the previous section. Three images are shown in Figure 1. The first image is a Brain MRI that consists four objects: CSF, white matter, grey matter and background from [19]. The second is

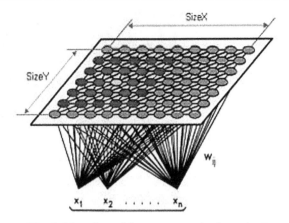

Fig. 1. Mapping of feature vector to the output

an X-ray image of a vessel with intensity inhomogeneity which consists of two objects: vessel and background from [20]. The target is to eliminate the vessel. The third is a camera man image which consists of three regions from [21].

These images are commonly used in papers [20–23] for image segmentation purposes and the algorithms compared have employed these images in their experiments. The original images are stored in grayscale space which take 8 bits and have the intensity range from 0 to 255. We have to cluster pixels of each image by our new algorithm and compare the result with K-Mean [24], FCM [25] and normal SOM [12] methods on image segmentation. In this paper, T1 is equal to 5% of image pixel's numbers, $T2 = 75$. Moreover, the maximum number of clusters is set 12 for experiments.

Figures 4 and 5 present the simulation results of three images corrupted with 15% and 25% salt and pepper noise respectively. Moreover, to show that the proposed method is robust to Gaussian noise, the next experiment is designed. We add the Gaussian noise with mean=0, variance=0.25 to the three images present in Figure 3 and presented the results in Figure 6. In the first column

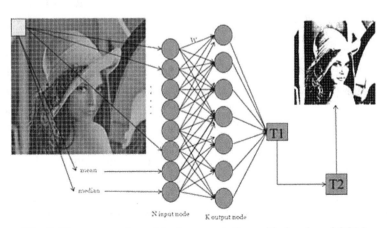

Fig. 2. The proposed model of segmentation with developed SOM

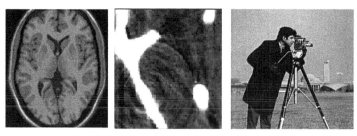

Fig. 3. Data set used in the experiment

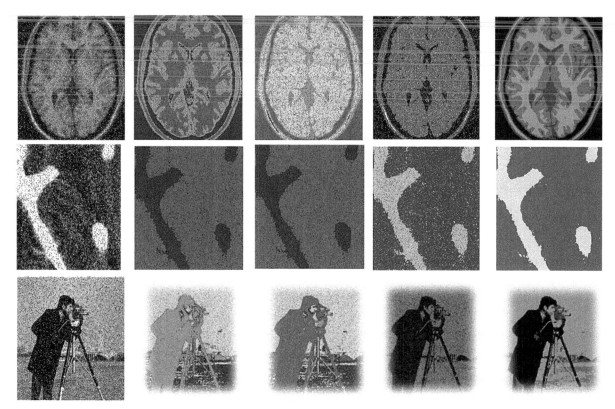

Fig. 4. The segmentation result of the three images contaminated with 15% salt and pepper noise in the first column was generated by the K-Mean (the second column), the FCM (the third column), the standard SOM (the fourth column) and the proposed SOM (fifth column)

of Figures 4–6 are the input noisy images; in the second, the third and the fourth columns are the segmentation results by the K-Mean, FCM and normal SOM respectively. The fifth column shows the results of the proposed SOM method.

From Figures 4–6, it can be seen that the proposed method performs well for all images. However, the rest fails in most situations. The reason is that the proposed SOM attempts to adjust weight vectors of the winning output neuron through spatial and statistical information of each pixel. Consequently, it shows lower susceptibility to noise. But, the standard SOM algorithm and also K-Mean and FCM methods are only concerned with intensity information and this information is changed by noise. Consequently, these algorithms are sensitive with respect to noise.

CONCLUSION

In this paper, we have presented a robust and effective approach for the segmentation of natural and medical images corrupted by different type of noise. For the segmentation of noisy images, the proposed approach utilized a SOM-based clustering with spatial and statistical information which are computed based on a block of each image pixel. In addition, using a two cycle thresholding process in the proposed method leads to an automatic segmentation which would not need to a prior knowledge about number of clusters. The efficiency and robustness of the proposed approach in segmenting both medical and natural images on different type and range of noise has been

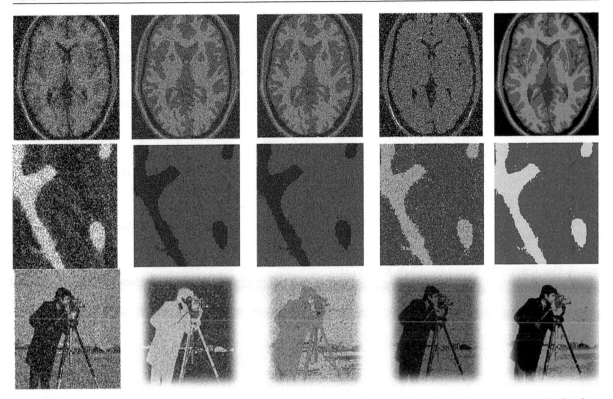

Fig. 5. The segmentation result of the three images contaminated with 25% salt and pepper noise in the first column was generated by the K-Mean (the second column), the FCM (the third column), the standard SOM (the fourth column) and the proposed SOM (fifth column)

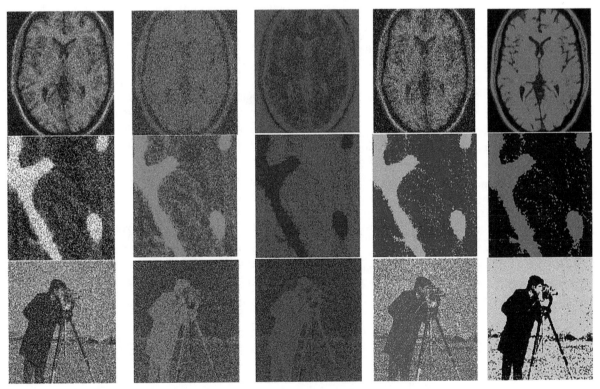

Fig. 6. The segmentation result of the three images contaminated with 25% Gaussian noise in the first column was generated by the K-Mean (the second column), the FCM (the third column), the standard SOM (the fourth column) and the proposed SOM (fifth column)

demonstrated using experimentation with several images corrupted with salt & pepper and Gaussian noises.

REFERENCES

1. Pratt W. , John Wiley & Sons, New York 1991.

2. Awad M., An unsupervised artificial neural network method for satellite image segmentation. The International Arab Journal of Information Technology, vol. 7, April 2010.

3. Awad M., Nasri A., Satellite image segmentation using self-organizing maps and fuzzy C-Means. IEEE, 2009, 398–402.

4. Jesna M., Raimond K., A survey on MR Brain image segmentation using SOM based strategies. International Journal of Computational Engineering Research, vol. 3, 2013.

5. Lopes A., Nezry E., Touzi R., Laur H., Maximum a posteriori speckle filtering and first order textural models in SAR images. [In:] Proceedings of International Geoscience and Remote Sensing Symposium, Maryland, 1990, 2409–2412.

6. Benediktsson J., Swain P., Ersoy O., Hong D., Neural network approaches versus statistical methods in classification of multisource remote sensing data. Computer Journal of Institute of Electrical and Electronics Engineers, 28(4), 1990, 540–551.

7. Perkins S., Theiler J., Brumby S., Harvey N., Porter R., Szymanski J., Bloch J., GENIE: A hybrid genetic algorithm for feature classification in multi spectral images. [In:] Proceedings of SPIE Applications and Science of Neural Networks, Fuzzy Systems and Evolutionary Computation III 4120, USA, 2000, 52–62.

8. Zhang P., Verma B., Kumar K., Neural vs statistical classifier in conjunction with genetic algorithm feature selection in digital mammography. IEEE, 2003.

9. Zhou Z., Wei S., Zhang X., Zhao X., Remote sensing image segmentation based on self organizing map at multiple scale. Proceedings of SPIE Geoinformatics: Remotely Sensed Data and Information, USA, 2007.

10. Kohonen T., Self-organizing maps. Computer Journal of Springer Series in Information Sciences 30(3), 2001, 501–505.

11. Wirjadi O., Survey of 3d image segmentation methods. 2010.

12. Tian D., Fan L. et al. MR images segmentation method based on SOM neural network. [In:] Proceedings of the First International Conference on Bioinformatics and Biomedical Engineering, ICB-BE, China, 2007, 686–689.

13. Kohonen T., Kaski S., Lagus K., Salojarvi J., Honkela J., Paatero V., Saarela A., Self organization of a massive document collection. IEEE Transactions on Neural Networks, vol. 11, 2000, 574–585.

14. Yeo N.C., Lee K.H., Venkatesh Y.V., Ong S.H., Colour image segmentation using the self-organizing map and adaptive resonance theory. Elsevier, 2005.

15. Demirhan A., Guler I. Combining stationary wavelet transform and self-organizing maps for brain MR image segmentation. Engineering Applications of Artificial Intelligence, vol. 24, 2011. 358–367.

16. Li Y., Chi Z., MR Brain image segmentation based on self-organizing map network. International Journal of Information Technology, vol. 11, 2005, 45–53.

17. Available insight segmentation and registration toolkit (ITK), an open source and cross platform system: http://www.itk.org/.

18. Alipour S., Shanbehzadeh J., Fast automatic medical image segmentation based on spatial kernel fuzzy c-means on level set method. Machine Vision and Applications, vol. 25, 2014, 1469–1488.

19. Gilboa G., Osher S., Nonlocal linear image regularization and supervised segmentation. SIAM Multiscale Modeling and Simulation, vol. 6, 2007, 595–630.

20. Nadernejad E., Sharifzadeh S., A new method for image segmentation based on Fuzzy C-means algorithm on pixonal images formed by bilateral filtering. Signal Image Video Process, vol. 7, 2013, 855–863.

21. Bernard O., Friboulet D., Thévenaz P., Fellow M., Variational B-spline leve l-set: a linear filtering approach for fast deformable model evolution. IEEE Trans. Image Process, vol. 18, 2009, 1179–1191.

22. Jain A., Dubes R., Algorithms for clustering data. Englewood Cliffs, NJ: Prentice–Hall, 1988.

23. Bezdek J.C., Pattern recognition with fuzzy objective function algorithms. Plenum Press, New York, 1981.

FLIGHT SIMULATORS – FROM ELECTROMECHANICAL ANALOGUE COMPUTERS TO MODERN LABORATORY OF FLYING

Adam Zazula[1], Dariusz Myszor[2], Oleg Antemijczuk[3], Krzysztof A. Cyran[4]

[1] Silesian University of Technology, Institute of Information Technologies, e-mail: a.zazula@polsl.pl
[2] Silesian University of Technology, Institute of Information Technologies, e-mail: d.myszor@polsl.pl
[3] Silesian University of Technology, Institute of Information Technologies, e-mail: o.antemijczuk@polsl.pl
[4] Silesian University of Technology, Institute of Information Technologies, e-mail: k.cyran@polsl.pl

ABSTRACT

This article presents discussion about flight simulators starting from training simulators, applied in military and civil training tasks, up to the domestic simulators. Article describes history of development of flight simulation equipment. At the end of this paper new unit of Silesian University of Technology – Virtual Flight Laboratory – is presented.

Keywords: flight simulator, history of flight simulators, virtual flight laboratory.

INTRODUCTION

The development of modern technology is closely dependent on computers and digital techniques. The use of proper tools allows for constructing new appliances and enables efficient trainings. Effective skill development is possible with different types of simulators [2]; they are incredibly significant in different branches of industry, as the only safe and effective method of training in many cases. Also in case of aviation industry the need for ground training was recognised very early. The history of flight simulators reaches the beginning of 20th c. and starts soon after the Wright brothers' first flight in a motor aeroplane [6]. One of the first available simulators reproduced the rudder elements of Antoinette 7 plane. It was made of two half-barrels piled in such a way that they were in a state of unsteady balance. Sitting in the cockpit, the pilot attempted to set the crosswise gauge in balance with the horizon with the use of rudder. The instructor observed the rudder, and on the basis of his own experience, decided about the position of the construction. The first milestone in the early years of

the development of such devices was the introduction of steering drives and mechanisms setting the position of the cabin. The first such construction was built in 1917 in France.

In 1929, along with the first commercial flight simulator called "Link Trainer" (and also "the Blue Box", due to its colour) made by Link Company, the branch of planes started its sudden development. This was caused by the interest of military commanders in the simulators. It was noticed that simulators allowed for trainee's adaptation to flight instruments, acquisition of habits and skills necessary during the flight but also allowed training for dangerous flights e.g. in a situation of limited visibility (what is particularly important in military situations) in safe circumstances.

After a series of primitive flight simulators in 1941 Wing Commander Iles constructed a fully automated pneumatic simulator Silloth trainer. One of the first devices of this series reflected a C100 DF plane and was used to train cabin crews in navigation. Later versions simulated two- or three-engined bombers. The flying fortresses of that time required a cabin crew of a number of people, therefore, it was essential to train the whole crews in communication techniques and their preparation to react appropriately in crisis situations.

The first drafts of electronic simulators were made as early as in 1929 in Germany. However, no simulator was build according to this project. In Great Britain, at more or less that time, a project by G.M. Hellings based on electromechanical analogue computer was designed. The project assumed simulating the characteristics of different types of planes. Mechanical version of this project was made by General Aircraft Limited and functioned in Empire Central Flying School. In 1943 Bell Telephone Laboratories produced a simulator of PBM-3 plane. It was built on the basis of the plane cockpit with rudder instruments operated with a primitive computer calculating the flight parameters. In the same year, Curtiss-Wright Corporation, headed by doctor Dehmelem, built an advanced simulator Z-1 of AT-6 plane, which was steered by a primitive analogue computer allowing flights on the basis of instruments.

Until 1949 Curtis-Wright sold thousands of their own simulators, with improved analogue computers to simulate different stages of flights and types of airframes. Up to then, all the available simulators were used for military purposes. The first civil simulator used by the airlines was a simulator designed in 1948, reflecting Boeing 377.

In 1950's and 1960's at University of Pennsylvania, simulator UDOFT (Universal Digital Operational Flight Trainer) was built. It offered elaborated possibilities to make calculations concerning the flight. More importantly, the calculations were made in real time. Unfortunately, a large problem in 1950's was high failure frequency of computers, therefore, the work with such simulators was interrupted by long service breaks.

the first visual simulators commonly used in civil simulators were based on physical model of the terrain and a TV camera that moved in above the terrain to generate views in the cockpit. The camera was initially black and white (1950's) and then colour (1960's). The first attempts to generate the image fully controlled by computer were made by General Electric. In 1971 McDommel-Douglas Electronics Corporation built a simulator Vital II, which simulated landing at night and screened the images in a fully vectored manner.

In 1980's a lot of flight simulators were designed on such computer models as VAX and SEL 32/77. This gave the foundations to build fully digital simulators, also the amateur. The first simulator for domestic use was designed at the turn of 1979. The project was started by Bruce Artwick, making the versions available for Apple and TRS-80 computers. The version from 1980 screened the world made of 36 squares sized c.a. 1 km making a grid 6x6. There was also a hangar with an airport and mountains.

In 1982 Microsoft started cooperation with Bruce Artwick and a company called Sublogic, what resulted in Microsoft Flight Simulator. The simulator had Cessna plane panel and the images of 5 cities (Chicago, Seattle, Los Angeles and New York/Boston). The simulator required an IBM PC class of computer with a processor clocked 4.77 MHz and 64K of RAM memory. In 1983 another version for Apple computers was released. It had the base of 80 airports, buildings and bridges. In 1984 the versions for Commodore and Atari computers were better developed and used 8 colours. Two years later the versions for Amiga and Atari ST, due to their better graphical processing units, worked in 320×240 dpi resolution and used 16 colours. In subsequent years graphics and the texturing were developed. Additional supplements were also released which allowed diversification of tasks during flights [4]. In 2006 a version of Microsoft Flight Simulator marked with X symbol was released (FSX). It showed the whole globe and all the communication airports in the world., e.g. all flying club airfields in Poland, what proves the coverage and detailed approach in the virtual world. It is considered to be one of the best simulators available for both professional and domestic use. After this release, Microsoft withdrew from simulator market, however the product was developed by Lockhead Martin under the name Prepar 3D.

Apart from the development of simulators and simulating software, there has been a lot of research aimed at improving the effectiveness of trainings [3] and lowering their costs [1, 7] as well as decreasing the tiresomeness of long-lasting trainings in such type of device [5].

DISCRIPTION OF SIMULATOR'S WORK

In order to describe the operations of simulators Microsoft Flight Simulator X will be used. The programme is well developed, uses a lot of modern solutions and is the most popular flight simulator in the world market. The popularity is caused by the fact that the simulator can be used for both professional and domestic uses.

Communication in the simulator

there is a number of methods of communications in FSX – the producer focused on the most realistic approach to the problem of communication. Due to lack of possibility to understand human speech by computers, the communication is made by selecting the text from the list proposed by the computer. Setting the radio frequency is done in the same way as in reality – by setting the right frequency on a radio panel it is possible to connect to the control tower for the area or the area control. Having selected the right frequency the pilot notifies their intention and, depending on the situation, obtains detailed instructions of taxiing and landing, with consideration for appropriate entry into airport circle (left or right) and the order of landing , due to the presence of other aircrafts. The simulator allows the pilot to contact ATIS services (providing information about the conditions in a given airport and a method of approach), what is required in contacts with the tower. What is more, advanced communication is possible after logging to VATSIM network, for example.

Navigation and navigation systems

In Microsoft simulator a full range of navigation aids are available: VOR, NDB and ILS. The frequencies of radio lanterns are exactly the same as in reality. Practical approach of the designers is manifested in the fact that after setting the frequency of radio lantern it is possible to overhear its signal in the Morse code, what allows checking the correctness of the setting. After selection of radio lantern, its signal appears in the navigation equipment, what allows training flights without visibility (IFR). The simulator provides also GPS aids – both in Civil aviation and in large airline planes. It is possible to set the flights on SID and STAR points (the points are exactly the same as in reality). Simulator producer attempted to reflect real air navigation. It is also possible to make VFR flights, however, they require the pilot to compare the maps with the ground images of the Earth. In real aviation navigation is based on characteristic objects such as chimneys, mines, power plants, lakes and rivers. Unfortunately, the simulator without extensions does not offer the precise reproduction of such objects. For this reason, extensions improving the view of the Earth and adding characteristic objects in the area of flights are advisable.

Another important addition is airports. The simulator was developed in 2006 and since then large number of airports were modified or rebuilt. In the original version there are, unfortunately, no airport buildings and some mistakes happen, what generate a lot of problems during flights with VASTIM network. A pilot, who does not have updated view of the airport can find himself in a situation of landing in the place with no runway in VATSIM network. That is why it is so important to have an updated data. A lot of airports are available in freeware version of the simulator. Virtually all Polish airports are also available. Yet, FSX was released 6 years ago thus it needs updating, as they do not reflect the current state.

VATSIM virtual space

VATSIM is a computer network, whose main objective is to ensure flight control to simulator pilots. After the connection the pilot receives instruction concerning the flight and sees the aircrafts of other users of VATSIM system. the communication with other controllers and pilots are also possible. All the procedures and regulation for aviation are also binding. VATSIM network counts presently c.a. 100 000 users, each with a unique identification number in PID system.

VATSIM system requires precision and piloting skills in such a degree that allows:
- moving on taxiing ways and leaving them,
- maintaining the altitude with the accuracy of 200 ft, the course accuracy of 10 degrees and speed accuracy of 10 knots,
- making appropriate manoeuvre of take-off and landing,
- the skill of map reading and ICAO alphabet.

SIMULATORS FROM THE CENTRE OF AVIATION TRAININGS AT SILESIAN UNIVERSITY OF TECHNOLOGY – VIRTUAL FLIGHT CENTRE

In 2011 The Faculty of Automation, Control, Electronics and Computer Science obtained a grant for the project of "Comprehensive modernization of auditorium halls in the culty of Automation, Control, Electronics and Computer Science in Gliwice and building a Virtual Flight Laboratory" in the framework of Regional Operational Programme of Śląskie Voivodeship for 2007 – 2013, Priority 8 "Educational infrastructure", Activity 8.1 "Infrastructure of higher education" – "Regional Operational Programme of Śląskie Voivodeship – real response for real needs", co-financed by European Union from European Fund of Regional Development for 2007–2013. As a result of the project, the University purchased certified cabin flight simulators. The equipment includes two mobile simulators by FlyIt and a few stationary simulators by Elite.

Mobile FlyIt simulators

Full-size helicopter cockpit simulators (PHS – Professional Helicopter Simulator) and plane simulators (PAS – Professional Aircraft Simulator). The cockpits and the surrounding infrastructure are built in trailers, thus they can be easily transported to the place of training. They are fully autonomic units that require only power source (in case of lack of it, the training can be run for 1.5 hrs with the use of built-in UPS's).

The simulators allow Visual Flight Rules (VFR) training and Instrument Flight Rules (IFR) trainings. The used software is based on Martin Lockhead Prepar3D (earlier version of Microsoft Flight Simulator X) therefore, terrain mapping is developed both visually and in terms of topology. The available database includes 24 000 airports with all navigation routes It is also possible to create own scenarios of flight. The realism of simulations may be proved by the fact that the software maps even the influence of air rush generated by the propeller, building the power to both the axes of motion and the elevator.

The sets have doubled controls for two pilots, intercom, headphones and are fully equipped with aviation instruments. Full IFR panel contains the indicators of motor controls, altimeter, speedometer, Vertical Speed Indicator, rotor speed meter (PHS). The cockpits are also equipped with compete radio panels containing navigation, NAV/COM, HSI, ADF, DME, transponder and radio communication panel.

Visual impressions are provided by rear projection system covering 90 degrees in perpendicular and 110 degrees in horizontal direction with the multimedia projectors of resolution of 1400×1050 dpi each, what allows to cover the whole are seen from the aircraft windows.

The control switches were located in exactly the same way as in the modelled aircraft. Helicopter simulator (PHS) ha 6 popular models of helicopters: Piston R-22, R-44 (VFR-IFR), Schweizer 300 (VFR-IFR), Enstrom 280 FX, Turbine-MD 500, Bell 206 (IFR), AS 350 B2.. It is worth to notice that the set contains helicopters with both piston and turbine engines. Plane simulator (PAS) allows to simulate flights in both single and double engined planes, what allows preparation for ME certificate (Multi Engine). In the list of available simulators there are most popular aircrafts in flying clubs and used for passenger transportation including Cessna 172, 182, 182RG, Piper Seneca III and Beach B 58 Baron.

The instructor owns an ICC-Instructor Command Center equipped with three (PAS) or four (PHS) LCD screens, which guarantee a full view over the situation in the air, all the gauges and their readings, as well as the map with the flight map. There are possibilities to simulate different weather conditions, rain, wind of any direction, height of fog and clouds. The instructor has also a possibility to trigger different types of failures, from equipment failures to engine failure. ICC stand allows for replaying the flight for further analysis of flight and the mistakes of the trainee pilot.

The simulator also has a four-core high performance computing unit with two graphic cards, which allow for projecting images in available screens and projectors. Moreover, it is equipped with a high class audio system allowing to play real sound effects, what enhances the impression of realism.

Elite simulators

Elite company delivered two simulators: S923 FNPT II MCC and S812 FNPT II. The cockpit of FNPT II MCC is a typical cockpit for training in multi-engine planes according to norms JAR STD 3A. The panel for pilot is equipped with a speedometer, turn coordinator, artificial horizon, altimeter, Vertical Speed Indicator and communication panel. The part responsible for engine control contains information about the temperature and oil pressure, fuel flow, engine revolution, head temperature. Moreover, there are indicators of trap trimmer and GPS according to Garmin standard. The simulator also have a transponder steering and autopilot. Technically, the pilot panel is projected on LCD screens, on which the mask can be placed with appropriate controls and switches. The instructor sitting in front of two ICC screens can regulate the current plane position and flight parameters. The multiplicity of the meteorological settings are worth mentioning. Weather conditions, such as wind, can be set for a particular height and direction; the turbulences can be set at the levels from 0 to 12. As for visual effects, it is possible to switch on the cloud cover from CAVOK – cloudless sky, to 1/1 – complete cloudiness; the visibility in meters and the time of the phenomenon from the take-off. Large configuration possibilities are also possible in the area of setting different failures of the aircraft, which may happen during the flight. Instructor can evoke certain conditions at a given moment or schedule the incidents ahead. Route view can be seen on a map, with the flight and its altitude. It also shows the airports and navigation tools with their descriptions and frequencies. Interestingly, the simulators detect the season, time of day and year as well as adapt visual and weather conditions.

Terrain mapping in the simulator is based on a grid sized 1 km. Consequently, the heights in the simulator may differ from the real data. The height of the airports, as primary training areas, is accurate to 50 ft. If larger accuracy is required in the place that is not a primary training area, the producer provides technical assistance and the possibility to develop the database. Projection is made with standard textures covering the area. The objects such as bays, rivers, roads are completely vectorial. The runways with approach lights,, central and side, and PAPI/VASI agreeing with the airport data are in vectors. It is possible to use a RealView database, based on VIRGIS – Virtual Reality Geographic Information System, made by the Institute of Technology in Zurich. The system is characterised by high accuracy of land coverage up to 25 m, and 75% of the land is covered with the precision of 10 m. The whole system responsible for graphics was developed on OpenGL in C^{++} language. Due to that the hardware requirements in visual part are relatively low. One characteristic feature of Elite simulators, which is worth mentioning, is that they are very well developed in terms of the aerodynamics and real reproduction of flight mechanics.

All the simulator parameters are coherent with JAR STD 3A, what enables running any partial training and the flying time necessary to obtain a licence/certification – flight in a simulator significantly lowers the costs of certified licences.

Currently, the simulators are used to train Information Technology students (specialisation in ICT systems in aviation) and unique programme of ICT in air transportation. During laboratory classes, students deepen that techniques of three-dimensional modelling of images used in the simulators and gain specialised knowledge on the construction and functioning of air controls. They also learn about pilotage, procedures and systems used in aviation. They will not only allow understanding the functioning of simulators but also learning about the procedures and rules during real flights. Consequently, students gain both knowledge and skills on aviation and the possibility to get employed in this dynamically developing branch of economy. Apart from training purposes, the simulators are also used in research projects financed by European Union, such as EGALITE, HEDGE NEXT and SHERPA.

Acknowledgement

The research leading to these results has received funding from the PEOPLE Programme (Marie Curie Actions) of the European Union's Seventh Framework Programme FP7/2007-2013/ under REA grant agreement no 285462.

REFERENCE

1. Van Heerden A.S.J., Lidbetter R., Liebenberg L., Mathews E.H., Meyer J.P., Development of a motion platform for an educational flight Simulator. Manchester University Press 39, 2011: 306-322.

2. Lozia Z., Praktyczne zastosowania symulatorów jazdy samochodem. Postępy Nauki i Techniki 14, 2012: 148-156.

3. Raisinghani M.S., Chowdhury M., Colquitt C., Reyes P.M., Bonakdar N., Ray J., Robles J. Distance Education in the Business Aviation Industry. Journal of Distance Education Technologies 3(1), 2005: 20-43.

4. Ruley J.D. Microsoft Combat Flight Simulator 3.0. Plane and Pilot 38, 2002: 66-67.

5. Stanney K.M., Kennedy R.S., Drexler J.M. Cybersickness is not simulator sickness. Proceedings of the Human Factors and Ergonomics Society 2, 1997: 1138-1142.

6. Wicks F. First flights. Mechanical Engineering 122, 2000: 60-65.

7. Yang H., Sackett P.R., Arvey R. D. Statistical power and cost in training evaluation: some new considerations. Personnel Psychology 49(3), 1996: 651-668.

24

ENHANCE PERFORMANCE OF WEB PROXY CACHE CLUSTER USING CLOUD COMPUTING

Najat O. Alsaiari[1], Ayman G. Fayoumi[2]

[1] Department of Computer Science, Faculty of Computing and Information Technology, King Abdulaziz University, Jeddah, Saudi Arabia, e-mail: nalsaiari@kau.edu.sa

[2] Department of Information System, Faculty of Computing and Information Technology, King Abdulaziz University, Jeddah, Saudi Arabia, e-mail: afayoumi@kau.edu.sa

ABSTRACT

Web caching is a crucial technology in Internet because it represents an effective means for reducing bandwidth demands, improving web server availability and reducing network latencies. However, Web cache cluster, which is a potent solution to enhance web cache system's capability, still, has limited capacity and cannot handle tremendous high workload. Maximizing resource utilization and system capability is a very important problem in Web cache cluster. This problem cannot be solved efficiently by merely using load balancing strategies. Thus, along with the advent of cloud computing, we can use cloud based proxies to achieve outstanding performance and higher resource efficiency, compared to traditional Web proxy cache clusters. In this paper, we propose an architecture for cloud based Web proxy cache cluster (CBWPCC) and test the effectiveness of the proposed architecture, compared with traditional one in term of response time ,resource utilization using CloudSim tool.

Keywords: Web proxy cache cluster, resource utilization, load balancing, cloud computing.

INTORDUCTION

Currently, the World Wide Web (WWW) is considered as the most successful application for providing simple access to a wide range of information and services. As a result, the amount of traffic over the Internet has experienced tremendous growth and most clients browsing the web and loading files through the Internet expect that they should obtain a fast service and one of the effective solutions of enhancing performance of the Internet services is using Web proxy cache. Proxy cache [1] is an important device to guarantee the quality of Web services, and it helps to lower the demand for bandwidth and improves request turnaround time by storing up the frequently referenced web objects in its local cache. However, in Web proxy system environments, load state changes frequently and we cannot predict the time or height of peak load. To overcome

this issue, more resources added to guarantee system has enough capacity in order to handle peak load and maintain service quality level [7]. But, adding more resource means lower resource utilization and higher the system cost. Thus, a conflict occurs in between enhancing service quality and excelling efficiency of resources in web proxy cache clusters. In this case, Web proxy cache system often adopt load balancing strategies for obtaining a trade-off between those two issues of the system. However, performance analysis of various loading balance techniques used in Web cache proxy systems was well presented in [8]. The analysis indicates that both static and dynamic loading balance have a common issue related to resource provision i.e. whenever the load is low, it causes wastage of resources, whereas for being high the service quality deteriorates. In extreme overloaded situation (worst case), the Web proxy cache cluster drops services entirely.

Therefore, the load balancing strategy alone is unable to solve the conflict between improving resource utilization and enhancing quality of service. This conflict brings about the need to have a proxy system which is dynamically scalable i.e. having the capacity to adapting to the load that is needed (makes use of new nodes when there is an overloaded and removes nodes when there is light load). This is where dynamic scalability or *cloud bursting* is needed.

Cloud computing [9] is "a new paradigm, a type of parallel and distributed system, consisting of a collection of interconnected and virtualized computers that are dynamically provisioned and presented as one or more unified computing resources based on service-level agreement". And Cloud bursting is a new paradigm that applies an old concept to cloud computing, it represents the dynamic part of computing in the cloud. It describes the procedure in which new nodes are rented if needed and returned if not needed anymore. In proxy cache systems, cloud bursting means that if the system is overloaded for any reason, the load balancer automatically integrates new nodes from the cloud. Our work makes the following contribution:

- proposing an architecture for a Cloud based Web Proxy cache cluster system (CBWPCC),
- extending the capability of the cloud broker (as a user-level broker) to make the migration decision based on the application performance,
- evaluating the proposed architecture using cloudsim toolkit by considering different performance metrics.

RELATED WORKS

Significant number of work has been traced out so far on exploiting cloud computing for applications of data-intensive systems and scientific purposes. Systems for retrieving images based on contents are comprised of tasks related to high computations, as algorithms of those problems are of higher orders of complexities and volume of data are bigger. Therefore, to put up an image retrieval system, NIR needs to utilize cloud resources [3].

NIR is a kind of open source cloud which facilitated content based image retrieving systems. In BPEL workflow systems, virtual machines play significant roles. Tim Dorneman [4]

employed it in Elastic Compute Cloud (Eci3 of Amazon) and hence, it was possible to provide new hosts in BPEL workflow systems and handle peak load situations there as well. Results obtained from experiments and assessments on applications of computationally intensive video analysis highlighted those solutions as feasible and competent. Several concerns were concentrated on "cloud bursting" compute model as throughput or response time of applications has been found improved through elastic allocation of cloud instances with local resources. Various job scheduling strategies have been considered by De Assuncao et al. and according to this concept computer nodes were integrated both at local site and the cloud [5].

There may stay possibilities of inclusion of time constraints with each job and jobs are vetted on submission following one of those job scheduling strategies. The decision is made by the system whether it needs the job to be executed on the cluster or the job is redirected to the cloud. Elastic sites (proposed by Marshall et al.) [6] maintain transparency in extending computational limitations of local clusters to the cloud. Computed decisions on EC2 for node (de)allocation are taken through middle-ware after assessing job queue of local clusters. In contrast, our proposed system makes calculated decisions on bursting requests to cloud proxies based on the requested documents type (miss/hit) and their average service time. Closely related research [7] considers integrating local proxy cluster in cloud environment.

In our study we present a fine grain architecture of cloud based proxy cache cluster and consider the response time, resource utilization and the cost of this integration.

THE PROPOSED SYSTEM

Figure 1 shows high level architecture for cloud based proxy system and its connections to the corresponding components that together represent an interoperable solution for establishing a cloud based web proxy cache cluster. There are basically four main entities involved:

1) Cloud Information Service Registry (CISRegistry).
2) The broker.
3) Virtual Machines.
4) Physical Machines.

Cloud Information Service Registry (CISRegistry)

Public datacenters register their information to the CISRegistry. It provides utility computing service to Cloud users/Brokers. The Broker in turn use the utility computing service provided by the CISRegistry to become SaaS providers and provide services to their end users.

The broker

It is the key player in this model would be able to make use of the results to provide means for disturb and burst requests and it consists of two components:

- **Load manager** – has three main functions: (1) It receives the user's requests and processes them on FCFS basis, distributes the load among its local/public proxies under round robin policy and queuing the tasks when there is a available capacity for them in the infrastructure. (2) It takes the responsibility of creating virtual machine image and their initiation on selected physical hosts. (3) It also keeps track of the execution progress of service requests i.e. the performance is periodically monitored to identify exceeding in the predefined threshold and thus send a notification trigger to Resource Allocator for taking appropriate action.

- **Resource Allocator** – its responsibility is to handle the state of an overloaded system. The allocator queries the CISRegistry for the datacenters information when utilization goes over the predefined threshold. The CISRegistry in turn responds by sending a list of available datacenters to the Resource Allocator in order to start bursting the requests to the selected public datacenter.

Virtual Machines

Multiple VMs can be started and stopped dynamically to meet accepted service requests. In addition, multiple VMs can concurrently run applications based on different operating system environments on a single physical machine since every VM is completely isolated from one another on the same physical machine. However, we assume that cache application is composed of one virtual machine that housed in local cluster (private datacenter), which offer mechanisms for dynamic scaling of server capacity.

Physical Machines

The cluster comprises multiple proxy servers that provide resources to meet service demands. CBWPCC has $n + m$ back ends (including n local nodes and m cloud nodes, where $n > 0$ and $m >= 0$). Local nodes remains as part of the CBWPCC as

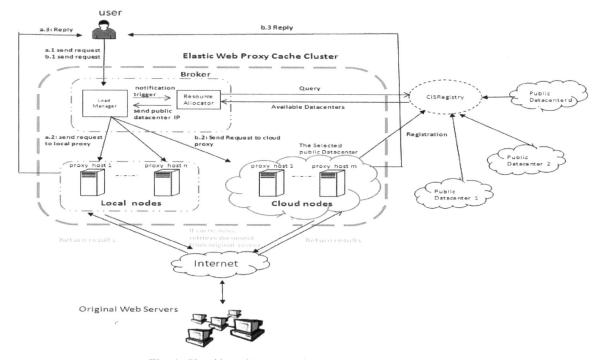

Fig. 1. Cloud based Proxy Web Cache Cluster Architecture

long as they work normally. Cloud nodes are constructed using cloud resources and they act same as local nodes functionally. The only difference is that the cloud node number changes with load status and the amount of available resources. In perspective of hybrid supply mode, CBWPP has the ability to use both local node and cloud node at the same time. Our system uses cloud resources for insuring of service quality and system performance in case of being overloaded and for providing reliability of CBWPCC, local nodes are used here. The proxies (local/cloud) retrieve and process the assigned requests. If the data is stored (i.e. hit cache), the requested document will be retrieved from the local proxy. If the requested document is not cached (i.e. misses cache), the proxy will redirect the request to the original Web server.

To ensure fast deployment of cache application in public cloud, we use fully configure image deployment method to construct cloud nodes for our system [13]. In this deployment method, the cache application is already installed and configured to create virtual machine in clouds.

PERFORMANCE METRICS

A number of metrics have been commonly used for evaluation of performance of the web cache. These metrics are related to cache efficiencies. Hit Rate (HR) which is the ratio of documents attained from usages of cashing mechanism against total documents required. Byte hit rate can be evaluated from the ratio of the number of bytes fetched from cache and the number of bytes that have been accessed. There are other two measures, named as user response time and bandwidth utilization, which can mitigate volume of bandwidth consumption. Besides, CPU and I/O system utilization , the fractional part of available CPU cycles or latency of disk and object retrieval got considerable attention to end users as other measures of the same objective.

In this paper, the response time is chosen for evaluation and assessment of the performance of web cache cluster. This performance metric is vastly used in this arena. However, from response time perspective, the existing web cache system may be considered in an ideal condition, as long as it can decrease the user's response time significantly. Still, because of the cache application's characteristic, some requests should be redirected

to the original server since their requested documents are not cached in the local disk of the proxy. These requests are termed as 'miss requests' whose response times are influenced with some attributes such as network conditions and process capacity of the original server. During the time of the congestion in the network or if the original server is overloaded, the response time of 'miss request' will be raised distinctly even if the load in CBWPCC is low. Thus, response time cannot be used as a direct performance index. Instead, we adopt a relative performance index R from [7]. it is the ratio of average service time of hit requests to original server average response time of miss requests in a given period of time.

$$R = \frac{AvgHitTime}{AvgMissTime} \quad (1)$$

$$AvgHitTime = \frac{\sum_1^{i=number\ of\ hits} service\ time\ of\ hit\ request\ i}{i} \quad (2)$$

$$AvgMissTime = \frac{\sum_1^{j=number\ of\ miss} response\ time\ of\ miss\ request\ j}{j} \quad (3)$$

While using R, a threshold range of values need to be set such that whenever the value of R goes beyond the threshold value, a new node is added to the cache cluster. In other cases, cloud nodes are removed from the cache cluster. However, setting the threshold value is an important issue and it should be decided at an optimum range for two reasons: the performance of the system should be maintained to an acceptance level and frequency of node number's alterations should be as low as possible to avoid performance jitter.

Assume that, a threshold range is set as $(t1, t2)$ where $t1$ is the lowest range value and $t2$ is the highest range value of the threshold value ranges. Now, if $R < t1$, the system will drop or release cloud resources if there are cloud nodes. If $R > t2$, the system will acquire cloud resources and build cloud nodes to increase proxy cache system's capacity. If R retains within this range, existing cloud nodes will be kept in rent and stream of incoming requests will be disturbed amongst local and cloud nodes. Figure 2 shows an activity diagram of our system.

COMMUNICATION AMONG ENTITIES

We modified the original CloudSim communication flow to another one shown in Figure 3. First, each public cloud datacenter registers itself with the CISRegistry (Cloud Information Service).

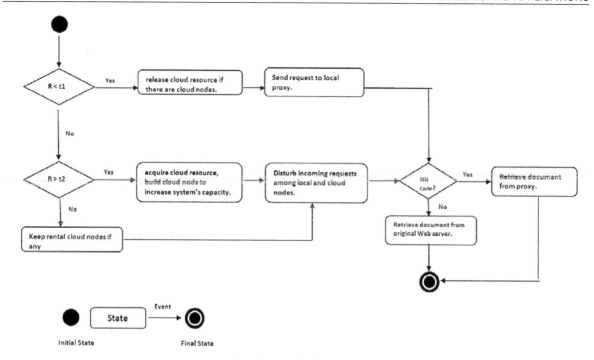

Fig. 2. Activity diagram

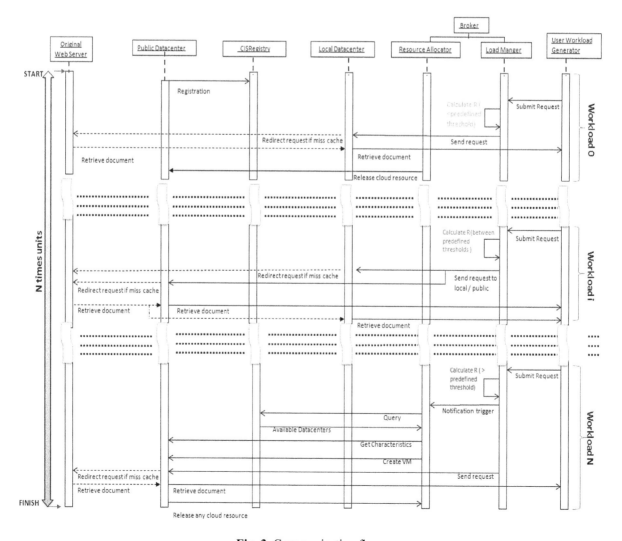

Fig. 3. Communication flow

CISRegistry provides database level match-making services for mapping user requests to suitable Cloud providers. The broker queries the CIS-Registry for a list of cloud datacenters which offer less latency and response time services. In case the match occurs and since we use an image fully install cluster the broker only needs to send requests directly to the selected Cloud datacenter. The simulation ends after this process has been completed in the original flow. Therefore, we added a new entity, called User Workload Generator, to periodically impose load on the system for N steps/periods (time unit = second). As can be seen from Figure 3, the performance index R is calculated at each step/period. The workload is defined as the number of requests from end users.

PERFORMCNE EVALUATION

This section describes results from a detailed evaluation study we performed. Particularly, we evaluated the feasibility and performance of CBWPCC.

Data Collection

In order to verify performance of the proposed architecture, we have implemented a trace-driven simulation of Web proxy cache cluster. We select squid access log of NLANR to be the trace in simulation compare CBWPCC with traditional Web proxy cache clusters (TWPCC) which have fixed node number and do not have the elasticity feature. The traces used for this study are downloaded from the NLANR website: ftp://ircache.nlanr.net/Traces. These one-day log traces were collected from the proxy locations in Palo Alto, CA. However, there are many possible responses that a Web proxy can provide to a client request [10], but we only considered GET requests such that the cache returned a "200" or "206" response code to its clients, Table 1.

Experimental Setup

This research utilizes a simulator environment where the CloudSim-2.1.1 is used as a framework [11] along with Java version 7 [12] and other necessary execution setup. We have set the threshold value R too (0.9, 1.2) and sample period to 120 seconds. The number for local nodes of CBW-PCC is fixed to 8.

In this simulation setup, a broker received the user's requests and processed (queue, execute) them on a FCFS basis. To evaluate the effectiveness of the proposed system in response time and resource utilization (CPU, memory and disk), two test scenarios were simulated: in the first scenario, all the workload was processed locally within the local proxy cluster (private cloud). In the second scenario, the workload (requests) could be migrated to public cloud in case the workload in local resources exceeds a predefined threshold. In other words, the second scenario simulated a CloudBurst by integrating the local private cloud with public cloud for handing peak in service demands. We assume that the broker migrate requests to a public cloud with minimum latency and response time.

In Figure 4, a comparison of performance result is depicted between the CBTWPCC and TWPCC, where number of fixed nodes were 8 and16. In this graph, from the initial point of 1000th period, the average response time curve of CBTWPCC is similar with that 8-node TWPCC. When the load of the system is enlarged, we can see that 8-nodes TWPCC cannot afford enough resources and its response time increased notably. While CBWPCC could get more resources from cloud and capacity of the system could be expanded dynamically. Therefore, the average response time of our system is maintained at a relatively lower level.

In case of the 16-node TWPCC, the beginning point at 1000th period, the response time of our system got raised as our system initially has 8 nodes only. After the beginning point, cloud

Table 1. HTTP Response Codes from [2]

Response Code	Description
TCP_HIT/200	valid document was made available to the client directly from the proxy cache
TCP_HIT/206	a partial transfer of the document directly from the proxy to the client
TCP_MISS/200	valid document was made available to the client by retrieving the document from another proxy cache or from the originating server
TCP_MISS/206	a partial transfer of the document from the originating server

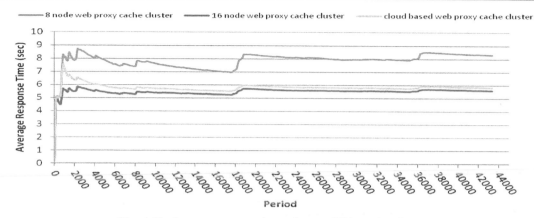

Fig. 4. Performance comparison of proxy Web cache cluster

nodes are added into the system dynamically and at the 18 000th period, the average response time of the system is going almost the same with that of 16-node TWPCC. It is noticeable that average response time curve of our system is slightly higher than 16-node TWPCC because of the latency incurred for those requests that are sent to public cloud.

In Figure 5, a comparison of CPU utilization is graphed depicting CBWPCC comparing with TWPCCs. CPU utilization of 8-nodes TWPCC is leading all, and all three curves are maintaining approximately a constant distance to each other. The curve of the TWPCC originated with the same point of that of the proposed system. After starting from the origin, curves of all three did not raise much with progression of the period. But from 0 to 1000 all of them raised sharply (with exponential rise). All 8-nodes TWPCC and CB-WPCC followed the same curve line rising sharply up to 65% CPU utilization at 1000 period. After that period, CPU utilization of 8-node WPCC goes little higher, as the curve raised very little, due to the cloud elasticity feature of our system cause the total number of requests processed locally less than total number of requests processed

in 8-node TWPCC in a given period of time. On the other hand, the curve of 16-nodes TWPCC is significantly lower than that of other two. Even up to 44 000 period of time, utilization of CPU did not go above 55%. While it reached 90% and 85% for 8-nodes TWPCC and CBWPCC respectively. CPU utilization of CBWPCC is significantly higher than 16-node TWPCC, since our system has only 8-fixed local nodes and thus they suffer CPU overhead higher than 16-nodes TWPCC which has 16-fixed nodes.

Functionally CPU and RAM are co-related to each other in a cache proxy systems. As CPU utilization as resource is lower in CBWPCC to 8-nodes TWPCC, the scenario is the same for utilization of memory as well, Figure 6. All three curves tend to be unchanged after 1000 period of time. However, sharp rising of edges were seen from the origin to 1000 period. As all requests are processed locally in 8-node TWPCC, it is getting higher overhead from requests that are consuming memory resources. While our CBWPCC has the ability to migrate part of incoming requests into cloud when R exceeds the predefined threshold, its local memory resources face little overhead because the number of requests processed locally

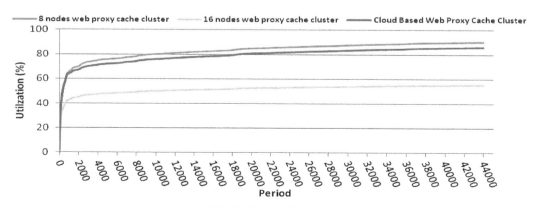

Fig. 5. CPU utilization

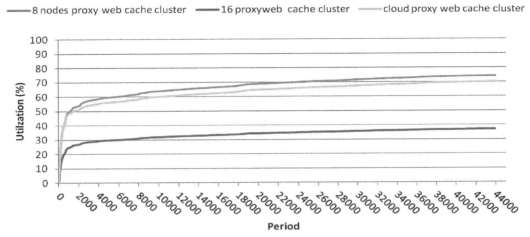

Fig. 6. RAM utilization

become approximately a half of total number of requests processed in 8-nodes TWPCC. In other hand and compared to 16-node TWPCC, our system has higher significant memory overhead since it has only 8 fixed local nodes with limited memory spaces.

In CBWPCC, we noticed that CPU and memory usage increases slightly to 65% and 50% respectively before acquiring new nodes from the cloud and both CPU and memory resources did not reach a critical overhead level. This is because our system is designed not to trigger on CPU/memory metrics but on another metric R crossing a threshold value.

In Figure 7, the utilization of I/O is much more effective in CBWPCC than in 8- and 16-node TWPCC. Though all three curves originated from the same point, with the gradual growth of workload rising, the curve of CBWPCC is higher than that of the two traditional web proxy cache clusters. Thus, our proposed system can handle more contents of bytes in a given period of time

since relieving workload on our local nodes cluster by bursting some requests to the cloud helps in enhance the disk I/O utilization of CBWPCC by 4.35%.

Result of VM cost with cost of data transfer and total cost of adding cloud nodes is depicted in a bar chart in Figure 8. The VM cost has four components:

- per processing cost,
- per unit cost of memory,
- per unit cost of storage and
- per unit cost of used bandwidth.

Cost per memory and cost per storages are incurred during creation of virtual machine. Cost per bandwidth occurs during transfer of data. Other costs, processing costs, are relevant to uses of processing of resources. The pricing policy was adopted from Amazon's business model of small instances ($0.06 per Standard On-Demand instance per hour) which means that cost per instances are charged hourly [14].

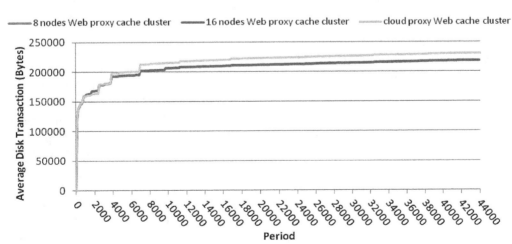

Fig. 7. I/O utilization

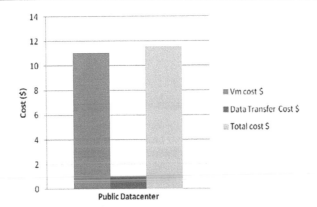

Fig. 8. Cost of bursting cache requests to public cloud

CONCLUSION

Load balancing strategies are adopted generally by traditional web proxy cache clusters to get a tradeoff in enhancing service qualities and resource efficiencies. Though, the solution seems to be reasonable, it will result in resource wasting when the load of the system is low. When the load is high, the service quality will be poor and it will be dropped in its worst case situation (when the system is exceedingly overloaded). To overcome this issue, this paper proposed an architecture for a cloud based Web proxy cache cluster. By using on demand cloud resources, the system to expands its capacity when the load goes beyond its local capacity and released them when the load gets down.

We evaluated the effectiveness of the proposed architecture comparing with traditional one which have fixed node number, in term of response time ,resource utilization. Results of the experiments shows that Cloud based Web proxy cache cluster performs better in obtaining of higher resource efficiency and lowering of system cost. And since we deploy the cache application in cloud environment, this may bring security issues. Therefore, our future direction will focus on presenting a solution to avoid the influence of cloud security for the proposed cloud based cache proxy system.

Acknowledgment

This paper contains the results and findings of a research project that is funded by King Abdulaziz City for Science and Technology (KACST), Grant No: T-T-12-0938.

REFERENCES

1. Zeng D., Wang F., Liu M. Efficient web content delivery using proxy caching techniques. Systems, Man, and Cybernetics, Part C: Applications and Reviews, IEEE Transactions on, Aug. 2004, 34(3): 270-280.

2. Mahanti A., Williamson C. Web proxy workload characterization. Technical Report, Department of Computer Science, University of Saskatchewan, February 1999, http://www.cs.usask.ca/faculty/carey/ papers/workloadstudy.ps

3. Yang Z., Kamata S., Ahrary A. NIR: Content based image retrieval on cloud computing. [In:] Proc. IEEE International Conference on Intelligent Computing and Intelligent Systems, 2009, IEEE Computer Society, Shanghai, China, 2009, p. 556-559.

4. Dornemann T., Juhnke E., Freisleben B. On-Demand Resource Provisioning for BPEL Workflows Using Amazon's Elastic Compute Cloud. [In:] Proc. of the 9th IEEElACM International Symposium on Cluster Computing and the Grid, IEEE, Shanghai, China, 2009, p. 140-147.

5. Assuncao M., Costanzo A., Buyya R. Evaluating the Cost- Benefit of Using Cloud Computing to Extend the Capacity of Clusters. [In:] Proc. of High Performance Distributed Computing (HPDC), June 2009, p. 141-150.

6. Marshall P., Keahey K., Freeman T. Elastic Site: Using Clouds to Elastically Extend Site Resources. [In:] Proc. of Conference on Cluster, Cloud, and Grid Computing (CCGRID), May 2010.

7. Duan Z.; Gu Z. EWPCC: An elastic Web proxy cache cluster basing on cloud computing. [In:] Proc. of the 3rd IEEE International Conference on Computer Science and Information Technology (ICCSIT), July 2010, 1(9-11): 85-88.

8. Alsaiari N., Fayoumi A. Load Balancing Techniques for Web Proxy Cache Clusters. International Journal of Advanced Research in Computer Science (IJARCS), Sep-Oct 2012, 3(5).

9. Buyya R., Yeo C.S., Venugopal S. Market oriented cloud computing: Vision, hype, and reality for delivering IT services as computing utilities. [In:] Proc. of the 10th IEEE International Conference on Advanced Learning Technologies, July 2010.

10. Rodriguez P., Spanner C., Biersack E.W. Analysis of Web caching architectures: hierarchical and distributed caching. Networking, IEEE/ACM Transactions on, Aug 2001, 9(4): 404-418.

11. CloudSim: A Framework for Modeling and Simulation of Cloud Computing Infrastructures and Services. The Cloud Computing and Distributed Systems (CLOUDS) Laboratory, University of Melbourne, 2011 (available from: http://www.cloudbus.org/cloudsim/)

12. Java software version 7 downloaded from: http://java.com/en/download/index.jsp (August 2013).

13. Krsul I., Ganguly A., Zhang J. VMPlants: Providing and Managing Virtual Machine Execution Environments for Grid Computing. [In:] Proc. of the ACM/IEEE Conference on Supercomputing, IEEE Computer Society, Pittsburg, PA, USA, 2004: 1-12.

14. Amazon EC2 Pricing. Pay as You Go for Cloud Computing Services. Amazon EC2, n.d. Web. 14 Sept. 2013. <http://aws.amazon.com/ec2/pricing/>

25

ROLE OF VISUALIZATION IN ENGINEERING EDUCATION

Renata Lis[1]

[1] Faculty of Fundamentals of Technology, Lublin University of Technology, Nadbystrzycka 38, 20-618 Lublin, Poland, e-mail: r.lis@pollub.pl

ABSTRACT

The article includes an analysis of the results of research on the influence of visualization on the effectiveness of training. It analyzes the application of visualization in engineering education with a particular focus on visual design principles. Examples of the use static and dynamic visualization in multimedia learning in technology and computer science are presented.

Keywords: visualization, visual design principles, multimedia education.

INTRODUCTION

The development of new information technologies affected the way of providing and assimilating information, focused on a monitor and digital environment rather than a book and a piece of paper. New media require having not only the abilities of reading and writing but also the so-called new abilities – visual literacy and digital literacy [8]. This situation forces a change of manner in conveying knowledge by education establishments. More and more information, provided in an inappropriate way, causes information overload. According to researches, information visualisation enables to convey knowledge in a condensed manner, increasing its assimilation, compared to traditional text transmission [15].

INFORMATION VISUALIZATION

The term 'visualisation' is defined in many ways [3]. However, the dominating one is that of perceiving it as a mental process occurring while thinking and as an iconic representation. The first case concerns a mentation which occurs during perception of visual phenomena supporting visual/spatial thinking; the second one – a presentation of information, knowledge, processes with the use of static and dynamic pictures. In both cases, we can distinguish the following types of visualization:

- infographics,
- visualization representation of numeric values,
- visualization concepts, procedures, processes,
- architectural visualization,
- 3D visualization [15].

The general distinction divides visualisation into a static and a dynamic one. Static visualisation includes:

- illustration – a presentation of visual elements using various media and such techniques as a hand drawing, a painting made with oil paint or a computer graphic;
- photograph – a faithful reflection of the state of affairs;
- 3D model – a digital reflection of the reality;

whereas the dynamic one consists of:

- animation, understood as a series of pictures simulating motion;
- video, which means a series of pictures in a video technique;
- interactions, i.e. pictures triggered by a user [3].

The sole ability of using advanced graphics software is not sufficient for correct designing education animations, drawings, diagrams and multimedia presentations. What is needed is the understanding of cognitive processes occurring while visualisation perception [5].

RULES OF VISUAL DESIGN

Rules of visual designing originated from the Mayer's theory of multimedia learning and gestalt psychology [11].

The theory of multimedia learning assumes that human brain receives information via two channels: a visual and a verbal one (see Figure 1). Such visual materials as: illustrations, photographs, charts and animations are processed in one channel and verbal information in the other. R.E. Mayer states that each channel has a limited capacity, therefore, it can process only limited amount of verbal and visual information in a specified time. Learning process occurs while processing information in information channels and organizing it into a comprehensive verbal or visual model and creating own knowledge in the final stage. However, cognitive overload often occurs, which is a result of inappropriate conveyance of knowledge by the teaching person.

According to the multimedia education theory, such rules as the following should be obeyed in the process of designing information visualisation:

- **the rule of contiguousness of visual and verbal contents** – visualisation helps the education process if the pictures and text layers of a message correspond to each other at the level of meanings [15];
- **the rule of personification** – didactic transmission should be personalised; messages should be written and spoken in the 1st and 2nd person and knowledge should be conveyed in a form of a dialogue;
- **the rule of modality** – visualisation is effective if supported by a narration; researches indicate that students who saw pictures and text and heard accompanying narration achieved

up to 50% higher scores in the subsequent knowledge tests, compared to those who only saw picture and the text which was to be read in the screen;

- **the rule of logicality** – the researches of Mayer reveal that better results of education are achieved if additional sounds, recordings, videos or narrations which are not a direct element of educational program, are removed; seemingly, it can attract the pupil, but it was proved that they do distract and dissuade from the main transmission of the content;
- **the rule of interactivity** – it relies on frequent overloading the presentation screens with information; if part of the elements are included in an interactive form – opened on a click – the learner controls his/her own cognitive processes, therefore increasing the effectiveness of learning;
- **the rule of redundancy** – the researches revealed that the use of visualisation containing text, picture and narration causes an effect of visual channel overload, thus the materials are less clear than those containing e.g. only a picture and text;
- **the rule of signalling** – the structure of education materials creates a specified space; to emphasize the crucial elements and relations between them, signalling certain terms and relations between them is important; the researches of the author of the theory of multimedia learning reveals that the examined ones achieved better effects when the education material was divided into signalled elements than in the situation without them;
- **the rule of parallelism** – effectiveness of learning increases if visualisation and verbal narration occur not subsequently but simultaneously; asynchronous and non-parallel

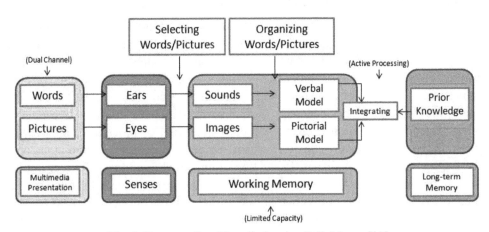

Fig. 1. Process of multimedia leaning R.E. Mayer [11]

occurrence of picture and verbal contents does not provide the learner a possibility of combining them in operating memory and relating them appropriately to the previous knowledge [9,11].

In the process of designing visualisations rules of perceptual grouping (which are described in laws of the gestalt psychology) are used.

- **Law of similarity** – elements with similar appearance are perceived as one. Eyesight groups unconditionally those elements which are characterised by similar relations resulting from the same shape, size or colour. This law is used quite often for selecting active links and buttons. Due to this issue, users have got no problem with navigation of these elements, they identify them upon the same features, e.g. colour which enables to combine them into groups.

- **Law of proximity** – the mind groups neighbouring elements. Approximation of appropriate elements increases the effectiveness of information perception. Application of such a mechanism improves the clarity of the material and facilitates the identification of the elements. The researches of G.H. Bower, M.B. Karlin and A. Dueck confirmed the suitability of using descriptions below pictures. Their experiment consisted in presenting pictures to a group of volunteers. Some of them only watched the presented works, whereas the second group not only saw the pictures but also had a possibility of reading their descriptions. The following stage of that experiment was to indicate the pictures which the participants saw among various ones. Obviously, the group who saw pictures with descriptions achieved better results. Due to the description, an observer can understand the presented content better [4].

- **Law of continuity** – it indicates that it is easier to perceive objects with soft shapes than those whose edges change sharply and rapidly. Objects creating lines or curves or any identifiable element, are perceived as connected with each other. A good composition is characterised by elements perceived as a whole despite the use of different colours or shapes. In this case, eyesight perception groups elements upon their location, not features. By using this law, recipient's attention can be directed towards specified elements [1].

Not only do the described rules and laws define how to design the visualisation. Having in mind the fact that every visualisation contains a picture, it is worth remembering the features of the picture which are related to strengthening the transmission.

EXAMPLES OF USES OF VISUALIZATION IN ENGINEERING EDUCATION

Visualisation is very significant in engineering education because this kind of education is a specific form which requires orienting towards the practical aspect of the described processes. For appropriate conveyance of knowledge a visualisation of a given process, e.g. friction one, is often necessary.

An example of application of visualisation in the education of future engineers in the technical and informatics education field of study is a multimedia course concerning technical mechanics with strength of materials created by a student of the above-mentioned field of study, as a part of its degree dissertation [7]. That course realises such issues as:

- calculation of friction factor with the use of inclined plane;
- calculation of efficiency of screw-nut system;
- analysis of stresses and calculation of G shear modulus (Kirchoff's) in a twisted pipe;
- examinations of deformations and stresses in a bent beam;
- static attempt of stretching the material;
- elastic buckling of a straight rods.

The course consists of many training screens containing static and dynamic visualisation in a form of photographs, illustrations and interactive pictures (Figure 2). It presents photographs and illustrations of research stations enabling conducting individual lab classes on technical mechanics. A simulation of operation of the individual research stations was included.

Another example is an interactive course of architectural modelling in Autodesk 3ds Max 2013 software, where an interactive visualisation and visualisation of procedures are very significant. Students deal with a simulation of operation of an actual 3ds Max software. Initial training screens have static visualisations in a form of screenshots of its interface, the next ones – interactive exercises relying on dynamic visualisation (Figure 3). This course requires a constant com-

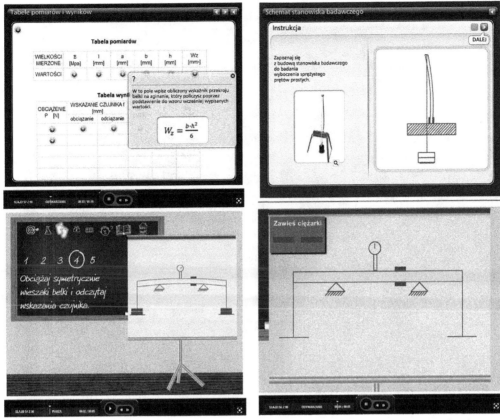

Fig. 2. Training screens containing visualisations from the course of technical mechanics
with strength of materials [7]

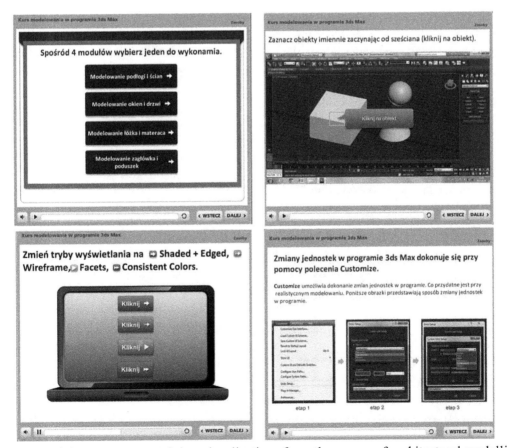

Fig. 3. Training screens containing visualisations from the course of architectural modelling
in Autodesk 3ds Max 2013 software [6]

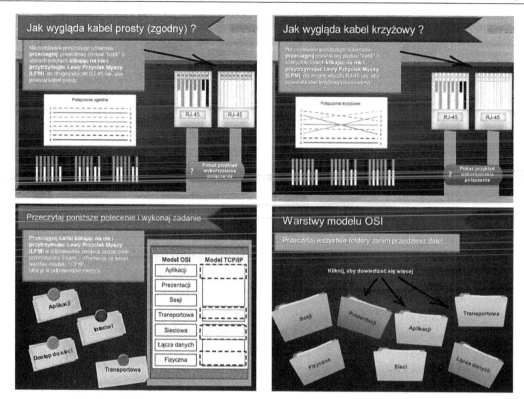

Fig. 4. Training screens from computer networks construction course [10]

mitment from students. If they do not click on the given option appropriately, they will not be able to proceed to the next screen, thus to complete the course. The range of the course comprises of basic knowledge on 3D modelling, 3ds Max 2013 software interface and utilitarian object and room modelling [6].

The last example of application of visualisation in engineering education concerns computer networks construction course [10]. It presents such issues as: computer networks topology and TCP/IP and OSI models, terminating cables, elementary hardware for designing the network, what an IP address and subnetwork mask are and area-based classification of computer networks.

The presented examples of multimedia courses became a subject of author's own researches, concerning the impact of visualisation on education effectiveness in technical and informatics courses.

VISUALISATION IMPACT ON EDUCATION EFFECTIVENESS RESEARCH

Education effectiveness is understood here as a level of implementation of the presumed didactic aims and the following knowledge increase indicator was used for measuring it [4]:

$$PW = \frac{Wpost - Wpre}{Wmax - Wpre} \times 100\%$$

where: PW – knowledge increase indicator,

$Wmax$ – possible maximal score of the researched one's competence measurement,

$Wpre$ – score of the researched one's competence measurement before the didactic process,

$Wpost$ – score of the researched one's competence measurement after the didactic process.

In the researches conducted by the author, the measurement of competence was made in a form of filling in a test of knowledge of a given range which was a part of the multimedia course. The researched ones had to fill it in before attending the course (a pre-test) and after it (a post-test). The acquired data were the basis for calculating the knowledge increase for each participant using the presented formula. Therefore, the data was averaged for the researched group.

In the case of multimedia course of technical mechanics [7], the researches were conducted in 2013 on a group of first-year students of the technical and information technology education first-cycle studies. Students were divided into two groups, one of which had got a task of acquainting with a course containing static visualisations in a form of photographs and illustrations as well as dynamic visualisations in a form of interactions and animations, and the second one – with materials containing the same issues but in a form of text. The test of initial knowledge (the pre-test) and of eventual knowledge (the post-test) was carried out in both groups. The tests were the same for each group and consisted of 9 questions. Single choice questions were used. For each correct answer a point could be scored. Maximal achievable amount of points were 9.

60 respondents participated in the research, 30 people per group. The first of the examined groups consisted of people who had got the task of completing the course containing visualisations in a form of pictures and interactions. The task of the second one was of completing the course including only text element. Essential content of both courses was the same.

Table 1 presents the average scores achieved by the researched in the pre-test and in the post-test as well as the percentage knowledge increase in the individual groups.

In the group participating in the course without visualisation, the result increased by 2.1 points, whereas the knowledge increase, calculated with the use of the formula presented earlier, was 43.6%. In the second one, which participated in the course with visualisation, the knowledge increase was very significant, because it was 82.35%. The points average increased by 4.7 points. Therefore, the impact of visualisation on the level of assimilated material in the range of technical mechanics is sig-

nificant. Students participating in the course with dynamic visualisation assimilated almost 40% more information than those in the one without it.

The next experiment concerned the impact of dynamic and static visualisation on the level of knowledge in the range of architectural modelling in Autodesk 3ds Max 2013 software [6]. Those were conducted in a computer room of The Faculty of Fundamentals of Technology at Lublin University of Technology with the participation of second-year students of the technical and information technology education first-cycle studies in the Spring Semester of 2014. Two lab groups were examined, a total of 33 people. The first group, 15 students, was asked to complete a course containing static visualisation in a form of illustrations and photographs; the second one, 18 people, attended to a course including dynamic visualisations in a form of animations and interactions. The test consisted of 7 single choice questions; maximum achievable amount of points was 7.

Table 2 presents the average scores achieved by the researched in the pre-test and in the post-test as well as the percentage knowledge increase in the individual groups.

The students participating in the course with static visualisation achieved 67.60% knowledge increase in the range of architectural modelling and the points average increased by 3.27. In the group with the course containing dynamic visualisations, increase of points was similar at 3.39 and the knowledge increase indicator equalled 69.63%. Therefore, students

Table 1. Average scores from the tests in the researched groups and percentage knowledge increase indicator after the participation in the course of technical mechanics

Type of educational material	Type of test	Average points scored (max=9)	Increase of knowledge
Course without visualization	Pre-test	2.4	43.60%
	Post-test	4.5	
Course with dynamic visualization	Pre-test	2.3	82.35%
	Post-test	7.0	

Table 2. Average scores from the tests in the researched groups and percentage knowledge increase indicator after the participation in the architectural modelling in Autodesk 3ds Max 2013 course

Type of educational material	Type of test	Average points scored (max=7)	Increase of knowledge
Course with static visualization	Pre-test	1.73	67.60%
	Post-test	5.0	
Course with static and dynamic visualization	Pre-test	1.61	69.63%
	Post-test	5.5	

Table 3. Average scores from the tests in the researched groups and percentage knowledge increase indicator after the participation in the computer network construction course

Type of educational material	Type of test	Average points scored (max=7)	Increase of knowledge
Course with dynamic visualization	Pre-test	0.9	86.35%
	Post-test	5.6	
Course without visualization	Pre-test	1	39.87%
	Post-test	3.56	

participating in the course with static visualisation achieved similar scores compared to those participating in the course with visualisations including not only illustrations but also animations and interactions. It can be concluded that – in the case of 3D modelling issues – the impact of introducing dynamic visualisation on the level of assimilating knowledge is minor, because it is quite expensive and time-consuming in its preparation.

The last course of the ones presented in this article concerned the computer network construction [10]. The research on visualisation impact on the level of knowledge in this range was conducted in the Spring Semester of 2014 at The Faculty of Fundamentals of Technology at Lublin University of Technology among the second-year students of the technical and informatics education first-cycle studies. They were divided into two groups which were independent from each other, each one having a task of completing a course containing dynamic visualisations or one without them. The text content of the course was the same in both cases. A total of 50 people participated in the research, 25 per each group. Table 3 presents the scores achieved by the researched in the pre-test and in the post-test, as well as the percentage knowledge increase in the individual groups.

The examined who participated in the course without visualisation in the range of computer network construction achieved an average knowledge increase by 2.56 points. The average knowledge increase was 39.87%. The second group, which was participating in the course with visualisation, raised its score by 4.7 and the knowledge increase was as high as 86.35%. Probably, numerous interactions and animations included in the course had a strong impact on that score.

The presented results of the researches have a preliminary and partial character. However, they can provide certain hints for designing visualisations and multimedia didactic materials.

CONCLUSIONS

The conducted researches aimed at specifying how the application of visuals in engineering education affects the effectiveness of acquiring knowledge and if dynamic visualisation is more effective than the static one.

The presented analyses reveal that the application of visualisation in the multimedia technical and informatics courses improved the assimilation of knowledge in that range significantly. In the case of the two courses, in which the scores of students participating in the course with visualisation and those in the one containing only a text version of the materials were compared, the average increase of knowledge equalled 40%. Whereas in the research carried out among the students participating in the courses including visualisations but varying in dynamicity no significant differences were observed. It can be presumed that a high importance on the level of knowledge increase among the participants of the courses containing visualisations was the sole matter of the courses, convergent with their field of studies as well as completing the courses in accordance with the rules of multimedia education.

REFERENCES

1. Anderson J.: Uczenie się i pamięć, integracja zagadnień. Warszawa 1998.

2. Arnheim R.: Sztuka i percepcja wzrokowa : psychologia twórczego oka. Gdańsk: Akademia Sztuk Pięknych 2004.

3. Bergström B.: Komunikacja wizualna. Wydaw. Naukowe PWN, Warszawa, 2009.

4. Bramley, Ocena efektywności szkoleń, Dom Wydawniczy ABC, Kraków 2001.

5. Dylak S.: Wizualizacja w kształceniu nauczycieli, Wydawnictwo Uniwersytetu im. Adama Mickiewicza, Poznań 1995.

6. Gąszczyk-Gołos K.: Analiza edukacyjnych determinantów efektywności kursów e-learningowych. Niepublikowana praca magisterska, Lublin 2014.

7. Kosicka E.: Projekt wizualizacji treści dydaktycznych z przedmiotu mechanika techniczna z wytrzymałością materiałów. Niepublikowana praca inżynierska, Lublin 2011.

8. Kress G., van Leeuwen T.: Reading images. The grammar of visual design. Routledge, New York 2008.

9. Leszkowicz M.: Komunikacja wizualna w edukacji. [In:] Skrzydlewski W., Dylak S. (Eds.) Media - edukacja - kultura. W stronę edukacji medialnej. Poznań – Rzeszów, Polskie Towarzystwo Technologii i Mediów Edukacyjnych Poznań 2012.

10. Łukanowski M.: Badanie wpływu interaktywnych form przekazywania wiedzy na efektywność kursów e-learningowych. Niepublikowana praca magisterska, Lublin 2014.

11. Mayer A.E.: The Cambridge handbook of multimedia learning. Cambridge University Press 2014.

12. Mączyńska-Frydryszek A.: Psychologia widzenia. Akademia Sztuk Pięknych w Poznaniu, Poznań 2002.

13. Pastuszka W.: Barwa w grafice komputerowej. Wydawnictwo Naukowe PWN, Warszawa 2000.

14. Pulak I., Tomaszewska M.: Visual literacy and teaching with infographics. [In:] Edukacja jutra. Edukacja w społeczeństwie wiedzy. Oficyna wydawnicza „Humanitas", Sosnowiec 2011.

15. Ware C.: Visual thinking for design. Burlington 2000.

26

REDUCED DATA FOR CURVE MODELING – APPLICATIONS IN GRAPHICS, COMPUTER VISION AND PHYSICS

Małgorzata Janik[1], Ryszard Kozera[1,2], Przemysław Kozioł[1]

[1] Faculty of Mathematics and Information, Warsaw University of Technology, Pl. Politechniki 1, 00-661 Warsaw, Poland, e-mail: majanik@if.pw.edu.pl, r.kozera@mini.pw.edu.pl, pkoziol@student.mini.pw.edu.pl

[2] Faculty of Applied Informatics and Mathematics, Warsaw University of Life Sciences – SGGW, Nowoursynowska 159, 02-776 Warsaw, Poland, e-mail: ryszard_kozera@sggw.edu.pl, ryszard.kozera@gmail.com

ABSTRACT

In this paper we consider the problem of modeling curves in R^n via interpolation without a priori specified *interpolation knots*. We discuss two approaches to estimate the missing knots $\{t_i\}_{i=0}^m$ for non-parametric data (i.e. collection of points $\{q_i\}_{i=0}^m$, where $q_i \in \mathbb{R}^n$). The first approach *(uniform evaluation)* is based on blind guess in which knots $\{\hat{t}_i\}_{i=0}^m$ are chosen uniformly. The second approach *(cumulative chord parameterization)* incorporates the geometry of the distribution of data points. More precisely, the difference $\hat{t}_{i+1} - \hat{t}_i$ is equal to the Euclidean distance between data points q_{i+1} and q_i. The second method partially compensates for the loss of the information carried by the reduced data. We also present the application of the above schemes for fitting non-parametric data in computer graphics (light-source motion rendering), in computer vision (image segmentation) and in physics (high velocity particles trajectory modeling). Though experiments are conducted for points in R^2 and R^3 the entire method is equally applicable in R^n.

Keywords: interpolation, computer vision, computer graphics, physics.

INTRODUCTION

In this paper we consider the problem of modeling curves via interpolation based on the so-called discrete *reduced data* $Q_m = (q_0, q_1, ..., q_m)$ (for i ∈ {0, 1, ..., m}), where $q_i \in R^n$. The term reduced data corresponds to the ordered sequence of $m+1$ input points in R^n stripped from the tabular parameters $\{t_i\}_{i=0}^m$. More precisely we obtain reduced data by sampling parametric curve $\gamma : [0, T] \to R^n$ with $\gamma(t_i) = q_i$ (where $0 \leq i \leq m$) in arbitrary Euclidian space without provision of the corresponding parameters $\{t_i\}_{i=0}^m$ (where $t_0 = 0 < t_1 < t_2 < ... < t_m = T < \infty$), usually referred in the literature as *interpolation knots*. To perform any interpolation scheme we need first to estimate the unknown knots t_i. One approach is to choose the parameters $\{\hat{t}_i\}_{i=0}^m \in [0, \hat{T}]^{m+1}$ blindly by assigning them e.g. natural numbers in the uniform manner: $\hat{t}_i = i$.

However, this simplistic method frequently renders surprisingly undesired results. Following discussion from [5] and [8] a strong indication exists that the method of *guessing* interpolation knots $\{t_i\}_{i=0}^m$ should incorporate the geometry of the distribution of sampling points Q_m. Such possible method is analyzed in [5] and [8], and is later referred to in our paper as *cumulative chord knot evaluation method*. In this approach we compensate for the loss of the information carried by the reduced data by calculating the distance between consecutive different points $\{q_i, q_{i+1}\}$ and use the cumulative distance as respective values for the unknown knots: i.e. $\hat{t}_0 = 0$ and $\hat{t}_{i+1} = \|q_{i+1} - q_i\| + \hat{t}_i$. The problem of fitting non-parametric data is not only an abstract mathematical concept, but can be applied in real life. The latter happens e.g. in computer graphics (motion rendering), computer vision (image segmentation) and other applications such as medical image processing or high-velocity particle trajectory modeling. Such examples are implemented here. The presented method can also be applied in modeling of different technical processes, i.e. [6] or [7, 9].

Concepts

Spline interpolation is a form of interpolation where the interpolant is a special type of piecewise polynomial called a spline (see e.g. [11]). A *cubic spline* is a piecewise cubic polynomial (see [2]) of class C^2. The essential idea is to fit the data $\gamma(t_0), \gamma(t_2), ..., \gamma(t_m)$ with a piecewise cubic $S : [0, T] \rightarrow \mathbb{R}^n$ of the form:

$$S(t) = \begin{cases} P_0(t); & t_0 \leq t \leq t_1 \\ \vdots & \vdots \\ P_{m-1}(t), & t_{m-1} \leq t \leq t_m \end{cases} \quad (1)$$

where each $P_i : [t_i, t_{i+1}] \rightarrow \mathbb{R}^n$ is a third degree polynomial defined by

$$P_i(t) = a_i(t - t_i)^3 + b_i(t - t_i)^2 + c_i(t - t_i) + d_i \quad (2)$$

with constant vectors $a_i, b_i, c_i, d_i \in \mathbb{R}^n$. Again by [2] the latter coefficients (with the aid of Newton's divided differences) read as:

$d_i = P_i(t_i) = \gamma(t_i), \quad c_i = P_i'(t_i) = s_i,$

$b_i = P_i''(t_i)/2 = [t_i, t_i, t_{i+1}]\gamma - \Delta t_i[t_i, t_i, t_{i+1}, t_{i+1}]\gamma,$

$= ([t_i, t_{i+1}]\gamma - s_i)/\Delta t_i - a_i\Delta t_i,$

$a_i = P_i'''(t_i)/6 = (s_i + s_{i+1} - 2[t_i, t_{i+1}]\gamma)/(\Delta t_i)^2,$

where $s_i = \dot{\gamma}(t_i)$ and $\Delta t_i = t_{i+1} - t_i$. There are two possible cases here: i.e. s_i are known (Hermite interpolation) and s_i are unknown (a common case in practice). The latter case is considered here. In doing so, we recall that values of s_i for $i = 1, ..., m - 1$ can be derived from: $P_i''(t_{i+1}) = P_{i+1}''(t_{i+1})$ (see also [2]). If s_0 and s_m are given then we deal with the so-called *complete spline*. On the other hand, if s_0 and s_m are also unknown, we can add constraints $\ddot{\gamma}(t_0) = \ddot{\gamma}(t_m) = 0$. Such boundary conditions render the so-called *natural splines* with $P_0''(t_0) = P_{i-1}''(t_m) = 0$. The natural spline determines the smoothest of all possible interpolating curves in the sense that it minimizes the integral of the square of the second derivative (see [2]).

NON-PARAMETRIC INTERPOLATION AND KNOT EVALUATION METHODS

Some practical problems exist while dealing with the incomplete data set. We can consider many problems where the sequence of points Q_m interpolates the unknown curve γ with no provision of *knot parameters* $\{t_i\}_{i=0}^m$. Such a task is coined as *fitting the reduced data* Q_m and any interpolation scheme based on such data is called *non-parametric interpolation*. In order to apply a scheme based on non-parametric interpolation, careful guessing of the knots $\{\hat{t}_i\}_{i=0}^m \in [0, \hat{T}]^{m+1}$ needs to be made so that the resulting interpolant $\tilde{\gamma}$ (here $\tilde{\gamma} = S$, see Eq. (1)) yields the best possible orders of convergence – see e.g. [5] and [8] for the analysis of C° piecewise-cubics and piecewise-quadratics or see [4] or [3] for C^1 or C^2 piecewise-cubics, respectively.

Uniform Knot Evaluation Method

The simple stand the most natural fashion of choosing the knots is to approximate the unknown $\{t_i\}_{i=0}^m \in [0, T]^{m+1}$ in the uniform manner:

$$\hat{t}_i = i, \quad (3)$$

with $\hat{T} = m$. The potential problems in selecting $\{\hat{t}_i\}_{i=0}^m$ blindly are illustrated in Figure 1 and Figure 2. We present here interpolation problems, that can arise while reproducing the sector of the circle. We specify two different set of point q_i. In the case, when the points are distributed in the regular, uniform manner the uniform evaluation method, not surprisingly, is able to reproduce the curve γ very well (see Figure 1). But in the case, when points are placed in irregular intervals along the circle, strong deviations from the original curve can be observed (see Figure 2).

a)   b)

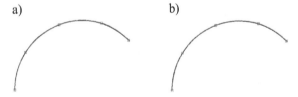

Fig. 1. Cubic spline interpolation with (a) a uniform knot evaluation method (red line) and (b) a cumulative chord knot evaluation method for uniformly distributed points

a)   b)

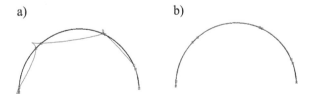

Fig. 2. Cubic spline interpolation with (a) a uniform knot evaluation (red line) and (b) a cumulative chord knot evaluation for points distributed in irregular fashion

Cumulative Chord Knot Evaluation Method

Following [5] or [8] instead of choosing the knots blindly (e.g. as by (3)) we can assign to them the values of the cumulative distance between the interpolated points:

$$\hat{t}_0 = 0, \quad \hat{t}_{i+1} = \|q_{i+1} - q_i\| + \hat{t}_i, \qquad (4)$$

for $i = 0, 1, ..., m - 1$ and $\hat{T} = \sum_{i=0}^{m-1} \|q_{i+1} - q_i\|$, where $\| \cdot \|$ denotes a standard Euclidean norm in R^n. Formula (4) for estimating knots t_i takes into account the geometrical distribution of the points Q_m for an arbitrary dimensions, what makes our procedure usable for any non-parametric interpolation problem. The results of the interpolation of the points placed on the sector of the circle can be compared in Figure 1 (for uniformly distributed points) and in Figure 2 (for data distributed in irregular manner).

Comparison of Knot Evaluation Methods – Examples

Following experiments performed here (see Figure 3) certain facts should be emphasized:
1. If the number of interpolation points Q_m is small and the data are distributed in highly irregular manner the uniform method creates irregularities in trajectory estimation, while the curve obtained by chord evaluation method maintains plain and smooth shape.
2. If the data are distributed in the uniform manner then both methods work equally well, since uniform distribution of knots reflects uniform distribution of the data.
3. If the number of points Q_m is large then the results from both methods appear to be very similar, but in fact the convergence order of the approximation to the trajectory is not fast for uniform knot evaluation method and would give big errors while estimating the length of the curve [5] or [8]. This does not happen with item 1 from above.

For data distributed in the uniform manner even for simple guess $\hat{t}_i = i$ we obtain desired results. However, there are some problems for which we do not have control over specifying interpolation points, or even if we have, we want to specify only small collection of points. In the latter case to correctly reproduce the curve we need to choose more points in the area where the curve is changing rapidly, than in places where it remain steady. Such procedure would result in increasing density of points in some regions, yielding in non-uniformly distributed data.

SPHERE ILLUMINATION (COMPUTER GRAPHICS)

The main goal of the sphere illumination module is to present the estimation of the trajectory of the light-source movement on the basis of a sparse sequence of observed frames, which are defined on the basis of the position of the light-source. Each frame is created by illuminating the same three dimensional object in the same place in space by light-source. Frames differ from each other only by the assigned a place in sequence and the position of a source of light in 3D space. The sphere illumination module estimates the position of a source of light in an exact number of frames placed between each frame of the input data. Therefore the resulting sequence of frames consists of the initial set of frames and the set of estimated frames forming altogether the estimation of the movement of the source flight. For sphere illumination, Phong reflection model [10] is used. To calculate the intensity of each pixel we apply:

$$I = I_a + I_d + I_s,$$

where I_a is the intensity of ambient colour of the pixel, the I_d is the intensity of colour for diffuse reflection of light at the pixel and I_s is the inten-

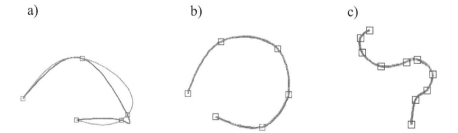

Fig. 3. Cubic spline interpolation using both knot evaluation methods: uniform (red line) and cumulative chord (green line). Example scenarios: (a) the number of interpolation points is small and the data are distributed in a highly irregular manner, (b) the data are distributed in a uniform manner, (c) the number of points is large

sity of colour for specular reflection of light at the pixel. The ambient colour parameters are constant for a particular object and do not depend on the position of the observer and the position of light-source. Therefore, the equation for the ambient property is of a form

$$I_a = k_a,$$

where k_a is a constant value of colour intensity. The I_d is the diffuse property of the material. The basic form of an equation for the I_d intensity of diffuse compound of colour for a given pixel is

$$I_a = k_a \cdot cos\vartheta,$$

where k_d^R is a constant value of the diffuse property and ϑ is the angle between the surface normal and the vector pointing from the surface point to the light source. The I_s is the specular property of the material. The basic form of the equation for the I_s intensity of specular compound of colour for a given pixel is

$$I_a = k_a \cdot (cos\varphi)^p,$$

where k_s is a constant value of specular property of a material, which is illuminated by the white light, p determines the size of the highlight spot and φ is an angle between the vector pointing from the specified point to the position of the observer and the ideal reflection vector.

Experimental Concept

In the sphere illumination model we implemented two different knot evaluation methods for determining the trajectory of the light-source, namely uniform and cumulative chord. The trajectory is obtained by interpolating the curve through specified points in the three dimensional space (see Figure 4). The experimental task was to study the differences between methods simulating the sphere illumination by the moving light-source, where the light-source travels with constant velocity.

Example

We prepared a set of input data consisting of points shown in Table 1. Those input data points

Table 1. Input data for sphere illumination module

Frame number	X	Y	Z
1	120	120	120
2	120	220	120
3	120	220	320
4	820	620	320
6	220	120	20

a)

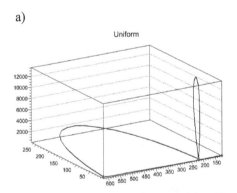

b)

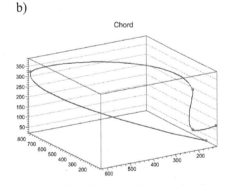

Fig. 4. Light-source trajectory: (a) uniform knot evaluation, (b) chord knot evaluation

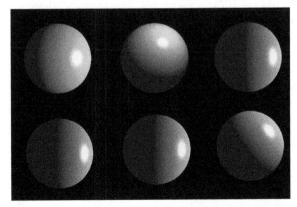

Fig. 5. Frames [8-13] rendered after interpolation for points from Table 1. Uniform evaluation

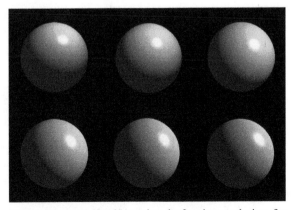

Fig. 6. Frames [8-13] rendered after interpolation for points from Table 1. Chord evaluation

define the position of the light-source, which illuminated the object in each of the frames. For this set of coordinates we simulated the movement of the light-source applying both knot evaluation methods (see Eqs (3) and (4)). The trajectories of the light-source for both methods are shown in Figure 4. More precisely, Figure 4a and 4b present the same set of frames, which were an input for the interpolation task. However, the images do not exactly match, as the scales on these picture differ. This difference originates from significant differences in coordinates of the estimated points on trajectories. Algorithms for Phong illumination model and spline interpolation are applied in exactly the same fashion. As a result we obtained two different sequences of images for the same frame sequences within the whole resulting set of frames. Figue 5 presents frames between 8 and 13 (row ordered) of the set obtained for a uniform evaluation of knots. Figure 6 presents the same set of frames obtained for the evaluation of knots based on the length of chord.

IMAGE SEGMENTATION (COMPUTER VISION)

The main goal of the *image segmentation* module is to present the border line surrounding a certain area in the picture on the basis of a sequence of points marked by the user as interpolation points. Each point that is marked by the user is drawn on the picture in real time and the current shape of the curve is plotted onto the image. As all of the significant points are marked user closes the curve by splitting the image into two regions. The user can calculate the number of pixels within or outside of the region closed by the curve, which is realized by the Flood Fill Algorithm [1], which counts all points of the area until it recognizes reaching the border. The border curve (see Eq. (2)) may be calculated by applying two different knot evaluation modules discussed herein.

Experiment Concept

In the image segmentation model two different knot evaluation methods are implemented for determining the shape of the curve (see Eqs (3) and (4)). The experimental task is to study the impact of the evaluation methods on curve's shape and the area of a region bounded by this curve.

Table 2. Input data for image segmentation module: left nasal canal

Point number	0	1	2	3	4	5	6	7	8	9
X	362	346	344	308	345	348	367	393	392	362
Y	354	359	405	375	318	222	139	325	443	354

Table 3. Input data for image segmentation module: right nasal canal

Point number	0	1	2	3	4	5	6
X	418	447	448	407	417	437	418
Y	365	272	232	142	186	248	365

Table 4. Input data for image segmentation module: cell image

Point number	0	1	2	3	4	5	6	7	8	9
X	402	485	421	375	346	261	255	228	300	402
Y	197	275	420	427	436	385	349	303	204	197

Example

We prepared two input images. Over the first one, we marked points as shown in Table 2 and 3. Over the second one, we marked points as indicated in Table 4. For this set of coordinates we evaluated the shape of the curve applying both knots evaluation methods. The coordinates for the first and the last points are identical, as the curve is closed. For both methods we also calculated the area within the selected region. Algorithms for the calculation of the area based on the Flood Fill Algorithm [1] with pixel count and spline interpolation are applied in exactly the same way. As a result we obtained two different shapes of unknown curve and consecutively two different sizes of a region bordered by the curve. Figure 7 presents the curve obtained for selected points with the uniform evaluation of knots applied. The computed size of the area within the curve is 10220 pixels and 1117 pixels for left and right canal respectively. Figure 7 presents the curve obtained for selected points with chord evaluation of the knots applied. The resulting size of the area within the curve was 10540 pixels (left canal) and 1366 pixels (right canal). Visibly the chord method outperforms the uniform one. The same observations originate from a comparison of curves bounding the cell, which is presented at Figure 8. The computed size of a cell within the curve was 44925 pixels using the uniform knot

a)   b)

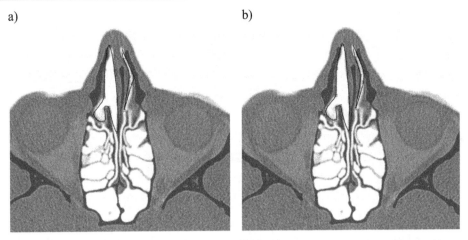

Fig. 7. Nose with area of nasal canals bounded by the curve obtained using (a) uniform knot evaluation (b) chord knot evaluation

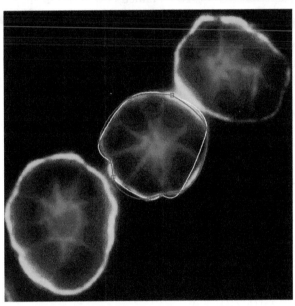

Fig. 8. A picture of call bounded with curves obtained using uniform knot evaluation (yellow) chord knot evaluation (pink)

evaluation method and 46701 pixels using the chord knot evaluation method.

TRAJECTORY MODELING (PHYSICS)

The main goal of the *trajectory modeling* module is to present the most accurate estimation of the shape of the trajectory obtained as an image of observed physical process and to provide analytical formula for estimated curve. The user is expected to mark points over the trajectory. Each point that is marked by the user is drawn on the picture in real time and the current shape of the curve is plotted onto the image. Therefore, the user can decide in which moment the whole trajectory is covered by the interpolating curve and perform the analysis of curve equations. The curve can be calculated by applying two different knot evaluation modules (i.e. uniform and cumulative chord).

Experiment Concept

As in the trajectory modeling, two different knot evaluation methods are implemented for determining the shape of the curve by interpolating the knots' values from the sequence of two dimensional points. The experimental task is to study the differences between the two methods to evaluate their impact on the analytical formulas obtained for both interpolants (serving as the boundary segmenting the image).

a)   b)

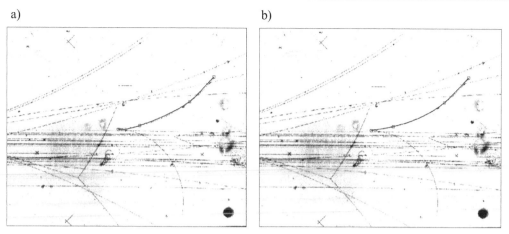

Fig. 9. Trajectory based on (a) uniform knot evaluation (b) chord knot evaluation

Example

We prepared an input image over which points as listed in Table 5 are marked. For this set of coordinates we evaluated the shape of the curve applying both knot evaluation methods.

Table 5. Input data for trajectory modeling

Point number	X	Y
0	371	408
1	443	395
2	611	318
3	691	238

For both methods we also calculated *the curvature* at points {(443, 395), (611, 318)}. The calculation is performed as presented below. Curvature $K(t)$ for curve $\gamma(t) = (x(t), y(t)) \in \mathbb{R}^2$ is defined as:

$$K(t) = \frac{x'(t)y''(t) - x''(t)y'(t)}{((x'(t))^2 + (y'(t))^2)^{3/2}}.$$

Momentum p of the particle of charge q moving within the magnetic field B reads as (see [12]):

$$p = (B \cdot q) \cdot r, \qquad (6)$$

where the circle radius r can be estimated by the curvature K:

$$r = \frac{1}{K}.$$

The analytical formula for $S(t) = (S_1(t), S_2(t))$ obtained from spline computation (see Eq. (1)) by (5) yields K. Since the charge q can be +1 or –1 the latter does not change the value of the momentum. Hence, (with aid of Eqs (6) and (7)) we obtain: $p = B/K$. The final unit of the momentum is $kg \cdot pixel/s$ (if the input value of the magnetic field B was given in T (Tesla)). As a result we ob-

tained two different shapes of the resulting curve and consecutively two different values of curvature. Figure 9a presents the curve obtained for selected points with a uniform evaluation of knots applied. The resulting curvature in point (443, 395) amounted to –0.0015 1/*pixel* and in point (611, 318) amounted to –0.0018 1/*pixel*. Figure 9b presents the curve obtained for selected points with applied chord evaluation of knots. The resulting curvature in the point (443, 395) amounted to –0.0003 1/*pixel* and in point (611, 318) amounted to –0,0011 1/*pixel*.

CONCLUSIONS

Our experiments show that one needs to be very careful while fitting non-parametric data. A proper knot parameterization must be selected with consideration for the geometrical distribution of data points. The experiments confirm the flexibility of cumulative chord knot parameterization. The latter is not preserved by a naive blind guess of the uniform parameterization.

REFERENCES

1. Bradski G., Kaehler A.: Learning OpenCV. O'Reilly Media 2008.

2. de Boor C.: A Practical Guide to Splines. Applied Mathematical Sciences, Springer 2001.

3. Floater M.S.: Chordal cubic spline interpolation is fourth order accurate. IMA Jouarnal of Numerical Analysis, 26, 2006, 25-33.

4. Kozera R., Noakes L.: C¹ interpolation with cumulative chord cubics. Fundamenta Informaticae, 31(3-4), 2004, 285-301.

5. Kozera R.: Curve modeling via interpolation based on multidimensional reduced data. Studia Informatica, 25(4B), 2004.

6. Lenik K., Korga S.: Deform 3D and SolidWorks FEM tests in conditions of sliding friction. Archives of Materials Science and Engineering, 56, 2012, 89-92.

7. Lenik K., Korga S.: The application of a tribotester prototype to sliding friction simulations and wear computations by means of FEM. Les problemes contemporains du technosphere et delaformation des cadres dingenieurs, 2011, 61-64.

8. Noakes L., Kozera R.: Cumulative chords and piecewise-quadratics and piecewise-cubics. In Geometric Properies of Incomplete Data, Eds R. Klette, R. Kozera, L. Noakes and J. Weickert, Computational Imaging and Vision. Springer, 31, 2006, 59-75.

9. Paliszewski P., Szczygiel I.: Modelowanie numeryczne procesu napełniania cylindra silnika ZI (in English: Flow simulation inside the IC engine). Postępy Nauki i Techniki – Advances in Science and Technology, 15, 2012, 116-122.

10. Phong B.T.: Illumination for Computer Generated Pictures Commun. ACM (1975).

11. Piegl L., Tiler W.: The NURBS Book. Springer, 1995.

12. Pinsky A.A., Yavorsky B.M.: Fundamentals of Physics. Volume II. MIR Publishers 1975.

27

DETERMINATION OF OPERATOR'S IMPACT ON THE MEASUREMENT DONE USING COORDINATE TECHNIQUE

Ksenia Ostrowska[1], Danuta Szewczyk[2], Jerzy Sładek[3]

[1] Laboratory of Coordinate Metrology, Mechanical Department, Cracow University of Technology, Al. Jana Pawła II 37, 31-864 Kraków, Poland, e-mail: kostrowska@mech.pk.edu.pl; dszewczyk@mech.pk.edu.pl; sladek@mech.pk.edu.pl

ABSTRACT

Coordinate measuring arms (CMAs) are devices which more and more often replace conventional coordinate measuring machines because of their undoubted advantages, such as mobility, the opportunity to increase the measuring volume, the opportunity to connect the optical probe, and above all, good price-quality ratio. Because these devices are handheld and redundant, what has the greatest impact on the measurement result accuracy are the operator, the machine kinematics and its ability to obtain repeatable measurement results; despite the fact that one point can be obtained from an infinite number of shoulders' positions. In this paper it was determined by using R&R method how significant are the impacts of both the operator and the measuring device on the accuracy of measurements done with CMA, both with rigid switch probe and optical probe.

Keywords: R&R method, coordinate measuring arms (CMA), operator impact, repeatability, reproducibility.

INTRODUCTION

Coordinate Metrology enables imaging objects by scanning surfaces and whole objects through the use of optical technique and computed tomography. Not long ago classical (contact) measuring machines were the main direction of development of the coordinate measuring technique. In recent years, however, growing interest in optical measuring devices of coordinate measuring technique was noted. Contactless measurement methods are characterized by: a very short measurement time, lack of necessity to program the machine, non-invasiveness and a large amount of data obtained for later analysis. The biggest disadvantage of this method is its small accuracy in comparison to contact coordinate measurements [6, 7, 9, 12].

Currently the coordinate measurements are the most advanced section in measuring technique used during quality control in the industry. Because of higher and higher requirements manufacturers of measuring instruments tend to continuously improve their devices. Coordinate Measuring Arms (CMAs)are among the most modern measuring devices. Their design makes it is possible to perform measurements of complex objects with high accuracy and in a very short time, what has a big impact on the quality of the product. CMAs cooperate with both switch probes, as well as contactless triangulation probes. Their undoubtedly biggest advantages are mobility and opportunity to increase their measuring volume up to 60 m through the use of systems, such as Gridlock or SpaceLock [5, 8, 11, 16, 19].

This paper presents the impact of the operator and of the measuring device using R&R method. The impact was determined both for CMA equipped with contact and contactless probe.

R&R METHOD

The "R&R" method (Repeatability and Reproducibility) is based on the calculation of repeatability and reproducibility of measurements, where reproducibility is, depending on the adopted set of variable conditions, a resultant of uncertainty including these conditions, while repeatability is an element of uncertainty derived from the gauge [10, 15].

In analysis by the "R&R" method, three basic concepts need to be used, such as: repeatability, reproducibility and inaccuracy. The definition of repeatability given as the standard uncertainty is determined in general as σ_g (gauge). The repeatability given as expanded uncertainty is in fact given as double expanded uncertainty (range of uncertainty) and is described as an abbreviation EV (equipment variation). A coverage factor $t = 2.575$ (level of confidence p = 99%) is most commonly used:

$$EV = 2t\,\sigma_g = 5.15\,\sigma_g \qquad (1)$$

Reproducibility of measurements [17] is the degree of compliance of the measurements results performed in variable conditions. To determine the reproducibility of the "R&R" method, following the experience gained in the industry, only the operator that performs measurements under repeatability conditions needs to be changed.

The reproducibility given as the standard uncertainty is usually determined as σ_a (appraiser – carrying measurement). Reproducibility expressed in the form of the expanded uncertainty is reported as double expanded uncertainty (range of uncertainty) and described as an acronym AV (appraiser variation). A coverage factor $t = 2.575$ is most commonly used:

$$AV = 2t\,\sigma_a = 5.15\,\sigma_a \qquad (2)$$

To interpret the difference between repeatability and reproducibility, definitions of the conditions of continuity need to be known, because all the cross between these concepts usually arise from the definition [10] (Figure 1).

According to [17] refractoriness is defined as a systematic error, i.e. the difference between the average of an infinite number of measurement results of the same size performed in terms of repeatability, and the true value measured quantity. Refractoriness is generally designated averaging the error of the appropriate number of repetitions of measurements.

Reproducibility conditions cause randomization of systematic error, but its expected value in

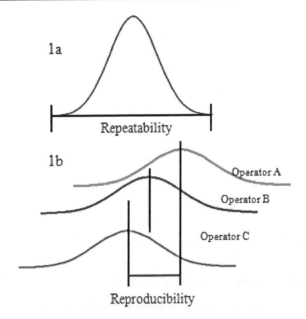

Fig. 1. Graphical interpretation of a) repeatability b) reproducibility of measurements

a hypothetical repetition of a series of measurements is zero. Analysis of R&R applies the same mathematical apparatus, which Shewhart used to develop his control cards, especially card $X_{cer} - R$ (therefore the „R&R" methodology is often called as the analysis of medium and stretch marks). This analysis is a tool to isolate and evaluate the participation of components of variation in the total scatter of measurements carried out during the monitoring of the manufacturing process.

Currently, the "R&R" analysis is a proven, recognized and required by many customers method (particularly the automotive industry). Till now, accepted procedures of "R&R" analysis have been introduced by the so-called "big three" (Ford, Chrysler, General Motors) in collaboration with Automotive of the American Society for Quality Control (ASQC) and the Automotive Industry Action Group (AIAG) under the requirements of the quality system QS-9000 [3, 10].

R&R METHOD (FORD-TYPE-2 FULL VERSION)

This method allows to determine the error of repeatability and reproducibility of the measuring gauge in a separated form (separately). The measurements were made by three operators, who measured ten parts (distance on step gauge ball-bar) in three trials. Measurement conditions were similar to the conditions of repeatability [1, 2, 3, 4, 13, 14, 17].

At the beginning the measurement was performed using CMA with rigid switch probe, where information of the contact was induced by an operator. The results were then processed in PC-Dmis metrological software (Figure 2).

Then the measurement was performed using CMA with a mounted R-Scan triangulation probe. As a result a cloud of points in 3DReashaper collaborative software was obtained, and then it was imported into Gom Inspect software provided by GOM, where data were processed and calculated (Figure 2).

Sequence of performed operations in R&R method for Coordinate Portable – Arm with switch probe

a) Each of the operators carried out the measurement of 10 different length of artefact (Figure 3).

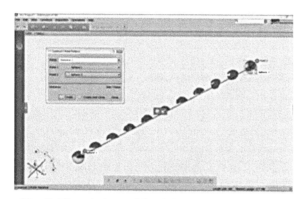

Fig. 2. The window of the GOM company software

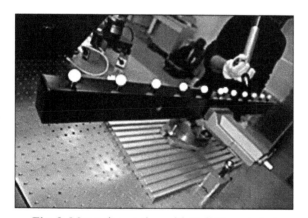

Fig. 3. Measuring station with Ball-Bar artefact

Fig. 4. Measuring CPA with optical probe [6]

b) Heave value (R) for each operator was calculated, as an absolute value of the difference between the value of maximum and minimum length of the measurement results:

$$R_J = \left| P_g - P_d \right| \qquad (3)$$

c) The sums of individual heave values were calculated (ΣR_A, ΣR_B, ΣR_C).

d) Average values of the heave sum of the individual operators were calculated:

$$R_{Acer} = \frac{\sum R_A}{L} = 0.0140 \qquad (4)$$

$$R_{Bcer} = \frac{\sum R_B}{L} = 0.0220 \qquad (5)$$

$$R_{Ccer} = \frac{\sum R_C}{L} = 0.0190 \qquad (6)$$

where: L – quantity of measured parts.

e) Average values from measurements of all trials for the individual operator were calculated:

$$X_{Acer} = \frac{\sum X_A}{I} = 549.7200 \qquad (7)$$

$$X_{Bcer} = \frac{\sum X_B}{I} = 549.7150 \qquad (8)$$

$$X_{Ccer} = \frac{\sum X_C}{I} = 549.7040 \qquad (9)$$

f) From average values (X_{Acer}, X_{Bcer}, X_{Ccer}) extreme values were chosen (Max_{Xcer}, Min_{Xcer}) and their differences were calculated (R_{Xcer}):

$$R_{Xcer} = Max_{Xcer} - Min_{Xcer} = 0.0160 \qquad (10)$$

g) The values of coefficients were determined D_4 and K_1 on the basis of Table 1, depending on the number of attempts.

Table 1. Values of coefficients D_4 and K_1

Number of attempts	D_4	K_1
2	3.27	4.56
3	2.58	3.05

h) Reproducibility of the measuring gauge was calculated ($E.V.$) as:

$$E.V. = R_{cer} \cdot K_1 = 0.000042 \qquad (11)$$

i) Percentage repeatability of the measuring gauge was calculated (E.V.%):

$$E.V\% = 100 \cdot \frac{E.V.}{Tolerance} = 0.0310\% \qquad (12)$$

j) The value of coefficient K_2 on the basis of Table 2 was determined:

Table 2. Values of coefficient K_2

Number of operators	K_2	Number of operators
2	3.65	2
3	2.70	3

k) Reproducibility of the measuring gauge was calculated ($A.V.$):

$$A.V. = \sqrt{\left(R_{Xcer} + K_2\right)^2 - \frac{E.V.^2}{(n \cdot r)}} = 0.0190 \quad (13)$$

where: n – number of parts,
   r – number of attempts.

l) Percentage reproducibility of the measuring gauge was calculated (A.V.%):

$$A.V.\% = 100 \cdot \frac{A.V.}{Tolerance} = 13.9950\% \quad (14)$$

m) Repeatability and reproducibility resultants of CMA (R&R):

$$R\&R = \sqrt{(AV.)^2 + (E.V.)^2} = 0.0190 \quad (15)$$

n) Percentage (R&R%):

$$R\&R\% = \sqrt{(AV.\%)^2 + (E.V.\%)^2} = 13.9951\% \quad (16)$$

Sequence of performed operations in R&R method, for Coordinate Portable – Arm with an optical probe

a) Each of the operators carried out the measurement of 10 different length of artefact (Figure 3).

b) Heave value (R) for each operator was calculated, as an absolute value of the difference between the value of maximum and minimum length of the measurement results:

$$R_J = \left| P_g - P_d \right| \quad (17)$$

c) The sums of individual heave values were calculated (ΣR_A, ΣR_B, ΣR_C).

d) Average values of the heave sum of the individual operators were calculated:

$$R_{Acer} = \frac{\sum R_A}{L} = 0.0710 \quad (18)$$

$$R_{Bcer} = \frac{\sum R_B}{L} = 0.0980 \quad (19)$$

$$R_{Ccer} = \frac{\sum R_C}{L} = 0.0930 \quad (20)$$

where: L – quantity of measured parts.

e) From average values (X_{Acer}, X_{Bcer}, X_{Ccer}) extreme values were chosen (Max_{Xcer}, Min_{Xcer}) and their differences were calculated (R_{Xcer}):

$$R_{Xcer} = Max_{Xcer} - Min_{Xcer} = 0.0270 \quad (21)$$

f) Reproducibility of the measuring gauge was calculated ($E.V.$) as:

$$E.V. = R_{cer} \cdot K_1 = 0.00026535 \quad (22)$$

g) Percentage repeatability of the measuring gauge was calculated ($E.V.\%$):

$$E.V.\% = 100 \cdot \frac{E.V.}{Tolerance} = 0.2110\% \quad (23)$$

h) Reproducibility of the measuring gauge was calculated ($A.V.$):

$$A.V. = \sqrt{\left(R_{Xcer} + K_2\right)^2 - \frac{E.V.^2}{(n \cdot r)}} = 0.0297 \quad (24)$$

where: n – number of parts;
   r – number of attempts.

i) Percentage reproducibility of the measuring gauge was calculated ($A.V.\%$):

$$A.V.\% = 100 \cdot \frac{A.V.}{Tolerance} = 22.5700\% \quad (25)$$

j) Repeatability and reproducibility resultants of CMA ($R\&R$):

$$R\&R = \sqrt{(AV.)^2 + (E.V.)^2} = 0.0297 \quad (26)$$

k) Percentage ($R\&R\%$):

$$R\&R\% = \sqrt{(AV.\%)^2 + (E.V.\%)^2} = 22.5701\% \quad (27)$$

INTERPRETATION OF RESULTS

The percentages obtained from the calculation of specific indicators of concern:
- E.V.% – gauge (repeatability),
- A.V.% – operator (reproducibility),
- R&R% – gauge and operator together (repeatability and reproducibility).
- below 10% – resultant error of repeatability and reproducibility (gauge and operator) is acceptable,
- 10–30% – resultant error of repeatability and reproducibility can be acceptable depending on the required accuracy of measurement,
- above 30% – resultant error of repeatability and reproducibility is too high, the system should not be allowed to use.

R&R method concerns the assessment of the measurement system through the analysis of repeatability, reproducibility and dispersion in a situation where measurements were carried out by different operators [15]. In both cases the operators have the biggest impact. This is not surprising because CPAs are manual machines, but the percentage of operator participation suggests that during calibration of given device it should be taken into account as a part of the system. Looking at Table 3 it can be seen, that after connection of the optical probe to CMA the error significantly increased, almost twice. This is related to the fact that probe errors propagate the device error. The device equipped both with contact and contactless probe can be used conditionally depending on what measurement we want to do.

Table 3. Summary of results

Parameter	CPA with switch probe (%)	CPA with optical probe (%)
E.V.%	0.0310	0.2110
A.V.%	13.9950	22.5700
R&R%	13.9951	22.5701

CONCLUSION

Taking into account PN-EN ISO 14253-1 standard (Figure 5) [18], it can be seen that with the increase of measurement uncertainty the field of compliance decreases, which may lead to go beyond the scope of the MPE of measuring device. For comparison the same measurements were carried out with the operators who use the CMA for the first time. AV% reproducibility error was over 18% [10].

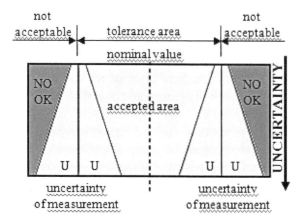

Fig. 5. Measurement uncertainty: the range of uncertainty reduces the fields of compliance and non-compliance [15]

Figure 6 shows how many factors affect the accuracy of measurement on CMA. These devices are largely dependent on the operator, its experience, software experience, manual efficiency, or ways of object attachment. Designated error of reproducibility of the measurement originating from the operator increases the range of maximum permissible error MPE of a measuring device, especially in hand-held devices for measurement, where the influence is dominant [10, 15].

Fig. 6. Ishikawa diagram developed for the process of assessment of measurement error [15]

Effect of operator can be reduced if we assume the measurement strategy that includes access to the measuring object on the same side, without changing significantly the characteristics of the distribution of encoders.

Acknowledgements

Reported research were realized within confines of project financed by Polish National Centre for Research and Development No: LIDER/06/117/L-3/11/NCBR/2012.

REFERENCES

1. Ermer D.S., Prond P.E. A Geometrical Analysis of Measurement System Variations. Annual Quality Congress Transactions, Boston 1993, p. 929-935.

2. Gawlik J., Rewilak J. Dobór i ocena zdolności wyposażenia pomiarowego w przemyśle maszy-

nowym. [In:] VI Sympozjum Klubu Polskie Forum ISO 9000 „Metrologia w systemach jakości", Kielce 2000.

3. Chrysler, Ford, General Motors: Measurements Systems Analysis, Southfield, MI, Automotive Industry Action Group, March 1998.

4. Ermer D.S. Improved Gage R&R Measurement Studies, Quality Progress 2006, p. 77-79.

5. Juras B., Szewczyk D. Dokładność pomiarów realizowanych skanerem optycznym. Postępy Nauki i Techniki, 2011, 7: 29-36.

6. Ostrowska K., Szewczyk D., Sładek J. Wzorcowanie systemów optycznych zgodnie z normami ISO i zaleceniami VDI/VDE. Czasopismo Techniczne, 2012, 26: 167-179.

7. Ratajczyk E., Zawacki M. Accuracy tests of measuring arms– is it possible to compare ASME and ISO standard requirements? Coordinate Measuring Technique. Problems and Implementations, Bielsko-Biała 2008, p. 137-146.

8. Sładek J. Ocena i modelowanie dokładności maszyn oraz pomiarów współrzędnościowych, Zeszyty naukowe seria Mechanika nr 87, Politechnika Krakowska, 2001.

9. Sładek J., Gąska A., Olszewska M., Ostrowska K., Ryniewicz A. Metoda oceny dokładności pomiarów realizowanych za pomocą ramion pomiarowych wyposażonych w optyczne głowice skanujące. Mechanik, 2012, 2.

10. Sładek J., Ostrowska K., Gacek K., Bryndza M. Designation of operator impact on errors of measurements realized by coordinate measuring arm. Advances in Coordinate Metrology, 2010, p. 130-137.

11. Sładek J., Ostrowska K., Gąska A. Modeling and identification of errors of coordinate measuring arms with the use of a metrological model. Measurement, 2013, 46: 667-679 www.elsevier.com/locate/measurement.

12. Sładek J., Sokal G., Kmita A., Ostrowska K. Wzorcowanie Współrzędnościowych Ramion Pomiarowych (WRP). Acta Mechanica et Automatica, 2007, 1(2).

13. Voelkel J.G. Gauge R&R analysis for two-dimensional data with circular tolerances. Journal of Quality Technology, 2003, 35: 153-167.

14. Duncan A.J. Quality Control and Industrial Statistics (fifth edition) Richard D. Irwin Inc., 1986.

15. Sładek J. Dokładność pomiarów współrzędnościowych. Wydawnictwo Politechniki Krakowskiej, Kraków 2011.

16. Ostrowska K. Metoda oceny dokładności pomiarów realizowanych za pomocą Współrzędnościowych Ramion Pomiarów, Praca Doktorska. Politechnika Krakowska 2009.

17. Rewilak J. Metoda doboru środków pomiarowych w Statystycznym Sterowaniu Procesem, Praca Doktorska. Politechnika Krakowska 2009.

18. PN-EN ISO 10360 14253-1 Kontrola wyrobów i sprzętu pomiarowego za pomocą pomiarów. Reguły orzekania zgodności lub niezgodności ze specyfikacją.

19. VDI VDE 2617 blat 9 - Accuracy of coordinate measuring machines Characteristics and their reverification Acceptance and reverification tests for articulated arm coordinate measuring machines – VDI VDE Dieseldorf 2009.

28

VIRTUALIZATION TECHNICAL THINKING WITHIN THE INFORMATION TECHNOLOGY

Robert Lis[1]

[1] Department of Teaching Methods and Strategies, Lublin University of Technology, Nadbystrzycka 38, 20-618 Lublin, Poland, e-mail: r.lis@pollub.pl

ABSTRACT

The article presents the possibilities of virtualization technical thinking within the information technology. This question expresses the need for virtualization of existing information systems to improve the conduct of business by the company. In resulting virtualization of the technical-computer thought on against existing needs of the functioning of 16-bit systems in 64-bit systems. Enables cost-effective use of excess capacity existing computing resources.

Keywords: virtualization, thinking technical-information.

INTRODUKCTION

The technical thinking consists in competent applying in intellectual activities both practical notions and judgements describing and clarifying the technique. To concern it can of different fields of technology. Nowadays almost an information technology is playing an important role in every field of technology and the human activity. She is developing at full speed. Is one of manifestations of this development virtualization of servers.

She evolved within a few last years from the technology being born to the seen function IT. Companies more and more often start using from her power to meet the changing business needs. Through virtualization of one's burdens, organizations can control and reduce costs, improving the scalability, the flexibility and the reach of computer systems simultaneously. Arising progress more and more is making aware, that virtualization alone in himself doesn't let companies build and perform business tasks. Denouement Hyper-V was first introduced as part of the system Windows Server 2008, and then extended and strengthened in the system Windows 2012. Hyper-V provides equipment investments of the server for business organizations of the tool for

the operational research through the consolidation of many functions of the server in the form of separate virtual machines started on the single machine of the physical host. It is possible also to use Hyper-V in order effectively to act on many operating systems, in it operating systems different from Windows, so like for example altogether DOS on one physical server, and also to exploit the 64-bit power of processors.

The purpose of this article is to signal the need to find an optimal solution to streamline the running of the business in its current form. The use of proven, high-performance 16-bit ERP applications running under the DOS operating system becomes more difficult due to technological advances and the lack of compatibility „down', current solutions. ERP software, particularly in a version for DOS systems have very specific requirements. It is eg. on the number of simultaneously open files.

DOS was able to open simultaneously to 255 files under the condition of proper configuring.

Parameter „files" required for the accomplishment it is possible to configure in the different way only on 32-bit systems. Rates offered at present of the proportion of the screen are an additional obstacle. In this case a resolution should be a standard in the 4:3 format. This

640x480 of pixels is most often, more rarely 800x600 of pixels. Such a resolution should be kept for right proportions of letters and the arrangement of windows. Direct reference to data saved onto the disk being a consequence of the application among others „only" 640 KB of the main memory in current systems very much was modernised by initial versions DOS. Applying SSD disks which can work with the speed will be a good example of memory towards creating the buffer called the RAM,, RAMdrive" in the destination of precipitating performing the operation you on very free at that time disks plate.

Every system of the ERP class performs operations, of which many times a document printout is a result. For a few years we have an already legally normalised possibility of the transmission of the documents for contracting parties without the signature and in an electronic form. However for the purposes of keeping records for the accountant and the possible tax audit documents having a force of law are most often printed on paper. Also tax documentation and less and less often tax declarations find their reflection in physics printouts. ERP systems designed for different sized companies usually implement sending codes to print directly to the printer via the parallel port. Unfortunately, the port has been almost entirely supplanted by USB, and multiple machines is no longer present. In addition, the matter is complicated by the fact that the use of heavy duty dot matrix printers have only LPT port. Operatings cost of these devices are limited to an exchange printing tapes every a few months or even years in case of occasional prints. Perhaps they aren't too fast, perhaps are too loud but the fact that they are able simultaneously to print a few copies of the same printout is also their advantage. For this reason users don't want to give these devices up.

Should also mention fiscal printouts which are a requirement of the completion of retail trades. Devices being used for it are communicating through a serial port. Even if a bought new

fiscal printer having a universal USB port will stay it still signals on this port will be emulating serial communication. Can see it in the system after installed drivers which are always visible as „high" COMM ports. it is necessary then to pay attention to the need for the change of the port number on one from acceptable through the ERP systems.

USE OF 16-BIT APPLICATIONS ERP

Some attempt to address the need for the use of ERP applications for DOS made Microsoft releasing system windows 7 in version 64-bit with additional software. Wanted to be able to work for applications that previously worked in the systems 16-bit to 32-bit. In order to keep the compatibility he suggested a solution named VirtualPC. was it is an ovule and simultaneously confession of the producer to the fact that he exists work opportunities need the behaviour with older applications. Virtual-PC was a simple concept of creating operating systems of guest ''in the system,, of host. The solution lived to see to become topical to version 2007, in which flat Aka a possibility was blocked virtualization of system windows 98. With next answer, revolutionary on account of the use free of charge, is HyperV. On purpose omitted dissolutions of other companies will stay for economic reasons.

Saying about virtualization as the indispensable tool enabling the service of ERP systems under DOS one should clarify this notion. On account of a lot of accessible definitions, I will use classifying solutions in terms of the running speed. With base wirtualizacji there were emula-

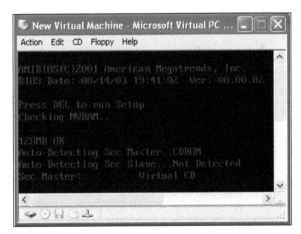

Fig. 2. Boot of the guest in the application Virtual PC

Fig. 1. Virtual machine in application Virtual PC

tors of operating systems which thanks enable applying interpreting the Instruction work of applications written to other system than installed in the computer. I will use the name here moderators because main games written under Atari, Commodore and many other computers but the PC started on the platform were their beneficiary. Their manner of the work caused the top-level emulation of the system of the guest what resulted up to 500 times in slower action than the system of the host. Next in virtualization Hypervisor is starting the special sequence of the VMXON instruction in the processor. In the native version virtualization in particular hypervisor – administrator virtualization, more efficient than the traditional emulation, the system of the guest is starting the host directly on the equipment this way, so that they as the most instruction make directly both he controls the equipment and is managing guest operating systems. Is maximizing in this way using the real equipment and providing software - machine virtualization only dangerous instructions. This model is a classic implementation of virtual machine architecture ; Primary hypervisors were used for testing. Modern equivalent enServer Citrix , VMware ESX / ESXi and Microsoft Hyper-V hypervisor.

The virtualization, in which hypervisors are in the traditional environment of the operating system and being on the next layer on the lower level of preference start the guest OS and hypervisor software running on the hardware allocates resources for running virtual systems. KVM, VirtualBox and Virtual PC are examples of virtualization hypervisor. As a result, Hyper -V works almost as good as the original system. However, it emulates a USB or audio inputs. If they are then you need to connect to the virtual machine via Remote Desktop.

USING THE EXCESS OF THE POWER IN CURRENT COMPUTERS

64-Bit architecture is being met today almost in every individual. 64-Bit processors and operating systems suiting them are a standard. Processors are characterized not one and a few not to say with a dozen or so physics cores. They often have a technology which is doubling the number of cores to several dozen logical cores.

Very much a lot of the main memory is in contemporary computers on account of for her relatively minimum price for the GB. a development of the so-called technology is supporting it double of the memory i.e. the memory put in pairs on the motherboard. Limiting to 4 GB 32-bit systems were able to address which was also changed on 64 TB in versions 64-bit.

The technological progress didn't pass bulk storages. The parallel record on magnetic plates increased "the packing density" causing information constant increasing the capacity and the price cutting. The development of the concept of very fast electronic disks of SSD caused, that very much a price for the megabyte magnetic disks offer which had diminished.

However the technological progress in this case a bit went too far ordering the operator using pointing devices as the feather, the mouse or the touch screen. Even harnessing bars code reader which by design entering the assortment into the system was supposed to hasten, in many cases will fail an examination for instance from the account of the lack of the bar code on goods.

A few ways to use the excess of accessible sources exist in contemporary computer machines. It is possible to distinguish:
- so-called virtualization „PC in PC" constituting emulation of equipment stores of the host with using the software started in specific

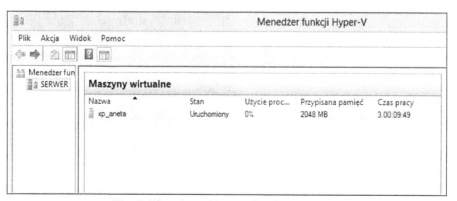

Fig. 3. Virtual machine application Hyper-V

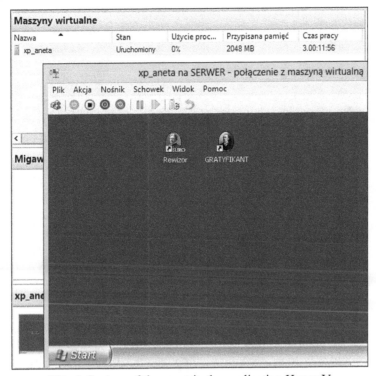

Fig. 4. System of the guest in the application Hyper-V

operating systems – very useful solution in testing purposes of the new software and the verification of saving viruses in terms of the presence;

- virtualization of application, that is making the application server available by hipervisor to the specific workstation and at using the desktop installed on operating systems of the software using it on the PC, what allows for the fast collective update or her blockade;

- client virtualization, which is the separation of the physical location of the server located on the hardware resources that reside on them, and client virtual machine images, from the place where the user is located and the use of so-called. thin clients – in the cur-

rent version outdated computers with weak resources connecting to the virtual desktop infrastructure by local – LAN or wide – WAN network with TCP / IP protocol with high throughput.

The most economically viable form of virtualization for the purpose of ERP applications running under DOS client virtualization, which from the server to the data repositories containing client virtual machines available on request to users for efficient use of existing resources, and often outdated information. therefore economically justified because the producer is providing with the version core of hypervisor Hyper-V system completely free of charge. It is fully functional platform of virtual machines.

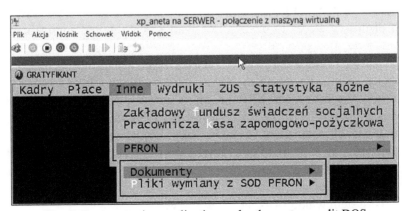

Fig. 5. Demonstration application under the system audit DOS

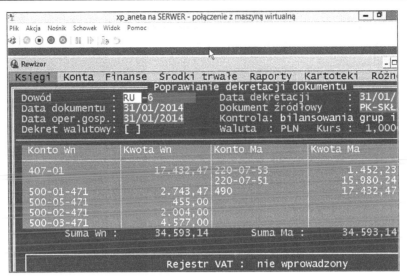

Fig. 6. Accounting application working under the DOS system audit without the graphic interface GUI

As a Windows PowerShell shell is enclosing with course books developed tools also free of charge enabling in the graphic way to create virtual machines and managing existing resources stayed. This system has both a Firewall and Defendera which are responsible for a safety.

However of scripts of such an application can be a few. Their choice is affecting the ergonomics from the side of the user or the administrator, the speed and the stability of action. As a result of run examinations I will focus on most optimum in terms of the productivity and the stability termination streamlining running a business in the current form.

The discussed solution is based on hipervisor in the version core. On account of as a rule very much big burdening the server with virtual machines isn't shown applying the graphical environment. Fully a management and a resource allocation of the host enable the operator Hypervisor. Existing tools are monitoring using resources by every customer. From here exceptionally effectively it is possible to exploit the entire power of the server and if some of systems of guests is turned off, to redirect dismissed stores to other virtual machine. The most he is an optimal system of the guest available for a dozen or so years Windows XP in the version 32-bit. His versatility consists in the service very much of many ERP applications working under control DOS and the possibility of configurations of parameters required by ERP. available tools of integration effectively are emulating action of the keyboard. Merging with such a virtual machine with the help available already from the system windows to get

98 client applications supporting the protocol of the RDP communication it is possible redirecting the customer of interrupts being responsible for parallel ports to the system and terrace. The printout which is being carried out on the machine of the host is staying in their result redirected to the printer connected in terms of physics to the port of the customer. To be redirected perhaps „move" both on parallel ports, privates as well as USB. using the redirection „of move" on a serial port to get it is possible fiscal printout at the ward with the help of the server being in a head office. Also bar code reader connected by a serial port, USB or keyboard to the computer of the guest will actually be active in the branch distant from the head office of the company.

On account of very long supporting by the producer the system windows XP his licence on the current computer it is possible virtualize and as operating systems of the so-called thin customer to use distribution free of charge of the system Linux. It will only be used to start the application communicating with hypervisor with the help of the RDP protocol. Many available tools exist free of charge as additional applications downloaded from appropriate repositories. A functionality of display layer which must provide the simultaneous access for users for everyone to many desktops of virtual machines is an important difference of such a solution simultaneously, in the opposite to layer visualization used at virtualization of very servers, where only an administrator is gaining access to the desktop of the system, whereas the user is using only services made available on the server.

CONCLUSIONS

Presented answers virtualization in the different form are ensuring benefits in the IT organization. many of mentioned above technologies connected mainly with the emulation are known and used in systems of the ERP class, some whereas, so like full virtualization of servers and desktops, are relatively new in terms of the realization in the business. virtualization to treat belongs not as the way to minimize the number of physical devices in the infrastructure of the business organization, but as the full support system delivering services backing the ERP software up under DOS in the effective way. Planning virtualization one should however choose stores of the IT infrastructure of the organization most appropriate in the current situation solution and to develop them in line with the earlier developed strategy virtualization. Such an approach will help to maximize swimming benefits from this technology.

REFERENCES

1. Popek G.J., Goldberg R.P.: Formal requirements for virtualizable third generation architectures. Communications of the ACM, Vol. 17 (7), 1974.

2. Promotional Materials Microsoft Corporation, VMware Inc., NetApp Corporatio.

29

VIRTUAL MACHINES IN EDUCATION – CNC MILLING MACHINE WITH SINUMERIK 840D CONTROL SYSTEM

Ireneusz Zagórski[1], Marcin Barszcz[2]

[1] Department of Production Engineering, Mechanical Engineering Faculty, Lublin University of Technology, 36 Nadbystrzycka Str., 20-618 Lublin, Poland, e-mail: i.zagorski@pollub.pl

[2] Department of Fundamentals of Technology, Technology Fundamentals Faculty, Lublin University of Technology, 38 Nadbystrzycka Str., 20-618 Lublin, Poland, e-mail: m.barszcz@pollub.pl

ABSTRACT

Machining process nowadays could not be conducted without its inseparable element: cutting edge and frequently numerically controlled milling machines. Milling and lathe machining centres comprise standard equipment in many companies of the machinery industry, *e.g.* automotive or aircraft. It is for that reason that tertiary education should account for this rising demand. This entails the introduction into the curricula the forms which enable visualisation of machining, milling process and virtual production as well as virtual machining centres simulation. Siemens Virtual Machine (Virtual Workshop) sets an example of such software, whose high functionality offers a range of learning experience, such as: learning the design of machine tools, their configuration, basic operation functions as well as basics of CNC.

Keywords: visualisation, virtual machine, milling machine, CNC.

INTRODUCTION, CURRENT STATE OF KNOWLEDGE

Constant development of computer and information technology is reflected in ever-growing interest of users in computer graphics. The self notion of computer graphics, however, is considerably broad and general and its division can be based on: the input format, the number of dimensions or the function it fulfils. According to the input format, we can distinguish the following types of graphics: vector, bitmap and fractal [1].

From the viewpoint of application of computer visualisation, of *e.g.* virtual machines or structural elements, vector graphics appears to be the most interesting. 2D vector graphics [1] can find application in recording technical configuration, whereas 3D vector graphics enables, for instance, modelling technical objects and model creation (of, for example machines, film or computer game characters), which through appropriate rendering and animation can create virtual reality.

The machine industry requires the work on such materials as aluminium, magnesium, titanium or nickel alloys. Frequently semi-finished products for such elements (automotive or aircraft) are made in the form of casts (Figure 1b) or plate of raw material (Figure 1a). Figure 1 presents such parts.

Manufacturing parts through machining demands application of modern machining tools. This requires effective milling techniques which would ensure optimum machine tool operation time, together with adequate quality, surface roughness to machining time correlation [10]. In milling the amount of material removed from a machined surface often amounts to 90%, for that reason certain machining methods appear of preference, for example: HSM (High Speed Machining), HPM (High Performance Machining), HPC (High Performance Cutting) or HSC (High Speed Cutting) [4, 5, 7, 9].

A modern engineer would not be able to fulfil his duties without computer aided designing

a)
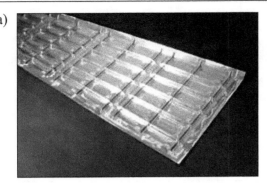

b)
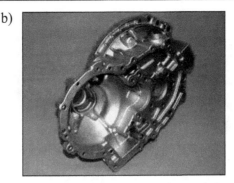

Fig. 1. Aircraft parts: a) aluminium alloy structural element, b) magnesium alloy transmission and clutch casing [12, 13]

software CAD/CAM/CAE. A particularly notable place among tools of this sort is occupied by Solid Edge or NX by Siemens PLM Software, which are particularly useful and widely employed in both industrial and educational applications. Computer aided designing and manufacturing are examples of functionalities offered by advanced functions of CAD and NX system CAM modules which are of high educational value. Building virtual machine parks allows designing technological processes that would serve as an experiment and would not require using an actual machine. This opens the possibility to build virtual laboratories for educational purposes. Kinematic simulation of 3D milling machine models provides a highly realistic reflection of a process realised physically on the machine [2, 3]. Figure 2 illustrates examples of modules and cabin, both designed in Modelling and NX Sheet Metal module of NX system.

Moreover, CAE computer software, using, *inter alia*, the finite element method (FEM), is capable of simulation (e.g. of external loads) and visualisation of conducted analyses, most frequently in a form of colour bitmaps, illustrating mesh nodes displacement or reduced stresses [6, 8]. Figure 3 presents model numerical simulations.

The presented examples derived from literature will provide the base for a more extensive analysis of potential of virtual machines and virtual machine parks at an introductory stage to courses discussing basics of numerically controlled machines.

VIRTUAL WORKSHOP – MILLING CENTRE WITH SINUMERIK 840D CONTROL SYSTEM

Modern aircraft elements are characterised by homogeneous structure, frequently made of monoblocks, manufactured on cutting edge numerically controlled machining centres [4]; hence the idea of introducing into the curriculum software enabling visualisation of a machining process in the form of virtual production and CNC machines. Figure 4 shows the main menu of Virtual Workshop. The software is available in two language versions – German and English. This is moreover the stage to select from two machining methods: turning or milling.

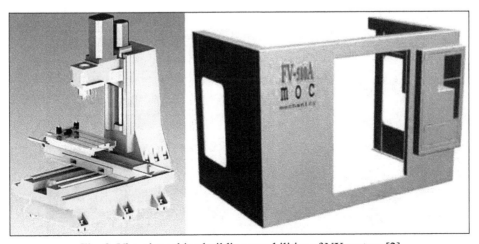

Fig. 2. Virtual machine building capabilities of NX system [2]

a)   b)

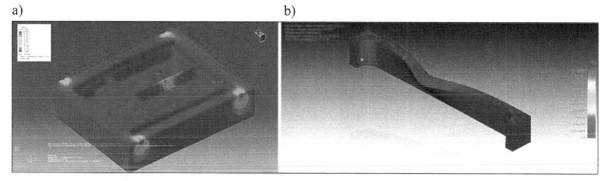

Fig. 3. FEM simulation on different software: a) Abaqus 6.9 EF1, b) Solid Edge ST4 (NX Nastran) [6, 8]

Fig. 4. Main menu [11]

The presented multimedia training software, Virtual Workshop, is available in the form of individual licenses for PC, and it is a tool for self-study in CBT (Computer Based Training), enabling independent training on the basics of numerically controlled machines design as well as CNC technology [11]. Figure 5 presents a milling machine equipped with SINUMERIK 840D control system and an operator panel, which is loaded with the start of the machine.

The selection of milling machine opens three stages of training to choose from, namely:
• Machine familiarisation (Familiarisation with milling machine),
• Machine set-up (Sinumerik 840D - Milling),
• CNC basics (Milling fundamentals).

Each task group contains expandable tabs, offering information on the progress in each particular task.

MACHINE FAMILIARISATION – FAMILIA-RISATION WITH MILLING MACHINE

The first stage of training available in Machine familiarisation concerns the design of numerically controlled machines. This tab expands into 10 sub-groups regarding, as follows:
• Complete machine,
• Control Panel (links the user to a help mode, where all buttons in the Control Panel are described),
• Machine Bed (Ball screw drive Y axis, Guide Y axis, Servo motor Y axis),
• Machine column (Ball screw drive Z axis, Guide Z axis, Measuring system Z axis),

Fig. 5. CNC machining centre and operator panel [11]

- Cross slide (Ball screw drive X axis, Guide X axis, Measuring system X axis),
- Spindle head (Main drive motor, Clamping cylinder, Centre sleeve),
- Clamping table (Vice, Clamping claws, Workpiece, Workpiece zero point, Machine zero point),
- Tool magazine (T1 Face-milling cutter d = 63 mm, T2 Slot milling tool d = 20 mm, T3 Slot milling tool d = 10 mm, T4 Spiral drilling tool d =8.5 mm, T5 Thread drilling tool M10, T6 Remote measuring probe),
- Switch cabinet (Supply module, Control with drive module, PLC),
- Components (Cabin, Main switch, RH maintenance flap, LH maintenance flap, Coolant lubricant basin, Sliding lubricant basin, RH chip basin, LH chip basin, Status light).

At any given stage of work we can see 3D visualisation of individual elements of the machine. A panoramic view is available from a desired perspective by turning around the machine and zooming, all performed with keyboard. Figures 6 and 7 present examples of views at the first stage of Machine familiarisation.

The next two stages of training revolve around the notion of virtual machine operation and operator panel procedures in Machine set-up menu, while CNC essentials can be found in CNC basics. Individual menus contain task sub-groups with expandable working tasks, as in the case with Machine familiarisation.

MACHINE SET-UP (SINUMERIK 840D – – MILLING)

As it has been mentioned, the second stage of training in Machine set-up consists of two main task sub-groups, which are as follows:
- Setting up the machine (Switching on, Manual movement, Tool compensations, Workpiece zero point),
- Programming (Write a program, Edit a program, Operate a program).

The training at this stage consists in the following subsequent tasks appearing in the Information box, 'i', *e.g.*: 'Turn on the machine using the main switch and wait until the control system has started,' as shown in Figure 8.

a)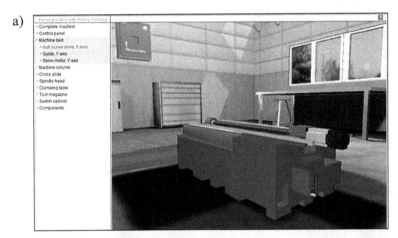

b)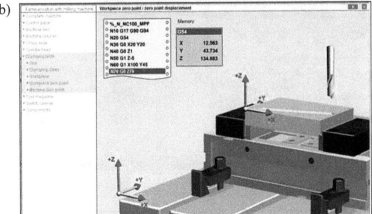

Fig. 6. Machine familiarization: a) Machine Bed and b) Clamping table (Workpiece zero point) [11]

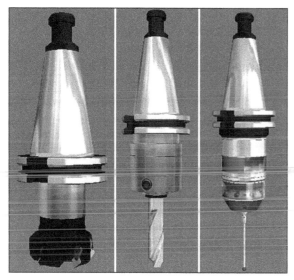

Fig. 7. Machine familiarization – Tool magazine: T1, T2, T6 [11]

We are given updates on completion of subsequent tasks within given task sub-groups, which are marked by ticking completed tasks.

CNC BASICS (MILLING FUNDAMENTALS)

The third, and final, stage of training, CNC basics, consists of four main task sub-groups, which, together with work tasks, describe the following:
- Training objective,
- Geometry (Coordinate systems, Points on workpiece, Absolute dimensions, Incremental dimensions, Polar dimensions, Contour setting),
- Technology (Speed, Cutting speed, Feed rate, Feed/tooth),
- Programming (Program configuration, Program header, Addresses, Travel commands, Tool path compensation, Tool offsets, Cycles/subroutines),
- Test it.

CONCLUSIONS

Dynamic development of computer graphics allows the creation of virtual models of machine parts, virtual technological machines, and consequently machine parks and virtual reality. Visualisation of machine parts geometry and virtual production (milling simulation) and virtual machines promotes our cognitive abilities. Therefore, it appears that this is the first step towards future stages of education and development of professional skills. The presented capabilities of Siemens software enable preliminary basic introduction of course participants into operation, programming and rudimentary knowledge regarding CNC machines.

Our future work will supplement the presented subject with available control functions in milling as well as the description of technological capabilities of the milling machine with the control system in question.

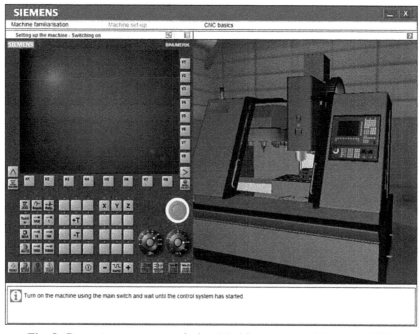

Fig. 8. Computer programme during Machine set-up training stage [11]

REFERENCES

1. Dziedzic K., Lis R., Montusiewicz J.: Bitmap graphics in teaching multimedia techniques. Postępy Nauki i Techniki, 2, 2008, 140–152.

2. Józwik J., Włodarczyk M., Ścierka T.: Geometric and kinematics model of vertical CNC machine centre FV-580A. Postępy Nauki i Techniki, 5, 2010, 85–96.

3. Józwik J., Włodarczyk M., Ścierka T.: Virtual controller VNC of vertical CNC machine center FV-580A. Postępy Nauki i Techniki, 5, 2010, 97–113.

4. Kuczmaszewski J.: Manufacturing effectiveness of aviation elements with aluminum and magnesium alloys. Komputerowo Zintegrowane Zarządzanie, Oficyna Wyd. Polskiego Towarzystwa Zarządzania Produkcją, Opole 2011, 7–18.

5. Oczoś K.E., Kawalec A.: Light metals forming. PWN, Warsaw 2012.

6. Pieśko P.: FEM analysis and experimental verification open and semi-open thin walls deformation. Report of the project No. POIG.01.01.02-00-015/08-00

7. Pieśko P., Zagórski I.: Comparative analysis of HSM, HPC and conventional milling methods of high-silicon aluminium. Postępy Nauki i Techniki, 7, 2011, 219–226.

8. Włodarczyk M.: Analysis of the influence of fixing and cutting forces on stress level in terms of the thickness of pocketing construction. Postępy Nauki i Techniki, 8, 2011, 82–92

9. Zagórski I., Kuczmaszewski J.: The study of cutting forces and their amplitudes during high-speed dry milling magnesium alloys. Advances in Science and Technology Research Journal, 7(20), 2013, 61–66.

10. Zagórski I., Pieśko P.: Comparative study of surface roughness of selected magnesium alloys after milling with carbide tool and PKD. Postępy Nauki i Techniki, 8, 2011, 53–58.

11. http://www.automatyka.siemens.pl, 2.06.2014.

12. http://agmetalminer.com/2010/03/29/new-airframe-construction-techniques-lowers-both-manufacturing-and-in-service-costs/, 4.07.2014.

13. Strazzi E., Ferrari Ch.: Low energy consumption and environmental friend process formagnesium anodizing, http://www.italfinish.com/public/images/lowenergy1.pdf, 9.04.2010.

30

THEORETICAL ANALYSIS OF THE FORGING PROCESS FOR PRODUCING HOLLOW BALLS

Grzegorz Winiarski[1]

[1] Department of Computer Modelling and Metal Forming Technologies, Mechanical Engineering Faculty, Lublin University of Technology, Nadbystrzycka 36, 20-618 Lublin, Poland, e-mail: g.winiarski@pollub.pl

ABSTRACT

Hollow balls are used in the production of various machines and devices. The technology for producing hollow balls by metal forming technologies poses numerous difficulties connected with the forming of a hollow billet. The billet, which is usually in the form of a rod, is subject to such processes as forging, helical rolling or cross-wedge rolling. The paper discusses a new method and conditions for producing a hollow ball. It was assumed that the ball would be produced in two forging operations: an initial forging operation and finish forging operation. The presented results are based on the FEM numerical analysis conducted using DEFORM-3D. It was assumed that the billet material was made from AISI 304 stainless steel used to produce balls for ball valves. Both the shape progression during the forging process and variations in the forming force were analyzed. Based on the conducted analyses, it can be claimed that hollow balls can be produced using the proposed forging method.

Keywords: die forging, hollow ball forging, FEM

INTRODUCTION

Hollow balls are mainly used in the agricultural industry (Fig. 1a) [2] and in the production of various ball valves (Fig. 1b) [1]. In the case of ball valves, one ball is usually used per one valve, while the number of balls used in the production of agricultural machinery, e.g. a three-point suspension system, ranges from 2 to 10 balls. Owing to the number of ball valves or said suspension systems that are manufactured, the demand for hollow balls is very high.

The so-far used metal forming methods for producing balls are mainly applied to the production of full balls. Hollow balls are obtained from full balls, and the holes are made by machining. Such a way of producing holes involves considerable material losses, which can be described by the formula:

$$S = \frac{\left(D - \sqrt{D^2 - d^2}\right)^2 \cdot \left(2D + \sqrt{D^2 - d^2}\right) + 3d^2\sqrt{D^2 - d^2}}{2D^3} \cdot 100\%,\qquad (1)$$

where the denotations used correspond to those in Figure 2.

For example, in order to produce a ball with a diameter of 80 mm and a hole of 50 mm, the percentage of the material loss amounts to 52.4%.

Nowadays there are numerous methods for producing full balls. The main metal forming methods for producing such products include die forging using forging machines, die forging using forging presses, helical rolling and cross-wedge rolling. Die casting and metal machining are also frequently used in the production of such balls.

When balls are produced by means of presses, the billet material is usually in a form of steel rods, whose diameters are smaller than the diameters of parts being formed. Hollow balls can be produced using forging machines, yet the production process of both full and hollow balls is then hindered. Balls

a)
b)

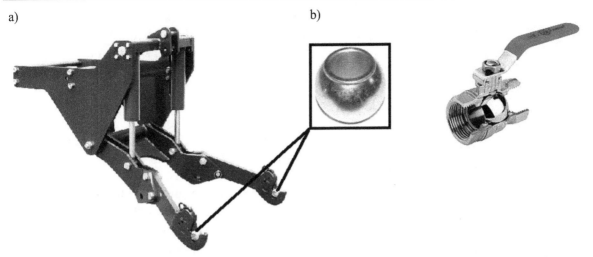

Fig. 1. Examples of applications of hollow balls: a) three-point suspension system in agricultural machinery,] b) ball valve [1, 2]

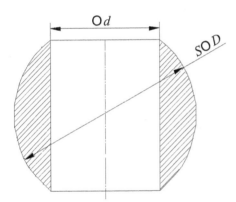

Fig. 2. Hollow ball cross section

with higher diameters are die forged, usually on a screw press equipped with a friction drive, using rods as the billet material.

Another method for producing balls is helical rolling, in which balls are first formed from a full rod by two skewly positioned rolls (equipped with helical impressions) and then separated from one another. Only one ball is formed at one rotation of the rolls [11]. The method is characterized by a very high efficiency, which depends on the speed of rolls.

Cross wedge rolling (CWR) is also used to produce balls, yet only the full ones. The process consists of axial forming symmetric parts with wedge-shaped tools. The tools are mounted either on the rolls or on flat or concave plates of the rolling mill [2].

Also, there are numerous innovative manners for producing balls by helical rolling, developed by the research team of the Department of Computer Modeling and Metal Forming Technologies at Lublin University of Technology. They include:

- rolling in helically-spiral impressions [5];
- rolling with two flat disks in spiral impressions [3, 4, 7];
- rolling with two conical disks in spiral impressions [8];
- rolling in a helical internal impression [9];
- helical rolling with three helical rolls [6].

However, it should be mentioned that the above rolling techniques are intended for the production of full balls with a relatively small diameter. On the whole, it can be stated that the above mentioned ball production methods do not allow effective formation of hollow balls. It is then justified to investigate new methods for producing hollow balls that would ensure lower material consumption and higher efficiency. For this reason, a new method for producing hollow balls is proposed and discussed in the present paper.

METHODOLOGY OF THE FORGING PROCESS FOR PRODUCING BALLS

The analysis of the forging process for producing hollow balls was conducted for a ball with a diameter of 80 mm and a hole of 50 mm. In the analysis, finish machining allowances were taken into account. The dimensions of the analyzed balls correspond to the dimensions of balls used in the production of selected ball valves. Both the shape and dimensions of the analyzed ball are shown in Figure 3. The figure also illustrates axial sections of ball 1 (with the predicted machining allowances) and finished product 2.

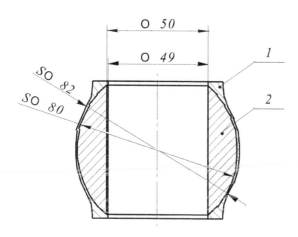

Fig. 3. Shape and dimensions of ball *1* and ball *2*

The forging process for producing hollow balls was realized according to the manner that is schematically illustrated in Figure 4 [13].

The proposed forging process consists of placing billet 2 in a form of a rod section in die 4, in which a preliminary impression has been made. In the first operation (Figure 4a) forging preform 5 is made from rod 2, and in the second operation (Figure 4b) the forging preform is used to produce a hollow ball. The ball forming is hence realized during two motions of punch 1. The punch travels with a constant linear speed along its own axis, causing the upsetting of the billet. The dies consist of two twin elements, and the parting plane between the dies goes through both the billet and punch axis. Owing to such

tool design, the dies can be parted to take the formed ball out of the tools once the process is completed. The dimensions of the billet (Figure 4a) were determined based on the constant volume conditions.

The numerical analysis of the forging process for producing balls was made using the FEM-based DEFORM-3D. In the simulations, it was assumed that both the punch and dies would be rigid objects, while the billet would be a discrete object divided into four-node tetragonal elements, described by a rigid-plastic material model. The material model (of the hollow ball to be formed) adopted in the simulations was AISI 304 stainless steel and the material data were taken from the library database of the applied software. This material type is used in the production of balls for ball valves. It was also assumed that the initial temperature of the tools would be 20 °C, while the billet temperature would be 900 °C. The simulations were performed at a constant punch speed of 10 mm/s. The punch translational motion continued until the complete filling of the impression. In the forging process schematically presented in the figure, the distance traveled by the punch was 22.3 mm and 25.1 mm for the initial forging and finish forging, respectively. The tool-billet contact conditions were described by the constant friction model, with the friction factor m set to 0.3 and the tool-billet heat transfer coefficient equal 10 W/m²K.

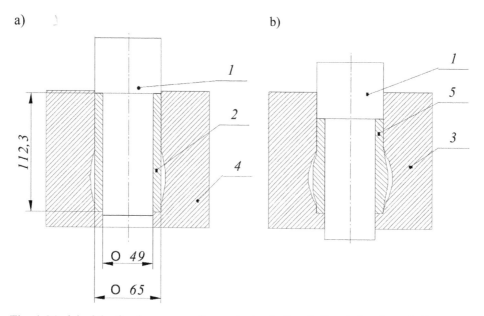

Fig. 4. Model of the forging process for producing hollow balls: a) forming a ball preform, b) finish forming a ball (described in the paper)

RESULTS

The process of forming balls from the billet in the form of a rod is schematically illustrated in Figures 5 and 6. The figures show the shape progression and damage function calculated for the ball preform and finished ball according to the Cockroft-Latham criterion, described by the equation [12]:

$$\int_{0}^{\varphi^*} \frac{\sigma_1}{\sigma_m} d\varphi = C , \qquad (2)$$

where: φ^* – denotes the limit fracture strain,
σ_1 – denotes the maximum principal stress,
σ_m – denotes the mean stresses,
C – denotes the material constant calculated in the simulations.

The forging process is realized in two operations, the first one consisting of forming a ball preform. The preform forming is necessary as the preliminary numerical simulations have proven that it is impossible to produce hollow balls in one forging operation, as can be seen in Figure 7. In the figure, the lappings that prevent the production of a correctly shaped part occur in the areas marked with letter A. They occur on both the external and internal surface of the ball, over its whole circumference.

If the forging process is realized in two operations, these lappings can be prevented and the formed ball can then undergo finishing. Owing to the use of a mandrel during initial forging (Figure 5), the material axial flow towards the symmetry axis can be prevented. As a result of upsetting, the rod diameter is increasing until the external billet surface contacts the die impression surface.

Due to the application of the preliminary impression, the maximum distance between the external billet surface and die impression surface is short, which means that the process is stable, strains are small and lapping is prevented. The low value of strain also prevents the occurrence of fracture on the external surface of the rod, where the damage function reaches the local maximum, which – according to the

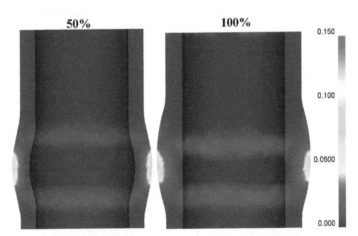

Fig. 5. Shape progression and damage function according to the Cockroft-Latham criterion in the axial section of a ball preform during initial forging

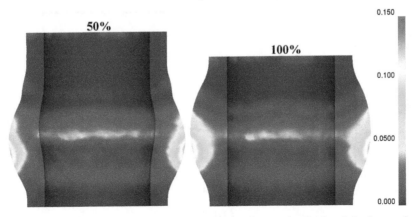

Fig. 6. Shape progression and damage function according to the Cockroft-Latham criterion in the axial section of a ball preform during finish forging

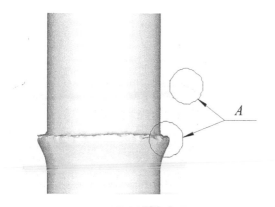

Fig. 7. Hollow ball forging in one operation
– the ball axial section profile when the
process realization is 80%

Cockroft-Latham criterion – does not exceed 0.15 (Figures 5 and 6).

The second forging operation to produce a hollow ball is similar to the process of forming the preform. Due to the punch action on the billet, the preform undergoes upsetting. At first, the material flows in a direction that is parallel to the punch axis; afterwards the external surface of the ball being formed contacts the impression surface. Once the material contacts the whole surface of the impression, it starts flowing towards the punch axis. Given the force parameters of the process, this phenomenon is desirable and advantageous.

Due to the billet-punch contact in the final stage of the forging process, the punch is reduced by the material in a short time. Therefore, the distance traveled by the punch working against the friction resistance is short; in effect, the fraction of the friction force occurring between the punch and material in the total force with which the punch acts on the billet is insignificant. Given the above, the friction forces have an insignificant effect on the maximum force value in the present process for producing balls.

Analyzing the variations of the forming force during initial forging (Figure 8), it can be observed that its increase is nearly linear until the force rapidly increases in the final stage of the process. This rapid increase is caused by the action of the above mentioned friction force on the

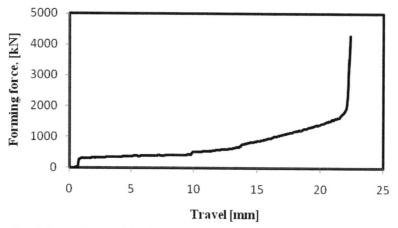

Fig. 8. Dependence of the forging force on punch travel in initial forging

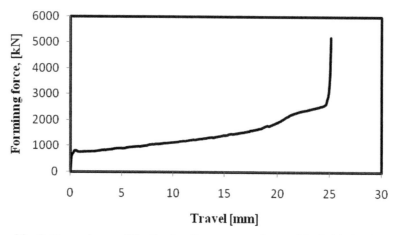

Fig. 9. Dependence of the forging force on punch travel in finish forging

punch and higher material resistances that occur in the final stage of filling the closed impression.

The forming force distribution during finish forging is shown in Figure 9. The maximum value of this force necessary to produce the preform is 4280 kN, while the force value required to form the ball is 5200 kN. Based on the chart shown in Figure 9, it can be observed that the force increases after the punch traveled a distance of approx. 20 mm. This is due to the contact between the billet material and the whole surface of the impression, which leads to an increase in the billet-punch contact area and the occurrence of the friction forces on the said surface.

CONCLUSIONS

The paper presented the numerical analysis results of the forging process for producing hollow balls. Based on the preliminary calculations, it was observed that forging balls in one operation would lead to lapping. For this reason, the process discussed in the paper was realized in two operations to ensure the production of good quality parts.

The results of the performed numerical simulations of the forging process prove that the proposed method is correct. They confirm that it is possible to produce a hollow ball in two forging operations. Such process requires that the tools with die impressions for both initial and finish forging be used. The tool kinematics and geometry are not complicated; therefore, experimental tests can be easily performed in a short time.

REFERENCES

1. http://upload.wikimedia.org/wikipedia/commons/thumb/5/52/Seccion_valvula_de_bola.jpg/220px-Seccion_valvula_de_bola.jpg

2. http://www.tenias.com/archivos/productos/enganche_delantero.jpg

3. Pater Z., Tomczak J. Narzędzie spiralne do walcowania poprzecznego kul. Polskie zgłoszenie patentowe nr P.399155, 2012.

4. Pater Z., Tomczak J. Narzędzie spiralne do walcowania poprzecznego wielokrotnego wyrobów typu kula. Polskie zgłoszenie patentowe nr P.399154, 2012.

5. Pater Z., Tomczak J. Sposób walcowania skośnego dwoma walcami spiralno-śrubowymi wyrobów typu kula. Polskie zgłoszenie patentowe nr P.398915, 2012.

6. Pater Z., Tomczak J. Sposób walcowania skośnego trzema walcami śrubowymi wyrobów typu kula. Polskie zgłoszenie patentowe nr P.400061, 2012.

7. Pater Z., Tomczak J. Sposób walcowania wyrobów typu kula, zwłaszcza w wykroju spiralnym dwoma dyskami. Polskie zgłoszenie patentowe nr P.399170, 2012.

8. Pater Z., Tomczak J. Sposób walcowania wyrobów typu kula, zwłaszcza w wykroju spiralnym dwoma dyskami stożkowymi. Polskie zgłoszenie patentowe nr P.399571, 2012.

9. Pater Z., Tomczak J. Sposób walcowania wyrobów typu kula, zwłaszcza w śrubowym wykroju wewnętrzno-zewnętrznym. Polskie zgłoszenie patentowe nr P.399529, 2012.

10. Pater Z., Tomczak J. Walcowanie poprzeczno-klinowe kul. Wydawnictwo Politechniki Lubelskiej, Lublin 2012.

11. Pater Z., Tomczak J. Walcowanie śrubowe kul do młynów kulowych. Wydawnictwo Politechniki Lubelskiej Lublin 2012.

12. Samołyk G., Bartnicki J., Gontarz A.: Fracture Model for FEM Modelling of Cold Metal Forging. Steel Research International, vol. 81, no 9, 2010, 302–305.

13. Winiarski G., Gontarz A., Pater Z., Tomczak J. Sposób i urządzenie do kucia kul. Polskie zgłoszenie patentowe nr P.403211, 2013.

Permissions

List of Contributors

Joanna Szulżyk-Cieplak
Faculty of Fundamentals of Technology, Lublin University of Technology, Nadbystrzycka 38, 20-618 Lublin, Poland

Aneta Duda
Faculty of Fundamentals of Technology, Lublin University of Technology, Nadbystrzycka 38, 20-618 Lublin, Poland

Bartłomiej Sidor
Renata Rososzczuk
Department of Applied Mathematics, Lublin University of Technology, Nadbystrzycka 38, 20-618 Lublin, Poland

Hamed Jelodar
Department of Computer, Science and Research, Islamic Azad University, Bushehr, Iran

Javad Aramideh
Department of Computer Engineering, Sari Branch, Islamic Azad University, Sari, Iran

Mehrnoosh Kheradmand
Student, Sari Branch, Islamic Azad University, Sari, Iran

Homayun Motameni
Sari Branch, Islamic Azad University, Sari, Iran

Artur Popko
Fundamentals of Technology Faculty, Lublin University of Technology, ul. Nadbystrzycka 38, 20-618 Lublin, Poland

Marek Jakubowski
Management Faculty, Lublin University of Technology, ul. Nadbystrzycka 38, 20-618 Lublin, Poland,

Rafał Wawer
University of Maria Curie Sklodowska, Multimedia Communications Lab. 20-011 Lublin ul. Narutowicza 12, Poland

Mariusz Śniadkowski
Fundamentals of Technology Faculty, Lublin University of Technology, 38 Nadbystrzycka Str., 20-618 Lublin, Poland

Agnieszka Jankowska
Student of Lublin University of Technology

Nadežda Čuboňová
Department of Automation and Production Systems, University of Zilina, SK-010 01 Zilina, Slovak Republic

Miroslav Císar
Department of Automation and Production Systems, University of Zilina, SK-010 01 Zilina, Slovak Republic

Konrad Gauda
Fundamentals of Technology Faculty, Lublin University of Technology, Nadbystrzycka 38, 20-618 Lublin, Poland

Monika Nowosad
Special Educational Centre, Kozice Dolne 33, 21-050 Piaski, Poland

Andrzej Jardzioch
Department of Mechanical Engineering and Mechatronics, West Pomeranian Technical University of Szczecin, al. Piastów 19, 72-300 Szczecin, Poland

Jędrzej Jaskowski
Department of Mechanical Engineering and Mechatronics, West Pomeranian Technical University of Szczecin, al. Piastów 19, 72-300 Szczecin, Poland

Dorota Wójcicka-Migasiuk
Faculty of Fundamentals of Technology, Lublin University of Technology, Nadbystrzycka 38, 20-618 Lublin, Poland

Arkadiusz Urzędowski
Faculty of Fundamentals of Technology, Lublin University of Technology, Nadbystrzycka 38, 20-618 Lublin, Poland

Javad Aramideh
Department of Computer Engineering, Sari Branch, Islamic Azad University, Sari, Iran

Hamed Jelodar
Department of Computer Engineering, Bushehr Branch, Islamic Azad University, Bushehr, Iran

Barbara Juras
Laboratory of Coordinate Metrology, Mechanical Department, Cracow University of Technology, 24 Warszawska Str., 31-155 Kraków, Poland

Danuta Szewczyk
Laboratory of Coordinate Metrology, Mechanical Department, Cracow University of Technology, 24 Warszawska Str., 31-155 Kraków, Poland

Jerzy Sładek
Laboratory of Coordinate Metrology, Mechanical Department, Cracow University of Technology, 24 Warszawska Str., 31-155 Kraków, Poland,

Marek A. Jakubowski
Management Faculty, Lublin University of Technology, Nadbystrzycka 38, 20-618 Lublin, Poland

Michał Charlak
Fundamentals of Technology Faculty, Lublin University of Technology, Nadbystrzycka 38, 20-618 Lublin, Poland

Michalina Gryniewicz-Jaworska
Faculty of Electrical Engineering and Computer Science, Lublin University of Technology, Nadbystrzycka 38A, 20-618 Lublin, Poland

Paweł Dzienis
Department of Mechanics and Applied Informatics, Faculty of Mechanical Engineering, Bialystok University of Technology, Wiejska 45c, 15-351 Bialystok, Poland

Romuald Mosdorf
Department of Mechanics and Applied Informatics, Faculty of Mechanical Engineering, Bialystok University of Technology, Wiejska 45c, 15-351 Bialystok, Poland

Mychaylo Paszeczko
Department of Fundamentals of Technology, Fundamentals of Technology Faculty, Lublin University of Technology, 38 Nadbystrzycka Str., 20-618 Lublin, Poland

Marcin Barszcz
Department of Fundamentals of Technology, Fundamentals of Technology Faculty, Lublin University of Technology, 38 Nadbystrzycka Str., 20-618 Lublin, Poland

Ireneusz Zagórski
Department of Production Engineering, Mechanical Engineering Faculty, Lublin University of Technology, 36 Nadbystrzycka Str., 20-618 Lublin, Poland

Marta Kowalik
The Department of Industrial Furnaces and Environmental Protection, The Faculty of Process & Material Engineering and Applied Physics, Technical University of Czestochowa, Al. Armii Krajowej 19, 42-200 Czestochowa, Poland

Jarosław Boryca
The Department of Industrial Furnaces and Environmental Protection, The Faculty of Process & Material Engineering and Applied Physics, Technical University of Czestochowa, Al. Armii Krajowej 19, 42-200 Czestochowa, Poland

Tomasz Cieplak
Department of Company Organisation, Lublin University of Technology, Nadbystrzycka 38, 20-618 Lublin, Poland

Mirosław Malec
Department of Fundamentals of Technology, Lublin University of Technology, Nadbystrzycka 38, 20-618 Lublin, Poland

Zbigniew Czyż
Department of Thermodynamics, Fluid Mechanics and Aviation Propulsion Systems, Faculty of Mechanical Engineering, Lublin University of Technology, 36 Nadbystrzycka Str., 20-618 Lublin, Poland

Konrad Pietrykowski
Department of Thermodynamics, Fluid Mechanics and Aviation Propulsion Systems, Faculty of Mechanical Engineering, Lublin University of Technology, 36 Nadbystrzycka Str., 20-618 Lublin, Poland

Mariusz Sosnowski
West Pomeranian University of Technology in Szczecin, Department of Automated Manufacturing Systems Engineering and Quality, Al. Piastów 19, 70-310 Szczecin, Poland

Jędrzej Jaskowski
West Pomeranian University of Technology in Szczecin, Department of Automated Manufacturing Systems Engineering and Quality, Al. Piastów 19, 70-310 Szczecin, Poland

Hadj Gharib
Mathematics laboratory, Djillali LIABES University, Sidi Bel Abbes, Algeria

Kamel Belloulata
RCAM laboratory, Djillali LIABES University, Sidi Bel Abbes, Algeria

Navid Khlilzadeh Sourati
Department of Computer Engineering, Sari Branch, Islamic Azad University, Sari, Iran

Farhad Ramezni
Department of Computer Engineering, Sari Branch, Islamic Azad University, Sari, Iran

Saleh Gorjizadeh
Student in the Department of Computer Engineering, Islamic Azad University, Sari, Iran

Sadegh Pasban
Department of Computer Engineering at Birjand University, Birjand, Iran

Siavash Alipour
Department of Electrical and Electronic Engineering at Malek-Ashtar University of Technology, Tehran, Iran

Adam Zazula
Silesian University of Technology, Institute of Information Technologies

Dariusz Myszor
Silesian University of Technology, Institute of Information Technologies

Oleg Antemijczuk
Silesian University of Technology, Institute of Information Technologies

Krzysztof A. Cyran
Silesian University of Technology, Institute of Information Technologies

Najat O. Alsaiari
Department of Computer Science, Faculty of Computing and Information Technology, King Abdulaziz University, Jeddah, Saudi Arabia

Ayman G. Fayoumi
Department of Information System, Faculty of Computing and Information Technology, King Abdulaziz University, Jeddah, Saudi Arabia

Renata Lis
Faculty of Fundamentals of Technology, Lublin University of Technology, Nadbystrzycka 38, 20-618 Lublin, Poland

Małgorzata Janik
Faculty of Mathematics and Information, Warsaw University of Technology, Pl. Politechniki 1, 00-661 Warsaw, Poland

Ryszard Kozera
Faculty of Mathematics and Information, Warsaw University of Technology, Pl. Politechniki 1, 00-661 Warsaw, Poland

Faculty of Applied Informatics and Mathematics, Warsaw University of Life Sciences – SGGW, Nowoursynowska 159, 02-776 Warsaw, Poland,

Przemysław Kozioł
Faculty of Mathematics and Information, Warsaw University of Technology, Pl. Politechniki 1, 00-661 Warsaw, Poland

Ksenia Ostrowska
Laboratory of Coordinate Metrology, Mechanical Department, Cracow University of Technology, Al. Jana Pawła II 37, 31-864 Kraków, Poland

Danuta Szewczyk
Jerzy Sładek
Robert Lis
Department of Teaching Methods and Strategies, Lublin University of Technology, Nadbystrzycka 38, 20-618 Lublin, Poland

Ireneusz Zagórski
Department of Production Engineering, Mechanical Engineering Faculty, Lublin University of Technology, 36 Nadbystrzycka Str., 20-618 Lublin, Poland

Marcin Barszcz
Department of Fundamentals of Technology, Technology Fundamentals Faculty, Lublin University of Technology, 38 Nadbystrzycka Str., 20-618 Lublin, Poland

Grzegorz Winiarski
Department of Computer Modelling and Metal Forming Technologies, Mechanical Engineering Faculty, Lublin University of Technology, Nadbystrzycka 36, 20-618 Lublin, Poland

Printed in the USA
CPSIA information can be obtained
at www.ICGtesting.com
JSHW051439221024
72173JS00006B/1520